Red Hot Marriage

MARRIAGE MANUAL

MAKE YOURS A

Red Hot Marriage

Made In Heaven Filled With Passion and Joy

R Lindemann

Aleph Publications
Wisconsin, USA

Aleph Publications
Manitowoc, WI

Paperback Edition
ISBN-13: 978-1-956814-16-3

32 31 30 29 28 27 26 25 24 23   1 2 3 4 5

Dedication

This book is dedicated to all those who have been living life feeling left out or shorted from suffering in their lackluster marriages. The pain felt by those who have drawn upon the short end of their marriage is not a pleasant experience. This pain often goes unseen by our spouse and the world. Trying to explain this to others often only invites ridicule, bad advice, and even more misery.

To those from the past, to those of you who live now, and to those who might experience the pain of a troubling marriage in the future, this book is for you. It is for your joy, for your comfort, and for your protection. Even though some who have suffered in such marriages are no longer here with us, this book is also dedicated to them as an acknowledgement to the world that the pain they felt is recognized.

This book is for all of you to make your life what it deserves to be, so that you can share a more robust and joy-filled life with your family and those around you. Now is your time to go and reclaim what has been taken from you. Your new life is waiting!

Disclaimer

Contents

Acknowledgments

Where does a person begin to express gratitude for all of the support they received from those dedicated souls around them who believe in the same goal? There is no perfect way to express the sentiment you feel when people believe in you. So, as I write this acknowledgement of your love and support, please know that all of you, who spoke encouragement and showed love and support as I wrote this book, are noticed and acknowledged. Special thanks to Amy Brocker for all of the thoughts and deep discussion as the book was edited. Thank you all for being there to discuss the content of this book, for your edits and reviews, for your suggestions and insights, and thank you most of all for your support and love as this book was being written.

Introduction

When dealing with people's feelings, many relationship books are written apologetically because our culture has caused us to be on defense due to religion, politics, race, gender, and our societal perceptions of "rights". This book is different; it is unapologetically honest and defies popular thinking while making all required statements. There is no pandering to anyone's fears, but rather, the rare commodity of blunt honesty about marriage relationships. This book is not about what we think or see as right or wrong, but rather explains why things are the way they are so that *you* have the power to change your circumstances for your own benefit and joy.

After having observed the effects that one generation's thinking has upon the next generation, I began to wonder if it is at all possible to stop the dangerous degenerative effects of humanity's thinking that damages each subsequent generation. And, if it is possible to stop this, then how do we do it?

From the stories of generations past, and in seeing what happened to those near to me, it became apparent that we often get caught in a destructive downward spiral in our relationships. Once we get caught in this lackluster spiral, it becomes difficult for us and our descendants to escape it.

Many of the attributes seen in the marriages of parents are often similar to the attributes seen in the marriages of their children. This can be especially true if the parents are dissatisfied but endure to a bitter end of "until death do us part". The fact that these similarities exist is not a bad thing in itself, but in many cases, when bad things happen to people, the attributes that are bad and similar to the parents' relationship have negative effects on the children of that marriage and on the children's marriages. In turn, this gets passed to each subsequent generation.

When a weak and misaligned marriage falls upon difficult circumstances, there is often undue stress within the relationship, and that stress causes a great deal of pain in the relationship and in the family. The children of the couple see their parents' examples, and then the children, more often than not, follow the same damaging pattern. This becomes a snare to them and they do not understand or realize that this is happening.

When the children of the couple grow older and marry, they exhibit similar behaviors within their own marriages. And if it goes unchecked, it's often even more damaging than the problem was in their parents' relationship. This unnecessary situation will be passed on to your children *if* allowed to continue. It is up to you and your spouse to defeat this unacceptable problem.

It's difficult to repair an item without the information written in the authorized repair manual for the item. Life is no different. If you have not been taught how to repair problems in a relationship then you are left to figure it out on your own. *The Marriage Repair Manual, Red Hot Marriage*, is that authorized manual for married life. This is not conventional information. It is point by point instructions allowing you to quickly repair your marriage problems. As you read, you will find many common and some not-so-common problems exposed, making them easier to see and understand. Exposing these problems allows you to be able to quickly define troubles when troubles come to your family and your marriage. When you recognize the root of a problem, you can quickly control and defeat it, something that many previous generations have been unable to accomplish.

The purpose of this information is to give *you* the power to overcome the difficulties you see within your own marriage. It is also to help you to better communicate with your spouse and to get your spouse to better communicate with you. This puts you in control of your life and of your environment. Your family can benefit from your knowledge, and your children can be saved from having their own marriages become troubled and unfair when you teach them the information.

After reading this unique and basic approach to extracting and disposing problems in your marriage, allow this message deep within your heart, and set out to live the life you were meant to live. Teach your children to do so as well!

In order to keep the message straightforward and easy for all to understand and relate to, this book is written using the typical husband and wife relationship model. But in many relationships, things are reversed with regard to men and women and the role each plays in the relationship. Adapt this message to what best fits your relationship and keep in mind that it is not one extreme or the other, but is more likely to be a mix of these situations in the way that they apply to you, your spouse, and your marriage.

In this book situations are often stated stereotypically about men and women because those impressions are quite accurate; however, they do not apply to everyone. For some couples, these stereotypical scenarios will be reversed. But the principle in this book does apply to everyone. For instance, stereotypically speaking, men are more intimately or sexually aggressive, and women are often portrayed as saying, "Go away, all you ever want is sex." While this is often true, there are many circumstances that are completely the opposite where the woman is sexually or intimately aggressive, and it's the man who says, "Go away." This can change over time and the roles may get reversed as a couple ages. In truth, there are no specific rules. But the stereotypes are very common, so we are using the stereotypes as broad examples in this book.

For the purpose of this book, I am trying to address as many questions and scenarios as possible, but I suppose there aren't enough pages in the world to address all of the questions and scenarios we create. There are certainly differences between the behavior and expectations of men and women; and typically these behaviors are consistent, but often the expectations will lean in the other direction. If this is your case, then you will need to do your best to imagine yourself in the other position while reading this book. There are parts of the book that are distinctive to men and there are parts that are distinctive to women, and these parts cannot be switched. You will need to blend the various scenarios and improvise your thinking by using the stereotypical examples, and then adapt them as best as is possible to relate to your own situation.

Some people have not been brought up with good examples around them. For those of you who have had only bad examples around you, some sections of this book might not seem to make sense until after you allow the principle in this book to become familiar to you. You can be certain that once you understand the root cause of a problem, then things will become much clearer to you, and far easier to correct.

Chapter 1

Building Your Marriage Foundation

Is your marriage what you expected when you decided to get married? Are you happy in your marriage? Are you getting what you want out of your relationship? For most of us, we never really thought much about what our married *future* would be like. We were in the moment and just wanted to be with who we believed was "the love of our life". There are those of us who have gone as far as making sure we had our finances in order and everything paid for before getting married in order to assure that financial matters would not spoil an otherwise good relationship. Yet, statistically, half of *all* marriages fail. Why is this? And what can be done about it? What can we do to make our own marriages better, or even great? How do we get what we want out of marriage? And is any of that even possible?

Clearing Your Head

Getting what we want out of marriage is not only possible, it is critical to your happiness and joy. For many people this expectation is in terms of getting enough sex or having your spouse actually listen to you. That of course is amongst the many other marriage complaints we so often have and hear. Most of us have not been taught how to make the problems in a marriage go away, or how to get our spouse to understand and properly respond to the way we feel about those problems.

We seek answers to our problems in the form of specific things to do in order to make life better, but the reality is that when we're experiencing problems it's more important to stop doing what caused our problems to begin with. Much information is available about relationships, yet so many people still suffer marriage troubles. This book exposes the causes of most troubles, but it can only offer thoughts for you to consider regarding solutions to the causes and their effects. After you have read and considered these thoughts then you can make better, more informed decisions as to what you can to do to remedy your situation if it is a well suited solution. Sometimes we can't control this because it's our spouse causing the problems that inflict so much pain on us.

The only way to truly remove problems is to stop the behaviors that caused the problems to begin with. Doing anything else only serves to further hide the problem. Anyone who has been emotionally beaten down for a long time by their spouse, or by any family member for that matter, must realize how valuable you are and you must learn that proper communication tools are your keys to success and joy. A great starting point is to make sure that *you* don't behave badly or do the same wrong things to others that they have been doing to you. The main problem that we have in dealing with our problems is that we don't understand our problems or where they come from. And we typically don't fully understand that our underlying problem is a problem to begin with.

Too many marriages are painful and end in divorce. Most people want their marriages to succeed and feel as if they've "tried everything possible" to get their spouse to understand how deeply they're hurting and how angry their spouse makes them feel.

As we age, our marriages change somewhat because life changes, but I believe that a marriage can and should be as exciting and active as it was when you first met. And that is your goal!

As we begin exploring how to make your relationship better and why relationships are all too often painful and fail, there are a few critical points that you must embrace in order to get the results you desire in your marriage. First, you must realize that your decision to read this book shows that, deep down inside, you're a good person and you want what is best for you and all of those around you. You must be willing to let go of all preconceptions about life and relationships in order to accomplish the sustained happiness and joy being discussed throughout this book.

You must regain the ability to clearly know what you want. Too often our world has dealt us unwanted and undesired misery, and this misery is often found in our marriages. The best way to begin to understand this point is by asking yourself "Do *I* want things better?"

Do I Want Things Better?

The primary question to ask yourself is, "Do I want things better?" It's likely that you're reading this book for one of three key reasons: You are hurting badly and want relief from the pain. Or possibly, someone gave this book to you and suggested you read it as preemptive information. Or maybe you're the curious type and like good information and love to learn. Personally acknowledging that you're reading this because you're hurting is a critical part in fixing your marriage problems. The pain we feel in a relationship is not to be taken lightly and it typically goes unacknowledged by our spouse and even by ourselves. This leaves us confused and feeling the brunt of the pain alone.

Without a good outlet to relieve ourselves of our pain, we become frustrated, which only serves to further deepen our pain. This leads us to a very critical and important question that we all need to answer. Make your choice below.

Do I want things better?
Yes____   No____

Commit to answering the question by marking your chosen answer. Answering it before you continue will be of great value to you and will assist you in more clearly understanding the remainder of this book.

The next point for you to make a decision about is also very important with regard to your marriage.

Do _I_ want to be right?
Yes____   No____

A and the third point to decide is:

Do I want to be true?
Yes____   No____

In order to make things better in your life you need to know the whole story. Commit to finishing this book sooner rather than later to get a better grasp on the whole story. By the time you're finished reading you'll have a completely new perspective on any unfair treatment that you have received over the years. You will also be able to effectively deal with the pain of those memories and put it behind you for good! When you're done, you'll regard those hurtful memories as important turning points in your life and will use those experiences and memories to guide your life to what it is meant to be as you navigate your future.

Before moving on, stop here for a moment and think carefully about how you answered the three questions.

Now that you have considered the questions and made key decisions, let's understand the meaning of the answers for each question.

The first question, "Do you want things better?" is very important. It's unlikely that anyone who is hurting would answer "No" to the first question. The first question is simple and straight forward, and there is little chance of misunderstanding it. If you are at all hurting, it is my hope that you have answered "Yes" to the first question.

As for the second question, "Do I want to be right?" well, this question is a bit more of a challenge; your answer to this question can mean different things. The way you have answered it, and what exactly is meant by your answer has everything to do with your life-experiences and the way you were brought up. Our initial answer to this question, tells much about the way each of us sees the world: There is only one proper answer to the question.

For many people, the third question, "Do I want to be true?" appears to be the same as the second, but it is not, and it is *not* easily misunderstood. This third question exposes why you answered the second question as you did. This last question "Do I want to be true?" has a great deal of meaning.

Think about it this way: If you answered "No" to the last question "Do I want to be true?" then you are actively saying that you are choosing to be wrong. This is because, if you are not true, then you have chosen to be false.

You cannot answer "Yes" to the question "Do I want to be right", and then answer "Yes" to "Do I want to be true?" without contradicting yourself at some point. This could be argued by many as semantics. But in truth, if you simply want to be right, it says nothing about your accuracy. What it does indicate is that you want to be right, and you want it *your* way.

The third question, "Do I want to be true?", has two elements. The first aspect of it is saying that you want to be true, and the second aspect is saying you understand that to be true you need to have your information correct. Whereas simply insisting on being "right" leaves your accuracy up for debate.

Why is this Important?

These questions are important to understand because when we're dealing with our feelings and emotions, it's our insistence on being "right" that gets in our way of completely understanding each other.

You might see this insistence in your spouse or even in yourself, where the end goal is that the person always insists on being right in an argument; that is to say—having it their way. This is one small part of a relationship, but it is an extremely important one.

If we're thinking wrong, but insist that we are right, then anything that we build upon our wrong thoughts will inherit the errors that were in that original wrong thinking that we set our foundation upon. Clearing your head with regard to your marriage is like clearing and preparing the land for the foundation of a new building. If the foundation is crooked, then the building will also be crooked. If it's built on faulty ground, then the building will shift and develop cracks in its foundation and will be compromised and eventually collapse.

Leveling the Land by Rethinking Your Answers

If you incorrectly answered the second question, "Do I want to be right?" as "Yes", then fear not! The good news is you can change your answer based on your new understanding of the question. You now know that you don't care if you are "right" but instead you understand that it's more important to be accurate, honest, and true.

The best part of life is that when we make mistakes, we can stop making those mistakes and immediately change our actions so that we are no longer making mistakes.

Don't Start Arguing, Understand First

If you read anything in this book and find that it falls in your favor as it exposes your spouse's bad behaviors, and you then proceed to pick a fight before you finish reading, then you obviously do not want your relationship to be better. If this is the case, then it's likely that many of your marriage and life problems are of your own making.

Think about it and understand what you have read *before* you engage in any conversation with your spouse about your marriage or relationship concerns. And if they're willing, then have your spouse read this book when you're done. Let the book sit for a few days or even a few weeks, and flip through it again with a fresh perspective. I assure you that you will have a very different perspective the second time through.

It's unwise to start any discussion about a sensitive topic before you are prepared with full understanding. Wait until you're ready and prepared with good, true, and proper information before engaging in dialogue about problems between you and your spouse, or anyone for that matter. Our goal should never be to force others to see it our way. The goal should always be to have others understand what is good and true so that they can see it for themselves. This is all part of your preparation for rebuilding your relationship, much like when you carefully plan things before building a new home—prepare first, and then build.

The Journey

Marriage is a journey through life that is supposed to be joyous and wonderful, but for many people this is seldom the case. With nearly half of all marriages ending in divorce, something clearly needs to be done—or said.

Marriages have been in peril since the dawn of civilization, and it seems that it worsens with each new generation, but that's not really the case. The truth is that the troubles we experience in our marriages today are common and have been around for a very long time. Oddly, even with all of the generations of marriage experience throughout the history of the world, it doesn't seem to get any better. We can figure out how to put a man on the moon, but we can't quite seem to conquer our own relationships.

Do we really want to live life feeling that we are connected to "The old ball and chain"? When our spouse isn't doing their part, then we experience a great deal of pain. When we have felt enough pain, then divorce is typically the result.

When allowed to freely answer without inhibition, each spouse in a marriage who is asked about the condition of their marriage typically responds with an answer that is different from their mate. These answer differences are greatly dependent upon the position and perception of each spouse. When the two answers are in utter disagreement with each other, then the marriage journey is very uncomfortable for at least one, if not both people. This unnecessary problem is easily corrected when you know why this happens to begin with.

Teach a Man to Fish

There is a saying that "if you give someone a fish, you feed them for a day, but if you teach them to fish then you feed them for life." While teaching a man to fish is good lesson, it's actually somewhat shortsighted.

A part of our marriage journey typically includes children. If I teach you to fish, then you and your family can eat and be satisfied, and that's good. But it's not good enough. If it were good enough, then there would be no more bad marriages.

I believe that we are better served to teach a man to teach men to fish so that the teaching propagates to each subsequent generation. Then the feeding part becomes a natural result and benefit of knowing how to fish and is no longer seen as the problem. In fact, the feeding part never has been the problem. The problem has always been humanity's inability to pass true wisdom and good knowledge to each subsequent generation.

Have you ever noticed that people who have divorced parents often end up divorced themselves? Why is this? And what can we do about it? When you understand how to have a great marriage, then you can teach your children to teach their children to also have great marriages. Doing this will bless your descendants with full, robust, and joyful lives. And it will do the same for you!

Chapter 2

How Do I Make My Marriage Better?

The holy grail of all questions is "How Do I Make My Marriage Better?" This question has been asked within the hearts and minds of married people for thousands of years. Even though many relationships appear to show otherwise, historical evidence indicates that only a relative few couples seem to have been able to successfully overcome *all* marital strife. In order to do so they had to find the answers to each of their questions to achieve marital bliss for their entire duration of "until death do us part."

Each marriage situation is unique. The pain felt by each of us has its own set of circumstances. We can group the basic elements of painful marriage relationships into stereotypical categories. And when these stereotyped categories that we're discussing here are addressed, it helps in holding further problems at bay by answering questions about basic behaviors. However, only speaking in stereotypes does not eliminate the problems we face, but it does aid us in *defining* those problems. To *eliminate* our problems, we must dig a bit deeper.

You will not find any recommendation to seek counseling here. In the event that you do decide to seek counseling, consider the following:

Sadly, relationship counseling is often needed, but it should not be. If you seek counseling at any point, be aware that there are glaring problems with the practices of a few in the counseling community.

When a marriage is facing serious issues, selecting a good and trustworthy counselor is vital to the survival of the marriage. Counselors are people too, and they have biases for good or for bad. A counselor with any agenda other than to make the marriage work is likely not right for anyone unless serious and dangerous abuse issues are included in the marriage problems.

You can think of a bad counselor in terms of having a bad lawyer who is greedy negotiating a business deal between two companies. When the companies are just about to come to an agreement, then the lawyer creates more contention to be worked out—for a hefty fee. It's good to cover all of the legal bases and make sure that each company's issues are all addressed, but it should stop there.

If the counsel mediating any relationship between two parties has an agenda of their own, then it's easy for them to stir up controversy just to keep the debate going. This happens both in business and in personal relationship mediation. There are people who thrive on this sort of behavior and a few of them actually counsel marriages.

Counselors should be impartial and caring. They should *not* want you to continue to see them once you have fully rectified your problems, other than to do an occasional checkup.

Remember this: Just because a person has credentials, it does not make what they preach accurate, helpful, or good. Counselors are people, not gods, and they have the same flaws, biases, and marriage problems that everyone else does.

The same holds true for relationship books. Many of these books are right-on-the-mark and are very useful, but the same type of counselor who counsels with an agenda, other than to rebuild a marriage, may also write books promoting their dangerous attitudes and agendas. Most books, such as this one, are only offering information, views, thoughts, and opinions for consideration and are not advice, directive, recommendation, counsel, or any other method of counsel for anyone to take any action other than being a suggestion to consider what is written and see how it compares to your life so that you can see potential problem areas and then work to correct those areas. So how do we tell which is good and which is bad? Simple, when you hear or read their words, do the words feed the problem, hide the problem, or expose the problem?

Exposing the Problem

Properly exposing the problem is the only appropriate answer to how we can tell which is which. Anything other than utter openness only serves to deepen the problems that arise between the two people in a marriage or any other relationship.

Utter openness is the beginning of what people fear the most—honesty! Full honesty in a marriage is a very rare thing. In fact, people typically use imbalanced compromise and silence to solve marital problems rather than proper full and open honesty. In saying this, I do not want being "honest" to be misinterpreted as meaning that you should say everything the moment that it pops into your mind. Making an uninvited comment such as, "That makes you look fat", or a comment like, "Why are you so lazy?" can be both rude and foolish. There are ways of addressing your feelings about these issues without inflicting deliberate emotional injury on the other person.

The answer to the chapter title *"How Do I Make My Marriage Better?"* is both simple and complex at the same time. To fully understand why it is both simple and complex you need to fully grasp the principles laid out in this book.

Sometimes we start to read a book of this nature and get hung up at some point and never go on to finish it. This is because we reach a point of conflict within ourselves due to what it points out about us, and we can't find our way clear to accept the truth that has been set down before us. We shy away from completing the book because it points out our errors, and so we hide. As you realize each aspect of the principle set forth in this book you will find that you have a few pieces of you to pick up afterward. Shedding these pieces in this way, and then reassembling them *properly*, offers you tremendous control over your life going forward.

Most of us want fast and easy answers. We want it simple and we want it now! But reality seldom offers simple-and-fast as a viable option for our marriage woes—there are no drive-thru solutions for marriage problems. There are too many complex aspects of personality to deal with in order to make quick work of marital problems. At least that's the way things appear.

It is *people* that cause our problems in *all* relationships. And it might even be ourselves causing those problems; knowing this, makes any marriage problems that you are experiencing far easier for you to understand and conquer. I would like to relate the fullest understanding of why we each personally have the problems within ourselves that we do, but that would distract from the basic message of this book. But there is another cornerstone book called *Hot Water* that goes in-depth into why we each are the way we are. "*Hot Water*" refers to the way we become conditioned to our environment and no longer specifically notice it. This is similar to when you put your hand in hot water until you are accustomed to it, and then place it into lukewarm water, making the lukewarm water feel cold. But when you put your hand in cold water until you become accustomed to it and then place your hand in the lukewarm water, the same lukewarm water, that felt cold before, will now feel hot to you. This is also how we experience our relationship environment and those around us. If you need deeper understanding regarding some of the personal behavioral questions you or your spouse may have that this book does not have room for, the cornerstone book *Hot Water* addresses some of those questions. The first trick in getting to the bottom of "How Do I Make My Marriage Better?" is to understand satisfaction.

Understanding Satisfaction

Words are very important ideas. We use them every day, but typically we do not fully understand the true meaning of many of them. Words hold the keys for the answers to most of our problems.

The reason this world has so many problems is because we do not properly understand the words we use when we communicate.

To understand *satisfaction* we need to understand the word "*satisfaction.*" *Satisfied* stems from the word *satis* which means enough. This is to say that when you are satisfied you have enough. *Satis* is where the words *sate* or *sated* come from.

Choose one of the two answers below:

A.) I am satisfied _____

B.) I am not satisfied _____

If you're reading this book, then it is likely that you are not fully satisfied in your marriage. This means that you are not getting enough of something that you need or want. And it very well may be that both of you are not getting enough of something. The *satisfaction level* is the one and only point of contention in any troubled marriage.

When gone unchecked, low satisfaction creates a great amount of unwanted, unseen, unnoticed, and unknown tit-for-tat between you and your spouse. In the early stages of marital troubles, these actions are typically not consciously deliberate, but they escalate nonetheless. For those of you who have children, you have probably seen frequent occurrences of this type of escalation when your children play. You probably even remember this happening to you as a child: You're happily playing with your sibling or friend and everything is fine until one of the children gets too rough; then a push back, and another push back, and, before you know it, there's an all-out brawl.

It's often difficult for us to put our finger on exactly what happened during these exchanges, making it hard to tell exactly whose fault it was that the fight started to begin with. This is because a fight that escalates from play is seldom a deliberate premeditated malicious attempt to harm someone. This kind of situation is often due to an excited child having a bit too much fun and not quite understanding the reasonable limits of play in the same way that their sibling or friend does.

Tit-for-tat is no different with a married couple, except that, for a couple, it is far more difficult to detect the action. This is because, with couples, the actions are usually not specifically physical actions as it is when two children are pushing one another. The subtleties of the these actions in a marriage are extremely difficult to place our finger on. This is true even when we are aware that something's not right and are specifically looking for the problem.

There are usually no malicious acts in the early stages of these tit-for-tat actions, and because they are usually not being done for vengeful purposes it's more difficult to detect them. When someone deliberately hurts us we can usually tell that it was intentional, but the tit-for-tat in a marriage is the subtle and unnoticed result of feeling hurt and unsatisfied. Properly addressing this satisfaction issue will solve all marital problems of those who understand and then *properly* implement the solutions.

What is Your Marriage Worth?

Reading this book and wanting things better, clearly indicates that you do not care about being right, but rather you want to be true. Since you're not fully satisfied in your marriage, let's examine the value of a marriage. What is Your Marriage Worth? This depends upon your life-view.

Consider this: If you have a rare classic car that needs repairs, then you need to decide if you should junk it (divorce it), or keep and repair it. If you choose to junk your car, then it's likely that you'll buy a new car. And, in a few years, because of the way you treated it, the new car will have all of the same problems the old one did. Eventually you will also want to junk the new car! At this point your problems will start all over again and again and again with each new car you get, distorting your life a little more with each purchase. After a few years of owning each car, you begin to have mechanical fatigue problems and the car begins to fall apart, *unless* you truly cherish your original classic! Then it's worth a complete rebuild and overhaul and all of the polishing that accompanies properly caring for it. If you buy a another new car, it's probably not going to be a classic, and in a few years it may be the laughing stock of the community because it was a very unpopular design that didn't properly suit your needs, causing those around you to think "I told you so."

Let's read that again but this time we'll change a few words: If you have a marriage that needs repairs, then you need to decide if you should divorce, or save the marriage. If you choose to quit your marriage, then it's likely that you'll marry again. And, in a few years, because of the way you treat your marriage, the new marriage will have all of the same problems the last one did. And then eventually you will want to also end the new marriage. At this point your problems will start all over again and again and again with each new marriage you get into, distorting your life a little more with each marriage. After a few years of being in each marriage, you begin to have relationship fatigue problems and the marriage begins to fall apart *unless* you truly cherish your original marriage! Then it's worth a complete rebuild and overhaul and all of the love that accompanies properly caring for your marriage. If you get into a another new marriage, it's probably not going to be a classic, and in a few years it may be the laughing stock of the community because it was a very unwise decision that didn't properly suit your needs, causing those around you to think "I told you so."

The value of your marriage is what you make it. It's your choice and you get to decide if you will restore your valuable classic or junk it. An important point to remember is that if you have help from your co-owner when polishing and caring for your classic, then you will find that you have far more time to drive around together in it and enjoy it! It will be done far better and faster when both of you want it to feel and look all shiny and new and you both work together to make it that way every day! Marriage is a journey on a two way street that is driven together *in harmony.*

Classics have a desirable value even when they are in poor condition. It is the effort that is put into the classic that gives it its high value—a value that others will envy! When both co-owners work together to make it the best classic ever, then it will run smoothly, dependably, and sparkle with a blinding shine. This kind of classic is rare and we would all enjoy having such a beautiful cherished classic marriage for ourselves.

There is an oversight in our understanding of classics: We have this tendency to assume that the classic will always be there and in good condition for us without us taking any time to care for it. We treat our classics poorly and we neglect to properly maintain them, yet we still expect them to reliably fulfill all of our needs. When you neglect a marriage, it starts to decay and show signs of wear and tear. Eventually parts fatigue, and if repairs are not made then those parts *will* fail. When the marriage goes through the rough and rocky roads of life, then maintenance *will* be required, and you *will* have maintenance work that you *need* to do in order to keep it functioning smoothly and in like-new condition! If you and your co-owner fail to discuss and fully address the maintenance schedule of your classic, then the fatigued parts will cause your classic to break down and fail when you need it most. Debating about whether or not to make the repairs will not get the repair work done.

This brings us to another misunderstood word—*work*. The word "work" does not mean slaving in torment as we typically think it does. The true root meaning of the word "work" is simply *activity*. So don't think of restoring your marriage as "work" in the modern sense of the word, where many of us hate our jobs and consider them to be hard "work". Instead, consider your classic marriage to be a hobby that you very much enjoy working on in your spare time. Enjoy polishing it and keeping it in tip-top condition so that you can take it around the block for joy-rides whenever you need or want to, without it being dirty and shabby from neglect. Give your marriage the attention it needs and deserves. Polishing and maintaining it together with your spouse can, and should be, an enjoyable task!

You need to cherish your marriage and keep it active so that it serves you well and pays you both great dividends of joy as you travel from point to point together in it. Your bodies are the tangible part of the marriage, so make sure you also give each other the needed physical care and attention. Later we will look at various ways of keeping your classic marriage active and getting your co-owner to also be excited to do their part.

Chapter 3

The Importance of Understanding Statistics

Statistics harm people, families, and marriages. Statistics are a medium of index that the world all too often sees abused. Statistics are commonly abused by those using the statistics to promote their own cause or agenda. To better understand the problems with statistics, we can compare the following: If you were to ask me the temperature and I took out a ruler to measure the length of the thermometer and told you the temperature was about six inches, I may be giving you an accurate number and measurement, but what good is that number to you? This is often how statistics are used. Yes, the thermometer is six inches long, but what has that to do with the temperature?

Let's consider the marriage statistic that indicates that half of all marriages end in divorce. Does this mean that you have a fifty percent chance of getting divorced? The answer to that question is "No, absolutely not!" Upon hearing this answer most people are confused, "Fifty percent is fifty percent, after all!" If fifty percent is true, then this means that your marriage has no better chance of lasting than the fifty-fifty chance found in the toss of a coin!

Most of us don't care about statistical math or feel that it matters, but understanding basics about statistics is very important in eliminating future misunderstandings in your overall life. Understanding the basics of statistical math is very important with regard to its effects on your marriage. Statistical surveys are seldom done scientifically proper. Typically, when surveys are done, they are done with an agenda to promote the cause of some group or person. Utilizing statistics to prove a point is fine, until your intent is to sway opinion through deceitful manipulation of the statistical facts.

When taking surveys, we can sway statistics by asking each survey question in a certain way. We can also sway the statistics by delivering the results a certain way. And with perhaps the most used abusive method of using statistics, we can sway statistics by outright deception. Our perception of statistics absolutely affects our actions, and therefore statistics can profoundly affect our lives, especially if we are complacent about those statistics.

It's not that the numbers are inaccurate in most statistics. But rather, it's the way the numbers are delivered to us that is all too often inaccurate and deceptive and deviates from the initial intention and purpose of the gathered information. For instance, if we discuss death statistics, and then abruptly begin discussing cancer and say that lung cancer is the leading cause of death, we should also very clearly show that it refers only to cancer deaths and not all deaths. This point should be *stressed* by the purveyor of the survey statistics in an effort to eliminate confusion for those who are receiving the information. An organization with an agenda for public attention will often use statistics for shock and awe value to bring attention to their cause.

When a particular disease or condition is on the rise, then, usually it is hyped as the "fastest growing." This may be true, but if one person has a particular disease and a second person also comes into the same condition, then the rate just doubled for that particular disease. However, the instances of cases is only two cases, while all other diseases, each by themselves, vastly exceeds two. This renders the two cases of the new disease insignificant in real-world numbers. So, even though the rate of new disease just doubled, it's still only two people. This alarmist method of getting attention is used on the public (that's us) on a regular basis.

Seldom do we take the time to verify the statistics that we see and hear. Instead, we blindly and dangerously trust those who are making their statistical claims. Our only protection against believing wrong information is to check the facts for ourselves with open eyes and an open mind. Making sure that you're interpreting the information correctly is your first step in doing so. If you are unable to understand the information clearly because something just doesn't seem to add up, then it's very likely that someone is being deceptive or manipulative with the information. Now let's connect this to marriage.

Marriage Statistics

So what does all of this statistics talk have to do with your marriage? With the information about the statistical accuracy in mind, here is a list of the few areas we are addressing:

- People who have sex more often have better marriages.
- People who go to church regularly have happier marriages.
- People who pray more have better marriages.
- Half of all marriages end in divorce.

Due to how commonly it is abused and misused, let's address the last item first because it is the most important to understand. The statistic that indicates that half of all marriages end in divorce is responsible for more divorces than most of us realize.

When a young couple is thinking about marriage and we tell them that their marriage has a fifty-fifty chance of ending in turmoil in five to ten years, it has a profound effect on their level of commitment. Further, when young people begin dating with this mindset, they hold little regard for a classic marriage. They begin to view marriage as a disposable item that only has a fifty-fifty chance of survival. Thus, they go into the relationship with the notion that it *will* likely fail in five to ten years at the flip of a coin.

Pre-conditioning someone's thoughts with a statistical flip of a coin, in itself, is tragic, and it places a great deal of stress on the relationship. When any rough roads are encountered by the couple, they are far more likely to have an attitude of, "Hey, it's a fifty-fifty chance, so what's the point of trying to make it work?" When young couples are dating and are taught this misrepresented statistic, it causes them to take less care in selecting their classic marriage, causing them to carelessly choose a less desirable marriage that will be of little value in their own future. You should be able to select yours by carefully studying its features; and when you find it to be agreeable, then you can make the final purchase (commitment).

By not believing in the true and priceless value of a proper classic, young couples are often smitten with that new couple smell and will carelessly set out and take the first one they find. Get to know someone before sealing the deal. Taking the first one that comes along is not always a bad thing, because the first one might be the best one for you. But often it's not the best because you haven't even read the brochure before test driving—failing to do so is reckless. "Testing" before marrying is the dating part, it is not sex.

You might still be wondering how this affects the statistics. Well to start, it unfairly influences and increases the statistical number because of the disregard to marriage being taught via the improper use or interpretation of the statistic itself. Let me explain: Going back to our thermometer example, the temperature was improperly measured with a ruler and determined to be six inches of temperature. We can all clearly understand why this is wrong and that it is not what was intended by the person requesting the temperature. We understand that what was intended, in the request, was the position of the mercury on the thermometer. It is the level of the mercury and the temperature calibration lines that indicate what the temperature of the air actually is. So how does this relate?

Well, if you ask "how many marriages end in divorce?", someone will accurately tell you, "About fifty percent of all marriages end in divorce." Thus, you assume that you have a fifty percent chance of divorcing. This seems logical, except for one important point— *You* are the air temperature that you are looking to get the statistic about.

The statistic, three inches of a six inch thermometer is fifty percent, it is length, not the temperature. So, ask yourself, "What have *I* to do with marriage statistics?"

Why is it important to know your connection to a marriage? Of the many people who divorce and go on to marry again, a certain amount of them divorce again and remarry again, and of those, a certain amount divorce and remarry yet again. This can go on four, five, six times and even more for one person.

So here is a proper way of understanding this statistic: *You are not a marriage.* A marriage is something that you can do more than one of. Thus, if you get married two times and divorced two times, then one hundred percent of *your* marriages failed.

This means that, statistically, two other couples will be married for life! That's right, for every marriage that fails there is a couple that is married for life. Further, when someone divorces more than once, then that alters the statistics. Yes, the fifty percent rate of marriages ending in divorce still applies, but what does not apply is the amount of *people* who divorce.

People who intend to never divorce, rarely divorce. But for those who consider that there is a fifty-fifty chance that divorce will happen in their marriage, they will likely get a divorce at some point in life because divorce is a personal choice of action and they are somewhat *expecting* it to happen. Divorce is a particular road *chosen* by the drivers of the classic. Let us also keep in mind that some divorces are not wanted and are done for protection in cases of financial protection when someone is dying, and in politics and other unwanted fame where the family of the famous spouse is being tormented because of the unwanted media attention that is typically very negative.

The following point is very important to know and remember: The "fifty percent of marriages end in divorce" statistic does not apply to *people*—It applies only to the people's *marriages!*

With regard to marriage, a point of further interest that's not able to be accurately recorded in statistics, is that many people who divorce choose to live with someone as if they are married, and then later they break off the relationship. This is the equivalent of getting a divorce without the legal and financial ramifications, and thus it is not statistically recorded. This would serve to increase the statistical divorce rate. When people are married for life, this cannot occur.

But because most of us do not want to be caught up in a nasty divorce, some of us choose to live together with no real commitment, usually ending in separating later.

The real percentage of married people who divorce from legal marriages is only about one third of *people*—it is not fifty percent of people. This is based on the fact that people who divorce often remarry, and many of those divorce again. Thus, their own statistic skews the perception of marriage for other people.

Of the eight marriages depicted above four have divorced. The figure indicates thirteen people, eight of which never divorce. Eight divided by thirteen is sixty-one percent, leaving only thirty-nine percent of the people being involved in divorce.

This means that roughly sixty to seventy percent of people remain married to the same person for the remainder of their lives. The statistic should be stated in terms of how many *people* who get married never divorce. This produces a far different and far more accurate impression, and it is the answer that truly matters to us when discussing marriage statistics. To add to this, some people will marry and divorce the same person multiple times skewing the statistic yet more.

To get a clear picture of why this is true, simply examine certain celebrities. There are some who have married seven times or more. This means that for each marriage that the one particular celebrity had, there are seven other marriages that will never divorce—ever! That is to say, there are seven marriages that will last the spouses' entire lifetime. When people go into a marriage *expecting* divorce, then it is likely they will eventually get divorced. So why is this important?

It's important because *you* are not a marriage and your marriage is only as good as what *you* go into it with. If we properly taught the meaning of these statistics to our children, then they would take getting married more seriously. A more serious approach to marriage serves to further reduce the divorce rate, thus increasing the amount of statistically successful marriages. It also causes the prospective owners of a marriage to thoroughly understand marriage before test driving. They would understand the maintenance needs before making their marriage purchase so that they fully understood the maintenance schedule needs of a classic valued marriage.

But let's not get too far ahead of ourselves here, because many of these "statistically successful" marriages are still *not* good marriages, which we will address in a later chapter.

Cause and Effect

The other statistics mentioned are more an issue of cause and effect:

- People who have sex more often have better marriages.
- People who go to church regularly have happier marriages.
- People who pray more have better marriages.

Based upon the same logic used when discussing various marriage statistics we could speculate that, because flowers open in the morning it causes the sun to rise.

The statistic that results in the conclusion of, "People who have sex more often have better marriages" is often promoted in just that way. Our marriage is suffering, so let's have more sex and then everything will be better. Right? Not so!

As a multitude of couples have discovered, the idea that "Having more sex improves your marriage" is not necessarily true. Similarly, the same incorrect thinking has gone into other statistical error, such as, "People who regularly attend church have happier marriages", "People who pray more have happier marriages", or even, "Having children can make your marriage last longer." The last one being a bit more complex. These statistics require the scrutiny of *cause* and *effect*.

Do people who have more sex have better marriages?
or
Do people who have better marriages have more sex?

The other questions are similar.
Do people who attend church more regularly have happier marriages?
or
Do people who have happier marriages attend church more regularly?

And last,
Do people who pray more have happier marriages?
or
Do people who have happier marriages pray more?

We will address the having children part a bit later.

Cause-and-effect is very important to understand and apply to our lives, especially to our marriages. Financial gain is usually the reason that statistics are misrepresented. Statistics are also misrepresented by people who do not understand the course of cause-and-effect.

Knowing, or even asking, which is the cause and which is the effect is important. You must ask yourself which is which when examining these and most other marriage statistics, or any other statistic.

People in happier marriages will typically have sex more frequently in the long run, than those who are in strained marriages. With this understanding about these often misunderstood statistics, we need to take it to the next level and ask why the marriages are better and happier.

If sex, children, prayer, and going to church were all answers to better marriages, then there would be no divorce in church-going folks who have children, pray, and have a lot of sex. There would have been far more of these couples married for life, but there are not.

Working it Backwards

You can't solve your marriage problems by working things backwards. Doing an end result first, won't make a problem go away. The final outcome has to be the effect; it cannot possibly ever be the cause. Though it must be said that in some rare cases, doing the effect first could snap people out of their rut and allow them to re-evaluate their lives and properly address the actual causes of their troubles. But this rarely works for long-term satisfaction and requires a lot more work and is far more painful than doing things in the proper order.

We create false hope for troubled couples when we imply that they can make their marriages better by doing an end result first. The staged and heavily-edited life versions we see in entertainment are of no assistance either. Telling a young couple that "having better sex more often will solve marital problems", only serves to mask their underlying issues. When troubled couples attempt end-result tactics first, they won't come to the understanding that their true problem is in *the actual cause* of the troubles that they are experiencing. Not understanding this hides the actual cause and allows us to believe that the effect is the problem. A good marriage is the *cause*, and it has the *effect* of better, adequate, and often breathtakingly great and frequent sex.

Chapter 4

Picking Compatible Companions

Because this book is about romantic relationships, it is appropriate to touch on dating. Every young couple should understand this chapter before marriage. Since most readers are already married, some of the points in this chapter are already past for you. But as you read, you'll begin to recall where some of your troubles began and you can then teach your children to avoid that uncomfortable path.

This chapter is very important for identifying the behaviors that often lay in wait to sabotage your relationship. Knowing that these behaviors exist *before* getting serious in a relationship is good because it gives you the power to end a troubled relationship before it gets too far down a painful and rocky path to a difficult future. Regardless of who we are with, most of us could joyfully coexist if we had a true desire to do so. However, due to the behaviors we each are personally accustomed to (our Hot Water), we typically will not coexist well with someone who is very different than us in their fundamental upbringing.

If you're already committed for the long haul, then the sources of these problems are especially important for you to understand.

You need to be able to clearly recognize these and other problems if you ever hope to make things better in your marriage.

The compatibility of the two people in a couple is not easily quantified. So how can you gauge compatibility? There is no quantifiable way to do it because it's a choice each person needs to make on their own. Understanding why each of us are the way we are, and why we behave as we do, making the decisions that we make, helps us (as discussed in the cornerstone book *Hot Water*).

We often select our mates based upon two primary criteria: Our excitement level and our comfort level. Excitement is usually the first thing we experience. You might see a person who you think is very attractive, where their attractiveness alone motivates you to take some action to be near the person for an opportunity to get to meet and know the person. The comfort criteria comes in to play once you have met and are getting to know each other better. If their ways are familiar to you, you will be comfortable with them. And because you see very few differences, you are not scared away.

This does not automatically make a couple compatible. The familiarity between them often becomes a trap for new couples because they are less likely to notice their incompatible aspects, until *after* they are married.

In many ways, the "compatibility" issue is misunderstood. While it can be of help, both people in the relationship do not need to share all of their interests. The real problem of compatibility goes far deeper, and usually has little to do with what we typically think it does.

Getting Out Before It's Too Late

"Getting out before it's too late" may seem to be a brutally difficult statement to accept, and doing so is a difficult thing for young dating couples to bring themselves to do. The sad fact is that, all too often, new couples date and quickly begin a physical relationship way too early. They get hooked on the feelings that accompany intimate situations (sex) that frequently result in unexpected and, all too often, unwanted pregnancies.

The rush of feelings and chemistry skews their perspective in judging whether or not they should continue their relationship.

Once the golden-seal is broken on the intimate aspects of their relationship, then much more is invested by each person. When we give up our most intimate parts we don't like to lose our investment. This tends to be especially important to women. Because of our investment, we often carry on a highly incompatible relationship for the sake of our lustful feelings, rather than for true love. Doing so creates a marriage that will likely end in divorce. But even so, a willing couple can easily overcome a troubled marriage that was primarily based only upon lust if and when they truly open their eyes to see and respect each other.

People often wonder what the Biblical perspective on separation and divorce is. Biblically there's nothing saying that you cannot depart from parents, siblings, or friends, and it is important to do so if parents, siblings, or friends are dragging you down or are selfishly having a negative effect on you and your marriage family, but with a spouse it's different. Once you have had sex with that person, you have made a promise through inviting them in or entering in. Violating that promise is an offense against that person and against the Creator's purpose for the "sex" parts of our bodies. We are designed to create and be committed to our creation just like the Creator has been to us and all of creation.

Sometimes some couples voluntarily and peacefully separate. This doesn't violate the Biblical laws when the two people stay single and don't have sex with anyone except each other, but seldom is that the case. Having a peaceful separation is not specifically Biblically restricted, but connecting with another mate afterwards is prohibited, and it is specifically called adultery and is mentioned in both the Old and New Testaments. In the New Testament, it is the Christ who makes the statement that whoever divorces and remarries commits adultery. This is not so if your spouse first dies, and then you remarry. So what does someone who had a past marriage do now that it's too late because they already remarried? There is nothing that you can do to change the past, but your past can give value to your future by dedicating yourself to your current spouse and living a full and joyful life with them by choosing to not repeat your past errors.

Encouraging teenage children to engage in premarital sex is both foolish and reckless! Typically, when parents do encourage premarital sex, their reasons stem from their own bad mistakes and experiences. They want their children to "shop around" for the right mate. "Shopping around" is okay, especially if you're only reading the brochures, but the "shopping" should not at all include engaging in sex. I understand that this is not a popular view, but it has repeatedly proven to be very effective in lending to better judgment of your compatibility when selecting a mate. I'm not referring to the teaching of abstinence, but rather the actual respect and practice of abstinence.

If the dating period of a relationship cannot survive on conversation alone, then one or both of the people are headed down a painful path and the marriage will struggle in the long run. The sex part of a relationship is a gift and it should not be thought of as a given part of *dating*. Understanding this allows the relationship to be tested for compatibility while the couple gets to know one another better. The couple can have all the sex they want *after* they have decided that their compatibility is adequate for marriage and *after* they have actually married. If a person in a dating relationship refuses sexual activity and the refusal causes problems in the relationship then that could be a clear sign that the marriage will likely experience problems.

Is Your Mate Compatible?

Does this mean that if you married someone who no longer appears compatible, that all hope is lost?

No, but such incompatibility is cause for a bit more effort on the part of both people in the couple. Some people believe that there is only one person that is meant for each of us and we must find that one person. There are certainly people who swear by soul-mate compatibility, and good for them! If they found that one person who they blend so well with, then we should not take away from what they have, because it is a true gift!

I lean towards the belief that, while you might not be compatible with everyone, you certainly are able to be compatible with many—meaning that your choice of partners is not limited to only one person on earth in order to achieve marital bliss. There are many people who are compatible with you. Selecting any one of them can allow you to achieve marital bliss if you're both willing to do your own parts in the relationship. I believe we can have such harmony when we select *a* correct mate—and maybe even *the* correct mate.

Compatibility is misunderstood because we usually look at the semi-tangible areas of life, such as our likes and dislikes, or the things that we like to do. But compatibility is simpler and goes far deeper than that.

Do You Love Them or do You Love the Way You Feel?

Backing up a step, when a young couple begins dating it is best for them to understand the difference between loving their mate, and loving the way their mate makes them feel.

Enjoying the physical rush that accompanies sexual intimacy before marriage, skews the judgment between loving them, versus loving the way you feel while being intimate with them. If all couples would reserve the gift of that sexual rush of feelings for after marriage it would make their marriage commitment that much more special. After all, why pay for, *or commit* to, what you can get for free? Many people do not agree with this, and, as the free flow of premarital sexual intercourse becomes more common, it's harder to find a person who is not battle-torn and worn out from being driven around the block with too many test rides. Being able to openly discuss these things, as a couple, before you get too deeply into a relationship is very important, which is why going without sex before marriage is generally a very good idea.

If you have children, properly teach them about this method of judgment. And if they are old enough and it is appropriate, then explain to them that you made some errors and how you fixed the problems brought on by the errors.

It's clear and easy to understand that intimacy at too early a stage in the relationship skews our perspective and makes it more difficult to detect proper long-term compatibility. So, how do we detect compatibility? So far, the statisticians have not attempted this one—thank God for that! Each couple's circumstances are different, but you can start with a few key points to understand your compatibility.

How Do They Make You Better?

Begin by asking yourself these questions: Does this person improve me? Do they make me a better person? Do they build me up, or do they tear me down? Do they care about my health, or disregard it and encourage bad habits?

Do They Inspire You?

Next, look at their emotional effect on you. Do they inspire you, or do they mock your ways? Do they encourage you, or discourage you?

Are They as Invested in the Relationship as You Are?

Be careful with this one because men are often the pursuers in the early days of the relationship. Actually, all of these points are not meant for first dates, but rather are meant for after you begin to know one another a bit.

Frequently, one of the people in a relationship is more interested than the other. If this does not equalize, then one of them is likely headed for a great deal of pain. If a potential lifelong mate is not putting a similar amount of effort into the relationship, then it is an indication that future problems will likely occur and the other mate will greatly suffer in the lackluster marriage.

This door swings both ways. You may be the one putting in less effort and be very comfortable with your arrangement, but I assure you, this will not go well with your mate in the long run. It is a rare few people who are not bothered by a heavily imbalanced relationship.

Don't Be Unequally Yoked

It is recommended in the Bible that we do not become "unequally yoked" to other people. What does this very wise statement mean? When oxen or other cattle are connected or harnessed together for work, it is called "yoked." Being unequally yoked would be to take two oxen that are very different in strength, and then place them on the same yoke side by side. This causes an excessive imbalance in the force on the yoke causing the weaker oxen to fall and drag the stronger down with them. Or it will cause them to veer towards the weaker oxen, thus, causing them to constantly go off course, and possibly end up going endlessly in circles and never actually getting anywhere while repeating the same mistakes over and over.

While it is referring to a believer being yoked to an unbeliever, marriage in general can be looked at in the same way as being yoked together. If you choose a mate who is in a far different mental place than you are, and they continually fall, then they will likely drag you down with them unless you are strong enough to keep them on a straight path. But, it could be you who is doing the dragging down. If the same person in the couple is always picking the other person up, then special effort should be taken to correct that situation. In a good balanced marriage, the two people will pick each other up if either of them falls, and they won't drag each other down.

Choosing a mate who works *equally* with you is a good way to grow together. This doesn't mean that you must both understand all things exactly the same way, but rather, that your willingness to put forth effort to work together is closely matched. Failing to do so is why there is often a clash when two people of differing socioeconomic classes pair up. The parents of the wealthy kids might have issues with an imbalanced match because it is thought that the poorer mate will degrade or drag down their child. There is good reason for this phenomenon, and the reason is that this can often be the case. But in truth, socioeconomic classes have little to do with a couple's actual compatibility. Position or birth order in their families can have more bearing on compatibility than economic class does. But in the end, none of those factors are as important as both spouses putting in full effort and being honest with each other without fear of attack from the other spouse.

Facing the Brutal Facts

The cold hard facts are difficult for us to face. In young dating relationships, these facts are obscured by the rush of intimacy and the familiarity we feel with the person. When we overlook the cold hard facts and invest ourselves in a marriage that is not equally yoked or well-balanced, then we have made some serious decisions that will have lasting and often difficult long-term ramifications.

In a dating relationship, getting out before you get in too deep seems to hurt a great deal, but getting out early pays both of you great dividends in your futures. Getting into a bad marriage situation drags you down to some very dark and painful places that often end in divorce and in broken lives for one or both people. So while it's painful to lose the investment in a young and troubled relationship, losing the investment is usually the wisest move to make. We see this all the time in long-term dating when unhappy couples break up, where immediately after the breakup one or both of them very quickly find their bliss in another person. But this does not mean that you should break up the moment you have a disagreement.

Facing the Brutal Fact of a Troubled Marriage

The decision to break up (divorce) is more difficult once you're married, and it's even more difficult after you have had children. The fallout from getting divorced follows you and your children *until the day you die!* Divorcing is a serious decision and must always be the last resort, and it should not be taken lightly.

Having children outside of marriage is technically not as *legally* invested as it is when you have children and then decide to get married. But in reality, with regard to the actual relationship and emotions, it is the same as being married when you have children before or outside of marriage. It's even more complicated when the relationship is a troubled one. Even in unwed situations the couple *can* work it out to achieve bliss. The fact that someone doesn't hold a marriage license has little to do with the actual relationship, because all of the same things still apply. The intention of marriage and its ceremony is an outward and public oath that you are committing to each other. Being unwilling to make such a public commitment is very revealing about the person or people who are unwilling to do so. This is something that should be thoroughly discussed early on in any relationship.

What's in a Ring?

During this public marriage oath it is customary to exchange Gold rings. It has come to be understood by our culture that it is the ring that is important. This has gotten to a point where people spend tens of thousands of dollars on a worthless diamond engagement ring, and are so concerned about *how it looks*, rather than *what it means*. Please take notice that the engagement ring is the meaningless expensive part, but it is the relatively inexpensive simple Gold wedding bands that are important. Yet, it is not even the round band that is important, but rather, it is the fact that it is made of gold and what that gold symbolizes that is of significance. I would venture to say that people who understand and accept this are far less likely to ever get divorced than those who do not understand this. Not because they chose to get silver or some other meaningless metal, but rather because they took no care in *why* they do what they do. Gold was originally symbolic of something, but I will leave that up to you to discover together with your spouse. It will mean more if you figure it out on your own. The circular form of the ring is meaningless, but it is believed to represent "continuousness" due to the fact that a circle has no end. In truth, the ring shape is only there because it makes holding onto the Gold without losing it far easier to do.

Where Did You Start?

There are two primary types of bad relationships: The type that already started off poorly *when you got married*, and the type that slowly got worse *after you married*. Both types usually continue to get worse with time, but the kind that starts off good usually takes less effort to correct in the future. Either way, even if you feel that you chose an incompatible mate, I believe that both types of bad relationships can and should be corrected in the long-run provided that *you both* want things better in the relationship.

This is not addressing physically abusive and dangerous relationships here. The answer is pretty clear in those situations. If you happen to be in that type of relationship, then, whether you are a woman or a man, consider promptly seeking safe and wise counsel, because no one deserves to be hurt.

Young Relationships, and Family and Friends

Young relationships are often influenced by family and friends. With regard to your own relationship, it's okay, and often good, to get opinions from parents and peers, but use caution in whose opinion you seek. Bad judgment and bad opinions tend to go hand in hand. That is to say, if you regularly get bad advice, then you will likely make bad decisions. Be objective to the advice given to you, and *discern for yourself* as to whether it is appropriate for *your own* life, rather than depending on other people's opinions of their own advice.

Family and friends also have other effects on your relationship. The effects that I'm referring to here are with regard to the way we perceive ourselves (our *Hot Water*). When we're accustomed to a certain way of life, then that is the only way of life that we know. The impact of this can have horrifying effects on your relationship and it cannot be understated.

The differences in the micro-culture of each spouse's family often only show up years after the rings go on their fingers. When we're in the early stages of a dating relationship or a marriage, we allow our mates a great deal of slack and tolerance with regard to their behavior. The reason that we do this is because, in general, we like the way they make us feel. Another reason is because we are tolerant and kind, and we hope that the person will change.

People do change, but in making the assumption that we actually need to change how we ourselves behave, we must realize that—changing the way we are because of how we were brought up—is the most difficult thing for any one of us to see our way clear to doing. This is because we don't specifically realize we're handling things and behaving in a bad way—it just feels normal to us. It's difficult to correct something that we cannot see, or that we are not fully aware we are doing.

The Importance of Trusting Your Spouse's Decisions

If you or your mate do not trust the other's judgment, then you are headed for some serious wrangling in your future. Being second-guessed is not pleasant, even if you deserve it.

Why would someone deserve to be second guessed? Because of repeated error. When someone keeps making the same errors over and over, they have earned being second-guessed by their spouse. But being second-guessed doesn't feel good for that person, even though they brought it on themselves by not being able to be trusted with the issue at hand.

The real problem comes in when you repeatedly prove your worth with good judgment, but then you are unfairly second-guessed regardless. If your spouse does not trust your good and wise decisions, then you will experience conflict and pain in your relationship.

Does Your Spouse Refuse to Know Your Heart?

If your spouse does not, will not, or cannot know your heart, then you are headed for conflict. A spouse who is too preoccupied with him- or herself is going to inflict a great deal of pain on their mate.

You cannot know the heart of your spouse if you do not get to know them by asking them their thoughts and opinions while, at the same time, you are open to receive what they have to say. When doing so, you must be willing to completely hear what they have to say, even if you know it will sting a bit or if you feel that you won't necessarily agree with them.

Many people think they know their spouse, but never actually ask what their spouse wants or likes. They go about life thinking that all is well and give their spouse whatever they themselves feel that their spouse wants or needs, rather than finding out what their spouse actually wants or needs by actually asking them. This is very common in life in general, but in a marriage relationship it touches all areas, from decorating your home to what you want to do in the bedroom—you will never know if you don't ask! When you do ask, then, when they respond, don't comment negatively about what they say that they want or need. Many marriages suffer a great deal because of failure to ask as well as then actually listening. And when people do ask, rarely do they allow their spouse free expression of thoughts and desires without throwing negativity and disapproval back in their spouse's face. You don't have to agree with what your spouse says, but you can certainly be kind, loving, and diplomatic with your replies. Shock and horror as a response to the wants and needs of your spouse are not the way to respond them.

Their Friends Reveal Them

It is said that you can tell the measure of a man by the friends he keeps. Setting aside the innocence of youth, this is typically very true. If you or your spouse associates with people who are divorced, and those people encourage divorce every time you and your spouse have an argument, then you're headed for trouble!

When we're hurting, we have a tendency to stay close to those who are willing to hear our pain and feed our current passion. Having someone whispering discord and divorce into the ear of you or your spouse whenever troubles arise is not good! If you're dating and you have a relationship where you or your mate are associating with this type of negative people, then expect trouble as long as those associations are active. Who we are friends with reveals a great deal about who we are and who we think we are. If you find that your associations are bad, then you should immediately begin to change who you are, and then your associations will begin to change in the same way. Who or how we are is our own *choice.*

Gratitude

If your spouse is ungrateful of you and what you bring to the relationship, then first examine what you actually bring to the relationship, and make sure that you are doing your part and more.

If you find that you are doing your full part of the relationship, but you are still being taken for granted, then it is a good sign that some changes need to be made somewhere in the relationship. A poor relationship causes you a great deal of pain. Gratitude in a relationship must not be assumed, it must be shown. If it is not shown, then selfishness exists within the relationship and you should work to remedy the circumstances.

Strategizing is Bad

If your mate strategizes on how they can get their way, then they are attempting to manipulate you. When manipulation is a regular part of a relationship it is not easily removed. Make sure that you yourself are not using manipulation in your relationship.

Often, people who manipulate grew up in a manipulative environment, and manipulation is the only way they know how to accomplish their desires. We could say, "They can't help it"; and while this may be true, it is not any less painful for you or your spouse as the manipulation continues.

Ending a manipulative relationship while dating, *before* getting married and having children, is a good choice. If you are already married or have children, you need to eradicate the manipulation problem in order to achieve your own long-term joy. In a marriage filled with manipulation, neither spouse can be truly happy even if only one spouse is doing the manipulating to always get their way. Manipulative people generally know what they are doing, and they don't feel good about themselves due to the fact that they manipulate others, only serving to put further strain on the relationship.

Don't be Hasty

Moving into a wrong relationship can cost you a great deal of pain. If you marry a person that you're not compatible with, it will cost you dearly all of your remaining days unless you are both aware and work together to create harmony in your relationship. However, if you patiently wait and find your compatible mate, who you can grow and learn with, then the wait will only cost you a little time and will pay you great dividends all of your remaining days.

It's different if you are already married. If you are already married you should not be hasty in terminating your relationship. Married people have a great deal to gain or lose in making a good or a wrong decision. Divorce is bitter and costly, and it typically follows you the rest of your life, which is especially true when children are involved.

Divorce typically involves an ex-spouse's new mate trying to be the parent to your child. At a minimum, this affects you until your children are on out their own, and usually far beyond that point. Both people putting adequate effort into your classic marriage to restore it to a beautiful, like-new condition is always the best option.

Signs of Problems

The cause of the trouble signs that are displayed by you or your spouse are hidden beneath layers of tit-for-tat, so be cautious in your judgments of each other's signs. You could be the cause of your signs and your spouse's signs, or your spouse might be the cause of yours, or maybe it's both of you creating the problems you face and the hurts you're feeling.

These signs might include drinking and drugs, working long hours, infidelity, depression, anger, constant frustration and even weight gain, and many more displeasing signs and behaviors. These signs are much like the warning lights on the instrument panel in your car. When the warning light goes on, you had better stop and give your car the needed and proper attention and care, or else be prepared for catastrophic failure. At times, these signs are deliberately done as revenge, but more often, they are done as an attempt at relief from the pain felt by the person who is exhibiting the signs.

It is seldom fully understood by the person who is exhibiting these signs that things are overheating. The fact that this is seldom known or understood is due to the person's undetected and unseen pain and frustration that is only shown by the warning signals. This is not excusing the behaviors or actions, but rather explaining *why* they occur, and that we should pay attention to the signs and take action based upon them. If your car's "Hot" engine warning-light is on, you take action by letting the car cool down before you drive it again. Use that same logic in your marriage and fix the problem that is causing the warning signs.

Compatibility in picking companions is wrapped up in all the sections in this chapter. If only we would properly teach these things to our children then the divorce rate would be almost zero in a single generation. Regularly look for signs of problems in your relationship and promptly take care of them *preemptively*. We typically do this with our cars and homes, but we fail to do so in our relationships when instead we should be even more vigilant with our more precious and impactful marriage.

Chapter 5

Marital Expectancy and Restoration

This chapter is where we begin getting into restoring your marriage. The pain we feel that was discussed at the end of the last chapter has a great deal to do with *marital expectancy*.

"Marital expectancy" is a very common set of expectations that accompany getting married. To better understand the term, we can refer to these *expectancies* as marital *assumptions*. Each spouse assumes that things will be a certain way when they get married. A good number of people would not have married their spouse if they had not made the assumptions about their spouse that they did when they decided to wed.

From a statistical perspective, we generalize and assume that a "failed" marriage is one that ended in divorce. While, in general, this is true, it is also true that there are many marriages that last until "death do us part" but are, or were, very painful for one or both of the spouses.

People who have deep religious beliefs do not like the thought of divorce; and to their credit, they are longsuffering with their efforts at kindness and tolerance. But, if they have a troubled marriage, then they still bear the pain felt in their relationship for what they feel was a "greater good" in staying together. When I say, "to their credit" I refer to their dedication to toughing it out to the end. However, at the same time, it's a sad testament to humanity, that people would be together so long and not experience the joy that we are all here for and which we all desire and deserve to experience.

Expectation is Natural and Proper

Expectation is an inherent part of humanity and without it life would stagnate. Expectation is the fuel that runs the world.

If we did not expect our car to bring us from point A to point B, then it is unlikely we would ever even get in it to attempt the drive. In fact, from the very moment you wake up in the morning you're filled with expectation. If you did not expect a surface beneath your feet, then it's unlikely you would place your feet on the floor when getting out of bed.

These fundamental expectations are set in place by our past experiences in life. We simply could not function without expectation. Expectation begins in the womb. Expectation is the prime cause of all things *creative* and *destructive*—that is to say *good* and *bad*.

People who are less active and do not achieve much, are that way because they have an expectation that either they will be stopped, or they simply have not been taught to expect much. Thus, they live their lives with low expectancy and then get what they expect or assume. In this way we are all largely the maker of our own futures.

Expectation in a relationship is no different. Expectation can be connected to the word "hope" in the way most people understand these two terms *hope* and *expectation*. Hope is positive expectation, but hope even goes a bit beyond that. Hope creates! Hope looks beyond expectation and enables us to see what can be, rather than what is. *What is*—is often our expectation, and often it is our expectation of bad behavior, but *what can be* is our hope!

Sadly, many people's hope is set only on what should be, and their hope has become nothing more than a mere expectation—an expectation that is often violated by their spouse. Always remember what you just read about *hope* and *expectation*.

Violations of expectation might seem to be a peculiar thing to be discussing in this way in the context of marriage. But consider the purpose of a business contract, in doing so you can see things more clearly without the emotional noise of a troubled relationship. Contracts are written because of expectation-violation. If people always did and expected what was agreed upon, then there would never be a need for a contract. It is because we frequently violate the expectations of others and/or expect more than we agreed to that these well-documented legal agreements are drafted. When contractual expectations are not adhered to, then the person whose expectation was violated has legal recourse in having that violation corrected or compensated for with the support of the legal system.

So how does this pertain to a marriage? Expectation in a marriage is the single most important reason that the couple married to begin with. If you expected a miserable and painful mountain of troubles before you got married, then would you have married? Not likely.

Since you committed to reading this entire book and have acknowledged that you want to be *true* rather than *right*, honesty and truth are what you seek and you understand that truth can be painful when you are on the wrong side of it.

Women and Men Kill Expectation

When couples begin dating, everything is typically very pleasant. If things were not pleasant, it is unlikely that there would have been subsequent dates, and as a result, the relationship would have promptly ended.

The reason that things are pleasant in the early days of dating and courtship is because *both* people have much hope or positive expectancy. Another reason is because our expectations of each other are typically being satisfied during that blissful period. As long as these two crucial requirements are being met, life will be very blissful for the couple.

Since this book is about making marriages better, we will advance to marriage and discuss marriage expectations and marriage hopes. Bluntly stated, women often kill expectation and then want to be served as royalty. Hang on ladies, there is another side to this story, but for now bear with and understand what you may be doing to harm your own marriage, and keep in mind that for some readers the situation will be opposite, where the husband is the offender.

Expectation plays an enormous role in marriages. If a wife tells her husband "No!" all the time, then she cannot expect him to be excited to do things for her, or to be excited to be with her. Eventually a wife's rejections of her husband's hopes and expectations, whether sexual or otherwise, are going to weigh too heavily on him. A wife's constant rejections slowly put out the flame of passion which her husband had towards her.

Similarly, if a husband continually fails to fulfill his wife's needs emotionally or around the house, then is it realistic for him to expect her to want to say "yes" to him? Not likely.

Hope and expectation are what life is all about. There is more depth to hope and expectation that will be discussed in later chapters. This "*hope* and *expectation*" issue is the unseen issue in the tumultuous veil of frustration in all relationships that are experiencing troubles.

Most people are unable to set aside their frustration long enough to think clearly about what's wrong in their relationship. In fact, most people don't understand that their frustration exists to begin with; and, obscuring the real source even more, the frustration is manifested in many different ways. A frustrated person will not necessarily display their frustration by acting in a way we typically see or think of as "frustrated."

Being Received

Marital *hope* and *expectancy* are key elements to having a great marriage, but it's a two-way street, or a door that swings both ways. What is the expectation that is so very important to us? What is the hope?

They are one and the same thing, and it is to be accepted and received by your mate. This is where the primary violation occurs. In fact, all other violations can be traced back to this one single violation. It is important to make your spouse feel wanted and desired.

Acceptance and *reception* are reasonable expectations by both spouses and are the hope of both spouses as well. *Hope* and *expectation* are what created the excitement for both of you when you first met. When hope and expectation get lost or badly damaged, then a relationship is in peril and you will need to restore them if you ever hope to regain a joyous relationship.

So how do problems happen to begin with? There are many reasons, but the tit-for-tat effect seems to be the most prominent. The part that's difficult and is the reason marriages often end badly, or painfully continue, is because we usually do not see through the "veil of frustration". *Being received* turns into *being rejected* after years, or even only months, of tit-for-tat.

A Broken Contract

Stereotypically, women break the expectation contract first, but they are not alone. Some men wrongly prefer their friends or sports, etc... over their spouse. Whether husband or wife, preferring anything over your spouse will end badly for you; and preferring other company or feeling that way is a clear indication that something urgently needs to be remedied in your relationship. Take the following examples into consideration. Each example has its own set of circumstances. Do any of these fit your life?

In the following examples of *The Shopkeeper and the Woman*, the customer is a lovely woman—she is the buyer or receiver. And a handsome man is the shopkeeper and is offering his goods—he is the seller. Each of these six versions is absolutely valid and could easily occur in life. All of our examples are of a male shopkeeper and a female customer.

The following stories of *The Shopkeeper and the Woman* put a non-romantic perspective on their relationship, thus allowing a clearer view of what is actually occurring in a relationship. Pay close attention to these six similar short stories, they have important differences that are critical to your relationship. They are written to be read independently from each other. Find the story that you feel best fits your situation and mark it. And then find the story that you feel your spouse would choose as the best fit and mark it. The rest of the stories do not matter to you. Take a moment to pause and then re-read your story and re-read your spouse's story.

The Shopkeeper and the Woman - Version 1

A shopkeeper who owns a small store has many good products to offer to his customers. He has a regular customer who is a lovely woman who happily purchases his fresh, quality goods. At the end of any one day they are both very pleased with the transaction, and both of them go their way completely satisfied.

One day, the woman was not in a good way and was feeling out of sorts. She came into the shopkeeper's store and decided that she did not want to purchase anything. The shopkeeper was perplexed because, up until this point, she had always been excited for and had need of his goods. He always gave her special deals and special care.

Being the understanding man that he is, he didn't give it much more thought, and his hopes went back to the lovely lady gracing his store with her presence on another day. The next day she came back and began to complain about his fresh, quality products and decided that she was unhappy with a product on the shopkeeper's shelf. The shopkeeper respected this lovely customer and immediately worked to accommodate all of her needs.

Now, over the course of months his lovely customer regularly returned to his store. Some days she was perfectly satisfied. It was these days that kept the shopkeeper excited with expectation and hope. However, some of the days the woman would come in and do nothing but complain and reject the quality goods on his shelves. She would frequently complain about what he had to offer.

This discouraged the shopkeeper from wanting to please this customer. Over time, he slowly stopped catering to the woman's needs. He didn't fully realize that his interest in his lovely customer had vanished, or that he no longer desired to have the woman as his favored customer. In fact, as time went on, the shopkeeper became frustrated with the woman and would go to work in the storage room whenever the woman came into his store.

The shopkeeper hid away in the back room so that he would not have to listen to her complaints and have her needlessly reject his quality goods. Both the shopkeeper and the woman had come to expect things to go poorly. The shopkeeper had become exhausted from the woman's constant rejecting of, and complaining about, his goods. He eventually asked her to find a different store and a different shopkeeper to bother, and requested that she never come back.

The woman sought out another store to fulfill her needs and all was well—at first. But, eventually, she repeated all of her behaviors and the same thing happened to her at the new shop. Eventually, her new shopkeeper also asked her to never come back. The only difference was that this shopkeeper was not as longsuffering as the first shopkeeper was, and he threw the woman out much earlier than the first shopkeeper did.

This happened repeatedly to this woman because she repeated her behavior at each shop. She had become so accustomed to the shopkeepers' desire to make her happy that she neglected being a kind and courteous customer. She became bitter towards all shopkeepers because they rejected her behavior.

With each shopkeeper, she had the expectation that she would always be appreciated as a valued customer, but disregarded her own behavior as a customer. This was her blind spot and her downfall, and it was unwelcome by all of the shopkeepers.

The Shopkeeper and the Woman - Version 2
In this version of our story things are a bit reversed.

A shopkeeper in a small community had a lovely woman customer who was a very faithful customer and always came in and bought his goods. She was so pleased with what the shopkeeper had to offer that she continued as a faithful customer for over a decade.

Now, the shopkeeper, being a man who feels the need to keep his profits high, decided to increase his profits by lowering the quality standards of what he had to offer. Since the woman had been coming in for decades, he made an unconscious assumption that she would always come to *his* store.

He began to make adjustments for rising costs so that his profits remained high; he did this by buying lower quality product to keep on his shelves. Because he did this, his goods were no longer of the same high quality that they previously had been. As he slowly reduced the quality of his goods, the woman's desire for his goods dropped.

Since what he had to offer was not of the same high quality that the lovely woman had come to expect, the things that she used his goods for were left wanting. This took away the lovely woman's desire to use his goods to fulfill all of her needs.

Now, since his goods were no longer of the same high quality that they used to be, her work with his goods reflected the quality and she began to lose interest in the tasks she used his goods for; and thus, her needs dropped considerably. Because her needs for the shopkeeper's goods dropped, there was not enough demand and the goods on his shelves became sour, which made his goods even less desirable to the woman.

The lovely woman faithfully continued buying her goods from his shop for another five years. In each of the five years the quality and freshness of what the shopkeeper had to offer her grew worse and worse.

One winter day, the woman had a very special occasion to prepare for. She got dressed up in her finest dress and went out to have her hair and makeup done for the special occasion. When it was nearing the time for her guests to arrive, she realized that she was missing some important items and the lovely woman had to make a trip to the nearest store for the needed goods.

As she approached the shopkeeper's store where she had done all of her shopping for so many years, she thought to herself, "This is a very special occasion and I want everything to be perfect. The goods where I normally shop are not as good as they used to be. So, I'll go to another shop a little further away to have my needs fulfilled with fresh quality goods—it will be worth the extra drive!"

When this lovely woman entered the next shopkeeper's store, she found a cheery and bright atmosphere with a friendly, handsome shopkeeper whose shelves were full of fresh, quality new product. The new shopkeeper greeted the lovely woman with much enthusiasm and welcomed her into his store. He showed her all of the quality goods that he had to offer her. The lovely woman was very pleased. She told the new shopkeeper that she may come visit his store more often; to which the shopkeeper replied, "I would very much appreciate that Miss. In fact, such a lovely customer as yourself would get treated very kindly and have other special advantages if you were to do all of your shopping in my store. I can supply all of the goods to fulfill all of your needs and I will do what I can to kindly service you! I will also give you a special discount if you do all of your shopping here."

From that day forward, the lovely woman found a new place to have her need for goods fulfilled. She forged a long and wonderful relationship with the new shopkeeper. She never returned to the other shopkeeper's store because he no longer was willing to fulfill her needs with quality goods.

The Shopkeeper and the Woman - Version 3

In a small general store in a tiny village, there was a very handsome and kind shopkeeper. This shopkeeper took much care in keeping his product fresh and making certain that all the goods he sold were of the highest quality.

One pleasant summer day, a lovely young woman came into his store and was very pleased with his goods. They were very good, indeed! The woman became a favored customer to the shopkeeper, and he enjoyed her company in his store.

After some time, he gave her special attention and offered her regular discounts because she was a very faithful customer. For years she had come into his store, and every time that she came in, the shopkeeper was excited to see her and he would joyfully greet her. He was always excited and hoped she would visit again, and he would do whatever he could to fulfill her needs.

The woman became very accustomed to his greetings and his kindness. Eventually she became so familiar with him that she no longer even noticed his eagerness to please her. Eventually the woman became complacent and no longer paid any attention to the shopkeeper, often ignoring him completely. The woman was not fully aware that she was doing this, so it continued for a long time.

Now, because the woman no longer noticed him, the shopkeeper was no longer able to offer his kindness to the woman and he began to lose interest in her as a customer. This went on for many years between the woman and the shopkeeper. He would greet the woman and she would barely notice him.

One beautiful fall day another stunning young woman came into his store. She was even more beautiful than the first woman. When the shopkeeper saw her, he hurried over to greet her with the same enthusiasm that he used to greet the first woman with. This second woman and the shopkeeper talked for a while, and then he gave her a tour of his store and showed her all of his quality goods. He explained how important he felt that it was to offer her the best quality that he possibly could so that she would want to come back repeatedly. The second woman purchased her goods that day and left.

On her next visit to his store, the second lovely woman told the handsome shopkeeper how pleased she was with his goods and how fine his quality was. He offered her special care and a special discount if she would do all of her shopping at his store. She agreed! In fact, her needs for his goods were even greater than the first woman's needs were.

Eventually the first woman noticed that the shopkeeper no longer paid her as much attention, but it was too late because the shopkeeper found a much lovelier customer whose need for his goods was far greater, and she always appreciated his warm greeting and the high quality goods he had to offer her.

The shopkeeper was quite pleased to fulfill the second woman's need for quality goods, and he joyfully fulfilled the needs of the second woman for the rest of his life.

The Shopkeeper and the Woman - Version 4

A shopkeeper in a small store had many good things to offer. He had a regular customer who was a very lovely woman who happily purchased his fresh, quality goods. At the end of any day they were both very pleased with their transaction and completely satisfied!

Now, one day the woman was not in a good way and was feeling out of sorts. She came in to the shopkeeper's store and decided that she did not want to purchase anything. The shopkeeper was perplexed because she had, up until this point, always been excited to utilize his services, and he always gave her special discounts. Being the understanding man that he was, he didn't give it much thought, and his hopes went back to the lovely lady gracing his store with her presence.

The next day she came back to his store and began to complain about his fresh, quality products, and decided that she was unhappy with a product on the shopkeeper's shelf. The shopkeeper respected his lovely lady customer and immediately worked to accommodate her needs.

Now, over the course of months, this lovely customer regularly returned to his store. Some days she was perfectly satisfied, and it was these days that kept the shopkeeper excited with hope and expectation! However, some of the days the woman would come in and do nothing but complain and reject the goods on his shelves. She would frequently complain about what he had to offer. This discouraged the shopkeeper from wanting to please this customer. And, over time, he slowly stopped catering to the woman's needs. He did not fully realize that his interest in his lovely customer had vanished. This was because he had slowly, over time, come to expect her negative tone and slowly his hope about her was lost.

He no longer desired to have the woman as his favored customer. In fact, as time went on, the shopkeeper became frustrated with the woman and would go to work in the back storage room whenever the woman came into his shop. He did this so that he would not have to listen to her complaints and hear her reject his quality goods.

Because they are from a very small community with only a few people, when the woman no longer bought as much, the shopkeeper's goods become outdated and bitter, and this caused the woman to complain even more. Both the shopkeeper and the woman had come to expect things to go poorly. The woman continued to frequent the store, but the shopkeeper would take refuge from the woman in his private storage room in the back of the store whenever the woman came in.

The woman's visits would change his disposition, and he did not like the way he felt when she came into his store. He continued to hide away whenever she came in to the store, and this made him feel even more badly. He was longsuffering and felt a sense of obligation to supply the woman's needs because she was a long-term and faithful customer who always came back. But every time she visited his store, she made it unpleasant for the shopkeeper. While he continued to bear with her unpleasant nature and complaining, he did not look forward to it.

For many years they each did the minimum to fulfill their own end of the transactions. She bought as little as she could and complained about it, while he would hide whenever he could to avoid her company. When he was forced to service her needs he would take her money for the goods and send her on her way with not so much as a, "Good day Miss." The shopkeeper longed for the day that he or the woman would retire and they would no longer have a need to see one another.

The Shopkeeper and the Woman - Version 5

A shopkeeper in a small community had a lovely woman customer who was a very faithful customer and always came in to buy his goods. She was so pleased with what the shopkeeper had to offer that she continued this for over a decade.

Now, the shopkeeper, being a man who felt the need to keep his profits high in order to run a successful shop, had decided to increase profits by lowering the quality standards of the goods he had to offer. Since the woman had been coming in for decades, he made an assumption, without realizing it, that she would always come to his store.

In an effort to keep his profits high, the shopkeeper began to make adjustments for inflation by buying lower-quality product to keep on his shelves. Now his goods were no longer of the same high quality that they previously had been. When he did this, the woman's desire for his products was greatly reduced.

Because what the shopkeeper now had to offer was no longer of the same high quality that the lovely woman had come to expect, the things that she used his goods for were lacking. This took away the lovely woman's desire to use his goods to fulfill her needs.

Since the woman's work with his goods was no longer what it had previously been, she began to lose interest in the tasks that she had used his goods for, and thus, her needs dropped considerably. Because her needs for the shopkeeper's goods had dropped, there was little demand for his goods. This caused the goods on his shelves to begin to expire and become bitter, making them even less desirable to her. But still, the lovely woman came faithfully into his shop to fulfill her needs.

With his sales lower, the shopkeeper's profits were also left wanting. Whenever this happened the shopkeeper tried to make adjustments so that he could continue to profit. Eventually, the woman's purchases dropped to a bare minimum and she reluctantly fulfilled her needs at the shopkeeper's store.

The woman came to dislike visiting the store, but continued to do so because it was convenient for her. Most of her shopping experiences were filled with much disappointment. This disappointment was taken wrongly by the savvy shopkeeper, and he began to lose interest and paid no attention to the woman.

She anticipated it as a good day when she no longer would have the need to shop in the shopkeeper's store. The dismal association of the shopkeeper and the lovely woman continued for the remainder of their lives.

The Shopkeeper and the Woman - Version 6

The final version.

A shopkeeper in a small community had a lovely woman customer. She was a very faithful customer and always came in and bought his goods. She was so pleased with what the shopkeeper had to offer that she continued this for over a decade.

Now, the shopkeeper, being a man who feels the need to keep his profits high, decided to increase profits by lowering the quality standards of the goods he had to offer to his lovely customer. Since the woman had been a dependable customer for a long time, the shopkeeper made an unconscious assumption that the lovely woman would always come back to his store.

As time progressed, he began to make adjustments for his changing costs so that he could keep his profits high. He began buying lower quality goods to keep on his shelves. This caused his goods to no longer be of the same high quality that they had previously been.

Slowly, the woman's desire for his goods dropped. This was because what he had to offer was not of the same high quality that the lovely woman had come to expect. The things that she used his goods for were now lacking because of the low quality goods he sold to her. This took away the lovely woman's desire to use his goods to fulfill her needs.

Since her work with his goods was no longer what it used to be due to the lowered quality, she began to lose interest in the tasks she had used his goods for; and this caused her needs for his goods to drop considerably.

Because her needs for his goods dropped, the shopkeeper's goods on his shelves began to expire because there was not enough demand for them. This made his goods even less desirable to the woman. Yet the lovely woman came into his shop faithfully for another five years. In each of the five years the quality and freshness of what the shopkeeper had to offer her got worse and worse.

The lovely woman politely commented on her concerns with regard to the poor quality of his goods, but nothing she said or did seemed to make any difference to the shopkeeper. Eventually, the lovely woman decided that she would no longer have any need for the shopkeeper's goods and she stopped shopping at his store altogether.

This ends the six versions of *The Shopkeeper and the Woman*. As stated at the beginning of this section: The stories of *The Shopkeeper and the Woman* put a non-romantic perspective on their relationship, thus allowing a clearer view of what is actually occurring in their relationship. Few, if any, couples are not in one or more of these examples. And only two examples turn into commercial bliss for the shopkeeper and a second woman.

Remember, the purpose of this section is for you to find the stories that best fit your current view and your spouse's current view of your relationship. Re-read those two stories a couple of times as you really think them through while reading this book.

Scratch That Itch and Hit The Spot!

In the various different versions of the story of *The Shopkeeper and the Woman*, we have seen the ways in which the interactions between them changed because of each of their own actions. Each of these simplistic scenarios is a realistic, viable possibility between a male shopkeeper and a female customer. It is up to you to decide what you feel would be a good or bad way for each of them to react.

Your thoughts or responses to these stories tells a great deal about you, the way you were bought up, and about why you have come into the situation that you now are in with your marriage relationship.

Meeting the needs of those around us seems to be a simple task. For instance, in a prominently known marital complaint, the wife should simply have sex with her husband more often. In some cases this may rekindle the fire in the relationship and then their needs would be satisfied, but this often falls short. Typically, when a spouse concedes to more sex it still leaves their mate *wanting*. Why is this?

Did you ever have an itch on that one spot of your back that you can't quite seem to reach? Most of us have had that problem at some point in life. We will often ask our spouse to scratch that evasive spot. And when our spouse hits the spot, then it's almost euphoric! But if they keep missing it, then it's torturous.

"To the left. No, not that far. No, more to the right."

"Whose right? My right or yours?"

"Up a little. No, not that much. Down a little..."

They never seem to be able to hit the spot. The itch is never fully satisfied! The person scratching is doing the right thing, but they are doing it incorrectly, thus leaving their spouse wanting.

Often when we offer something to our spouse, we want them to take things the way we offer it to them, and that's that! After all, *we are offering* to do something *for them*, so then they should take what they were offered... Right? This sort of thinking is dangerous, and in the long-run it will always lead to great disappointment for both spouses.

Since most everyone is familiar a car, I will use a car as a clear example of this problem. Let's say that your car needs a filter and oil change, so you bring it in to the garage to have the work done. The service mechanic drains the old oil out, and then changes the filter and puts in new oil.

The mechanic did everything *exactly* as you asked them to. They changed your oil and filter, and you paid them for their service—a done deal! Right? You drive away only to find that a couple of days later, your engine's oil light goes on because it's low on oil. Upon further investigation, you find that the type of oil used in the oil change was not engine oil. This caused your engine to use oil very quickly in a way that it should not, and now you're unhappy. Yet, the mechanic did everything that you had asked them to do.

Doing only the things that are asked of you is not a guarantee of satisfying the other person. Similar to missing the spot when scratching an itch, the mechanic clearly got something wrong and it caused problems with your car.

We expect the people who service our car to understand our full needs and use the proper oil when they change the oil in our engine. We also expect someone to hit the spot when we ask them to scratch that impossible to reach itch. This reciprocal expectation and the following proper fulfillment of that expectation are paramount to a great relationship! When this breaks down, then troubles *will* creep into your marriage.

The problem that we face in our quest to "hit the spot" when we "scratch that itch" is in finding the spot. The problem with finding the spot is that we are often too preoccupied to begin with, to notice that we are missing their spot. We must come to understand exactly what that spot is for our mate. In the next chapter we begin exploring those "spots" that we keep missing.

When marital expectancy and marital hope are shattered by repeatedly missing the spot, then several basic scenarios will occur, and each of them in varying degrees.

Depending upon each person's upbringing and tolerance level, the following basic scenarios will occur:

Our first scenario of divorce is the chosen method in about half of all marriages.

Our second scenario occurs when tolerance runs high and your upbringing was similarly tolerant, then people often slump into complacency and suffer a lackluster marriage that just seems to survive as it mires through the muck. And neither spouse experiences much joy if they experience any at all.

The last scenario is that of infidelity. Infidelity can be a very confusing and painful situation for both spouses, but it occurs because we fail to address and deal with our spouse's "spot".

Summing Up Expectancy and Hope

Expectancy and *hope* are inherent in our nature, and men have different expectancies than women, and women have different expectancies than men. Most of those expectancies are founded upon our physical designs, which are founded upon what we are modeled after. Women are built to receive and men are built to offer. That undeniable fact is built into our physical structure. Reserve all of your conclusions until you complete this book because the conclusions are likely not what you might be expecting at this point.

I do believe that women can do most anything that men can do, and that men can do most anything that women can do. But there is a simple truth, which is: men and women by and large do not want to do the tasks that seem to come with the territory of the opposite gender. If we all did want that, then the roles would be reversed overnight.

The subtleties of marital expectancy go undetected by most people all during our lives. This is because most of us don't spend our time wondering why things are the way they are. The world typically has its way with us and buries us in tasks that distract us from better understanding our personal relationships. This makes our awareness mostly nonexistent. Often, we only become aware that there is a problem after it's too late, and then seldom do we become fully aware of what the true problem actually was or is. If we all became aware of what the true problem was, then divorce would be nonexistent.

Chapter 6

Prelude to Rejection

When discussing relationships it is important for the person who is falling short in the relationship exchange to understand a few things.

When the other person in an imbalanced relationship receives no rewards or joy for their actions in regard to their spouse, then there is little incentive for that person to continue offering the actions or services in the long-run. With the understanding that marriage is not a business, you could think of this in terms of doing business with a company who will not pay you for your services; at some point you will refuse to offer your services to them any longer because you cannot afford to because they do not do their part to pay you.

Imbalanced exchange is not a very good way to function in a romantic relationship, and it's painful for the person who is being shorted. The business comparison is somewhat up to the perception and purpose of the person being shorted in the relationship. If the person is not doing things solely with the expectation that their spouse must return the favor for fairness, then it changes the comparison greatly, and is no longer a business-like relationship. In this case, the person is being shorted in the free exchange of heart and action. It hurts a great deal for the person being shorted. But, being shorted in the free exchange of heart and action is not the biggest problem in most relationships.

In an imbalanced relationship it is common that there is also *penalty* involved rather than only the other person's failure to do their reasonably expected part. When a person strives to share of themselves with their spouse or to share in a part of their spouse, then the heart of that person who desires to share is easily violated by the offending spouse. In many relationships, this is most notoriously experienced in the somewhat higher sexual desires of only one spouse in the relationship, and is a prominent area that we frequently see portrayed as the primary subject in many movies. An important part of any relationship is to make sure that you are not making your spouse feel unwanted and undesired.

By *"penalty"* I'm referring to the fact that when the person wants to share of themselves, or share in their spouse, that there is a heavy cost of condemnation or ridicule to the person who wants to share. What often occurs is that the person will make an attempt to share themselves with, or share-in, their spouse, but then they find themselves being the victim of accusations, rejection, and hostility and often are berated by their spouse for even thinking such thoughts. This is most notably reflected in the above mentioned entertainment where they jest with the general message of "All you ever want is sex." While it appears that the person who is wanting to share is only fixated on sex, they feel the pain of rejection and mockery nonetheless. When speaking of sex, fixation is a common and a fair complaint given by the rejecting spouse, however, while the rejecting spouse may have a legitimate complaint, the rejection of sexual-advances often reflects the overall relationship. In other words, if it is done with the sex part of a relationship, then it is most likely done in many or most other areas of the relationship as well.

When a person feels rejected, then that rejection is a severe penalty to them. There are times where the rejection fits the crime, however, more often than not, the rejection is unfounded, selfish, and cruel. If a person is helping a friend just because they want to help a friend and the friend mocks them for no reason, and tells them to go away, then the person will likely do so and find a new friend or assist another existing friend who will not treat them that way. When hearing this we might think, "why would a so called 'friend' do this when someone is helping them?" That's exactly the point, why would they do that? This is what occurs in most troubled relationships: one person offers, and the other person rejects. In many cases, the person who is doing the rejecting thinks that they are in control of the relationship, and the person who is offended mistakenly *also* thinks that the other person is in control. However, the reality is reverse; the person who has control of the relationship is the one who is bearing the burden of rejection. This is because that person is trying to endure because they are hoping that their oblivious spouse will eventually change and, at some point, actually have the same or similar desire to please each other.

Every person has a different level of tolerance for this sort of behavioral rejection, and if they don't settle into long-term mundane dissatisfaction, which typically includes frequent arguments, then eventually, they will leave the rejecting spouse to find acceptance elsewhere for what they seek to offer to someone. And if they don't leave, they might find another means of acceptance elsewhere while at the same time staying in the relationship; but in many ways when that's the case they have, in heart, already left their spouse.

When a person is negatively conditioned long enough in this sort of situation, they either leave, or learn to ignore. Most people have heard of the famous "Pavlov's dogs experiment" where Pavlov fed the dogs and rang a bell. Pavlov quickly got the dogs to salivate in anticipation of being allowed to eat the food that awaited them. After changing the order of things in the training of the dogs, Pavlov would ring the bell first and then the dogs began to associate the ring of a bell with being fed and would begin to salivate at the mere sound of the bell. The dogs had the ultimate assumption that they would be receiving food, which is made evident by the fact that they salivated at the sound of a bell. Rejection in a relationship is no different, though is it reverse in incentive. When a person is rejected long enough, they eventually learn or become conditioned to not do anything at all. It may seem advantageous to one spouse to be in the perceived power position as they continually reject their mate, but eventually they will no longer be sought after by their mate, and as often occurs, their mate will seek the desired type of companionship elsewhere.

Depending upon who you are in this scenario, you might think that it is wrong for the person to reject you or you may feel like it is wrong that your spouse decided to seek affection elsewhere. But regardless of what you think or what you want, the underlying truth of this cannot be avoided. In this case, the burden of correcting the problem is in the hands of the person who is doing the rejecting. The person who is seeking and desires sharing and companionship cannot control the rejecting spouse without manipulating them, and thus they might choose to seek satisfaction with someone who they do not have to pay a penalty to when making an attempt to share *with and in* them physically or emotionally. Our hurts, pains, emotions, and how we feel about this will not change the reality of it occurring in our own relationship when we repeatedly reject our spouse's desire to share with or in us.

Rejection and expectancy go hand-in-hand and cannot be separated. It is the *"what we expect"* part that determines the amount of pain felt in rejection, and in many instances, our particular expectation is the factor that makes an action feel like rejection even if it was not intended so.

What we expect in our relationship is each our own personal vision of our marriage. Our vision is made up of what we *want* and what we *hope* the other person will do to, with, and for us.

In the previous chapter, we read six different versions of *The Shopkeeper and the Woman*. In each of these common troubled relationship situations there were offerings and rejections. In the simplest sense, we see that the shopkeeper offered his goods to the woman and she either accepted or rejected those goods, but there is a twist to rejection that few of us ever notice. These veiled rejections are particularly difficult for us to put our finger on in order to be able to point out and define the actual problem.

There's a big difference between *wanting* someone to touch you versus *allowing* someone to touch you. And there's a big difference between wanting someone to succeed because you want the fruits of their success, versus wanting someone to succeed because you believe in them and what they do.

Rating a Marriage

To better understand rejection in a marriage let's break things down by rating marriages. Relationships can't specifically be quantified, so rating a marriage can be a misnomer, but doing this paints a clearer picture for you by simplifying and placing marriage scenarios into a short set of commonalities. There are two views of the same rating: The view from the *husband's* perspective, and the view of the *wife's* perspective.

Husband's rating view

Marital Bliss: He offers - She wants him to offer and she accepts
Good Marriage: He offers - She accepts
Surviving Marriage: He offers - She reluctantly accepts
Unhappy Marriage: He offers - She declines
Poor Marriage: He offers and begs her to accept - She declines
Downright unpleasant: He doesn't offer - She won't accept

Wife's rating view

Marital Bliss: She wants to accept and does - He wants to offer
Good Marriage: She accepts - He offers
Surviving Marriage: She reluctantly accepts -He pushes
Unhappy Marriage: She says leave me alone - He pushes
Poor Marriage: She says he never leaves me alone - He begs her to accept
Downright unpleasant: She says leave me alone - He won't offer

Remember, there is a big difference between *someone allowing you* to do something, versus *someone wanting you* to do something. Both of these rating charts are related to the stereotypical view of marriage needs in a relationship, but one set is from the wife's perspective and the other is from the husband's perspective. With some couples it is the wife who is doing the offering; but either way, it is unpleasant to be anywhere near the bottom of these ratings.

Moms and Sex

If your friends are more important to you than your spouse is, then you will have problems. This doesn't mean you shouldn't have friends. But if you choose your friends over your spouse, then you need to spend some time reflecting on why this is so. You have to make the time for each other as a couple. If both spouses don't put in the effort to make time for each other or put in the effort to think about each other romantically, then you can *expect* problems. We get so busy dealing with the day-to-day annoyances, struggles, and stress that we forget to regularly take some time to think about and accommodate our spouse's needs. Doing things like making discrete provocative comments to each other, or even respectful but not so discrete comments of an intimate nature shows that you are thinking about each other. If we fail to make these simple efforts then we can expect troubles and pain in the relationship.

This happens to mothers of young children when they get wore down and are tired of having their children and other people tugging at their pants legs all day long. A spouse who stays home with the children all day will have a deep love for their children, but will take the earliest opportunity for a little time alone, away from the children and spouse. We should all understand this, but often we do not. We come home from a "hard day at work" and can't cope with the children, and in doing this we somehow forget that our mate was with them all day long and needs some time to him- or herself. To all of you who work and have a spouse who cares for children all day long, make sure to be keenly aware that your mate needs some relief. Children are *on* all day long and can't just be shut off like a toy or ignored like a pet. Children are wonderful, but can take an enormous toll on the energy of a person, causing a need—yes a *need*—for a brief reprieve for the primary caregiver of the children.

For those brave and valiant women who choose to stay at home and rear their own offspring, alone-time is very important! Many women get conditioned, over time, by an oblivious spouse, to want and have a deep longing for space—alone. This can become habitual and then becomes a long-term part of the tit-for-tat that occurs in marriage. Make sure that you don't cause the problem with your spouse who cares for, or cared for, your children twenty-four hours a day, seven days a week. Doing so can surely reduce your spouse's desire to satisfy your needs and wants.

As a side note: To deal with this and similar problems, our culture has addressed this by creating yet another set of sexual dysfunction drugs. The drug companies are now wrongly telling women that there is something physically wrong with them, and that they have a sexual dysfunction requiring pharmaceutical medication with side-effects that would frighten evil itself, when, in reality, the only thing wrong is in our thinking. Let us not be deceived.

If a mate fails to grant any relief to their spouse, over a span of twenty plus years, then what can we expect but to have the wife (or husband) be conditioned to not want to be touched by anyone— Think Pavlov's dogs here. When the husband finally figures this out, it's often too late and the conditioning is deeply impressed into the wife's heart. She has become conditioned to not even think about being close to him any longer.

Most people fail to acknowledge how much dedication, as a full time occupation, it takes to bring up a family. Stay-at-home moms (or dads) are underrated and underpaid. For about twenty years the primary childcare parent dedicates themselves to child rearing with very few breaks. So-called "vacations" normally include taking the children to some place such as an amusement park. We all know that is not really a "vacation" for the primary care parent; typically it is quite the opposite unless the other parent truly carries most of the burden when on vacation.

If you're the fulltime caregiver of your children and your mate finally figures out and acknowledges the needs of the fulltime caregiver and you then fail or refuse to entertain ideas about them and sexuality with them, then you fail your spouse and yourself. This is imbalanced and unfair, but in the end, you will be with that person for a very long time. And if you recall how you felt when you first began dating, you must understand that you will be cheating yourself out of ever feeling that way again when you refuse to entertain and invite their sexual advances or neglect making *authentic* sexual advances towards them of your own desires.

If both spouses truly are pleased with their relationship, then imbalanced intimate desire is not an issue and is of no concern. The problem that typically occurs is that seldom will a person who is feeling rejected actually speak up and say what's really hurting them. This becomes somewhat difficult to discern because moms fail to *express*, and dads fail to *interpret* what the mom is feeling regardless of whether or not she expresses it properly. Thus, both spouses are not being attentive to each other in their selfishness. In this case it is much more the husband's fault than it is the mom's. Though, she should clearly deliver this message to him because sometimes people just don't see the obvious, and it needs to be carefully and politely spelled out for them.

Our biggest fear is rejection. Even if the less attentive spouse asks the neglected spouse if something is wrong, it is very likely that the neglected spouse will not want to speak freely because fully revealing their inner thoughts potentially opens them up to even deeper rejection from their neglectful spouse. The rejection is an even more powerful fear when the rejection comes from someone who we want to deeply love. When we open ourselves up to other people in a very deep and personal way, as we do in marital relationships, then we leave ourselves very vulnerable. It is good and proper to be open, but sometimes it can be painful.

People, both men and women, are often jaded in life from constant rejection due to less-than-good relationships while growing up around family and friends. By the time we finally find a person we love enough to open ourselves up to the risk of rejection, we have become so accustomed to withholding ourselves that we never fully trust our spouse. We don't allow them to ever see us when we are vulnerable. In the common lights-out bedroom scenario, lack of trust from your spouse is the primary cause of the problem. Most people ultimately prefer that their spouses look good and be fit and in good shape, but most people ultimately don't care all that much to where it would actually cause them to not want to see their spouse naked. Rather, they just want to be freely open with their spouse without their spouse always hiding from them. Again, this is one of those areas that when asking someone what they want, the true feelings are usually hidden for self-protection. Either spouse deliberately hiding themselves when the other obviously wants to see them is a serious breach of reasonable marriage expectations and is a very cruel behavior when it persists.

Stereotypically, it's the female who hides herself for self-protection. If a wife has been very self-conscious, but finally asks her husband what he would like her to do *to*, or *for*, him, then he is most likely going to be very reserved in his answer to her. This is because if he requests something that is too much for her to mentally handle, then she may crawl back into the safe fortress she hides in. Often, this is done by her displaying a look of horror, and then shock and awe, where she cannot believe he would request such things. And make no mistake about it, this is a two-way street. There are many women in this world who far outstrip their husbands in creative intimate desire, where *she* will be the one who wants more, but is reluctant to speak openly with her husband for her fear of him rejecting her again.

Wanting More or Better Sex in Your Marriage Bed

As the years pass, this subject becomes more of a problem due to what people are exposed to via entertainment, and then subsequently want to duplicate. The duplication is not a problem, but your intimate explorations should be your own creation, and should be *uninhibited* as you think of new and exciting ways to explore, and then do, your intimacy with your spouse. The problem with seeing everything on television, movies, and the internet is that people end up doing it all before they even get married and they become unnecessarily bored because they did life in the wrong order. Additionally, men who get it all *before* marriage are being taught by the women they're with, that commitment doesn't matter. Save your explorations for after commitment, and then take your time exploring and enjoy the gift of exploration that was granted to you by the Creator. There is a lot to explore and you should both enjoy doing so!

When the subject of sex is discussed, it's somewhat common for women to think their husbands are saying that their wives should just "lie down and spread their legs and then everything will be okay." This copout attitude tries to put the blame on the husbands. While it's true that there are men and women who want more intimacy and believe that doing so would serve their purpose, nothing could be further from the truth.

It is the offering, the willingness, the desire to actually want it, and the desire to want to share it that are truly desirable to the other person. The offering of self, the freewill choice of willingness to share, the desire to want it for yourself, and the desire to want to do it to please your spouse must all be there. If any of those four attitudes are missing, then someone in the relationship is going to feel shorted in the exchange.

We can get away with doing the minimum and just "spread our legs." But whether you are the man or the woman who is falling short with this sort of attitude in the relationship, it accumulates like a debt that you owe. And when you continually fail to actually desire to pay the reasonably-expected physical and spiritual love-and-affection debt that you owe to your spouse, you will feel the mounting debt in your relationship with your spouse.

Everything in life has a balance, and at some point the required adjustments will be made in some way. The part of this that's frightening is that many of us have slipped into utter complacency and never notice that our spouse has shut down and withdrawn into a lackluster existence that they wish would soon end. You need not go far to see this, all that you need to do is to listen to people talk and you quickly find this to be all too common.

As discussed in the cornerstone book *Hot Water*, our customary way of life is so accustomed to abusing the affection of our spouse in this way that we don't notice that we're doing so, we do not notice the slow progression of our spouse's withdrawal and ultimate rejection of us. Their rejection of the offending spouse is inevitable and typically is not specifically deliberate. As mentioned, the effect is similar to Pavlov's dogs, and it becomes critical to understand in this sort of situation. Slowly but surely, the offended spouse is trained to no longer care or desire. And if their desire is strong enough to still *want*, then they will either live a very dissatisfied and potentially hostile life, or they will look elsewhere when seeking the satisfaction of love that they desire and deserve and then possibly leave their spouse.

There is a difference between saying "would you like me to..." versus "I want to do..." This is enormously important to understand. But what is more important is actually meaning it when you say it.

"Would you like me to?" implies doing a favor for someone, versus saying "I want to do..." which implies your desire to do something to them. There's a third attitude which is "I am going to do..." that implies doing so without full consideration of the other person. And then there is "Can I do...?" which implies a request. None of these are wrong or bad when used properly. In fact, in most relationships, all of these are helpful in their proper time and place. With regard to intimacy, all of the perspectives are likely welcome at one point or another. The problem is that most of us do not realize the distinction between each of these.

The "Me", "I", and "You" in the following are you and your spouse. And each of these has two sides.

First is the offering side:

Would you like me to...? asks if you would like me to do something specific.

I want to... states that I have a desire to do something specific to you.

I am going to... says that I am doing something to you no matter what.

Will you let me...? asks if you will allow me to do something to you at an appointed time.

The other is the receiving side:

Would you do to me...? asks if you would theoretically ever be willing to please me in a particular manner.

I want you to... indicates that I want you to do something specific to me.

You are going to... Demands that you will do something specific to me.

Will you do it...? asks if you would actually carry out the task at some appointed time.

In both of these perspectives, the first and last items are very similar, but there is a difference between knowing whether someone says that they would theoretically do it, versus actually carrying out the task.

Joy in a relationship is achieved when these two perspectives are in harmony throughout all aspects of the marriage. Sometimes a bit of resistance is okay, and may even be somewhat enjoyably playful for a couple, similar to the coyness seen when you began dating. The problem with this in relationships that have a long history is that the playfulness is typically misread when any of these perspectives are abused.

Since it is probably easiest to view these in a sexual nature with regard to a marriage, try to put yourself in each position and then imagine being rejected by your spouse. Do you like the way it feels? Of course if you're the type who has taken a position to not enjoy intimacy and sex in your relationship, then ask yourself these questions about an area that you actually care about in your relationship. Eventually you will understand how your spouse feels about you rejecting them.

If you fail to have a genuine desire for your spouse, and if you fail to seek out and ask about their desires, then you *can* expect problems in your future. This applies until death do you part, that is to say, throughout your entire relationship far into the future until the day you die.

Turning your spouse into a complacent passionless being might seem desirable to you, but it is not desirable to your spouse. And when they finally decide that they have had enough, if it should occur before either of your deaths, then they will find satisfaction of their passions from someone or something other than you.

Does this make them unfaithful? I suppose by definition we can pin the blame on the spouse who strays, but, in truth, the unfaithful spouse is the spouse who fails to desire their mate. To commit to a relationship and then not fulfill the reasonably expected desires of companionship in body, heart, mind, and soul is indeed a cruel gesture that lasts a *very* long time. And the worst part about this is that low-desire people are often either unrepentant in this regard, insisting that their mate is "needy", or worse, they don't even realize that there's a problem to begin with. How often it has happened that a spouse disappeared seemingly without reason, when in truth they could no longer bear the penalty of rejection that they felt from their non-passionate and complacent spouse, and so they left them without notice. Make sure you don't make it hard for your spouse to love you.

If anyone imagines that a price will not be paid at some point for their own complacency with regard to their spouse and relationship, then they must understand that any human can only tolerate so much rejection before they crumble under the weight of the rejection of complacency. At some point and in some way, all things will be brought to a balance.

If a complacent person reads this and finally understands why their husband or wife seems to no longer have interest in them or in their relationship, then that is good. But there are still realizations that need to be made. If the spouse that has been feeling deprived too long finally breaks down and gets empty satisfaction from another source, and then the complacent spouse proceeds to suddenly change, then the change will typically be welcome. But, in other cases it's going to take a true and passionate desire for your spouse, *by you*, in order to begin to get your spouse to care about you again and bring their heart back to *you*. It takes time and must be a habit as a result of your true desire. If you fail to do this, then it is possible that you do not deserve your spouse. Keep in mind that many weeks of proper behavior can be undone by a single instance of recurring bad behavior.

If, in our selfishness, we fail to desire our spouse physically, emotionally, and mentally, then we must expect a price will be paid. That price has already begun to be paid by you and your spouse, which is something that complacent people do not take much notice of, and/or it is going to contaminate subsequent generations—that's your children!

Earlier I mentioned the key desire points in a relationship, but here I am pointing out the spouse's desire of the same:

First is the offering side:
I want you to ask "**Would you like me to...?**"
I want you to say "**I want to...**"
I want you to say "**I am going to...**"
I want you to ask "**Can I do...?**"

And the other is the receiving side:
I want you to want "**Would you do to me...?**"
I want you to want "**I want you to...**"
I want you to want "**You are going to...**"
I want you to want "**Will you do...?**"

This applies to all areas of a relationship, but again, it is most obvious in the bedroom. This is where the so-called "dirty talk" or "talk dirty to me" sentiment is from. Whether it is moans of pleasure or distinct specific verbal queues, it all comes down to letting your spouse know *that* you want, *what* you want, *how* you want it, *that you like* it, *why you like* it, and *how you like* it. As you defeat your complacent bedroom inhibitions and truly share in one another, these things begin to become a natural part of your relationship. But sadly, we have allowed other people (Church, government, schools, television, movies, etc.) to influence what occurs in the privacy of our own marriage bed. Some of the influence is inhibiting and other influence is un-inhibiting, and some influence is potentially damaging to our physical and emotional well-being. Turn away from such negative influences and disregard the unappealing distortion that loud-mouthed people place on intimacy.

The Bible says little about what should or should not occur in the sexual relationship between a husband and wife; yet, people have this terrible tendency to interpret the Bible to say things that it does not actually say or address.

What goes on in the privacy of your own bedroom between you and your spouse is of no concern to anyone else provided that there is no physical harm and that you are doing it for both spouses' joy and love. Enjoy yourselves and be thankful for each other and for the creativity that sexuality brings about when you allow it to. It is the Creator's gift to husband and wife, use it well and be creative in your mutual sexual and emotional exploration of each other!

Release Your Unhelpful Inhibitions

Due to people's inhibitions, often caused from a multitude of sources of outside incorrect information as well as some natural inhibitions, people often utilize alcohol as an inhibition reducer. For many people this is an okay thing, provided it's not abused, because it brings them out of their shell, but for others alcohol causes tremendous problems making them dangerous to themselves and others through poor and foolish judgment. With regard to consuming *any* mind altering substance to release inhibition, while it may be a good for some people in order to help them let go of all of the wrong teaching that stops them from being themselves, it is better and more fair to both spouses if the release of inhibition is purely from love rather than from having to consume alcohol in order to do so. A spouse who is willing to completely release him- or herself freely to their mate, without being under the influence of any substance, is giving a far more pure and loving offering than when they are overcome by intoxication.

A spouse, who is the recipient of intoxicated affection, will seldom resist what they desire. Thus, the intoxicated offering is seen by the intoxicated spouse as being fully accepted and a fully acceptable offering to their more desirous spouse.

If the offering is made while the inhibited spouse is intoxicated, the offering is typically going to be well liked by the more desirous spouse regardless, but it is certainly better if it is offered in purity, free of intoxication. Our society (including schools, churches, parents, etc.) has damaged marriages immensely by telling people what is right or wrong in the bedroom. Sometimes this occurs when we check our own curiosity by asking these people or seeking information from such sources. We wonder if something is okay and we seek advice and information on our question, but then we get an answer that often is inaccurate or outright distorted. What we have actually received is someone else's answer, which is interpreted from their own understanding of the Bible and life in general. The point here is that we need *not* ask about what is okay to do in *our own* marriage bed. It is each couple's own business. And our own guilt and/or the opinions of others about what should or should not go on in our own marriage bed does not have any right to be in our bedrooms. The only book you should look to in this regard is the Bible, and the Bible is *very limited* in expressing the private doings of husband and wife. The little that is said is typically misinterpreted by preachers and people in general. Read it for yourselves and then decide for yourselves.

In the end, it comes down to this: If you cannot release your inhibitions with your mate and overcome your fears and the noise of the world, then you do not deserve your mate and you can expect problems in the long-run because of your fear and inhibitions. You promised to give yourself to your spouse when you wed, so do it. As a couple, you should be able to freely speak about your desires and arrive at mutual guidelines of intimate exploration that you invent *together* as a team going forward in life.

Please do not misunderstand this; this is not saying a married couple should never drink and become experimentally amorous now and then by means of alcohol's release of inhibition. But rather, we are establishing how much more meaningful and pure it is when it's done of pure love, truth, and passion for one another.

Bring back the passion in both the physically-sexual side and in the rest of your relationship; because, if you're missing it in one area of your relationship, then you are also likely faking it in many other areas of your relationship.

In regard to this section and low desire, when we choose to not desire our spouses, then it is our spouse who controls the relationship in reality. Our delusion that we are in control is in error. If you or your spouse lives and behaves in this manner, then a price *will* be paid at the needless expense of your marriage. And as discussed in detail in the cornerstone book *Hot Water*, this will unavoidably affect your children's relationships with their spouses when their time comes. If they see a lackluster relationship when they look at their parents, then they will typically become conditioned to seek that same type of lackluster relationship as they grow up, unless they are lucky enough to stumble across information that breaks the mold for them.

Let's Talk Sex—What Is It?

There is an erred notion that some people are "stuffy" regarding sexuality, and that those stuffy people only have sex in one position, "missionary style." This notion is often accompanied by an incorrect belief that it is a more "conservative" mindset that is stuffy in this way. But it must be pointed out that, just because people who appear "stuffy" don't go around bragging about their sexuality and their sexual conquests, does not mean that these people are stuffy in any way. In truth, it is the people who feel that they must proclaim their sexual endeavors to the world who truly suffer from being stuffy. It goes under the heading of: Those who do—do, and those who don't—brag.

Let's talk sex, or rather, the physically intimate part of a male-female relationship. Do we really understand what sex is?

For thousands of years, committed couples have come at odds with one another. Prior to the notion that humans are derived from something primordial, there was a simpler view of what humanity was. Since the relatively modern view of life's primordial origins has become predominant, it is best to use the natural order of the way things work for our foundational understanding; though, the following does not necessarily support the idea of primordial origins.

While the order of things is said to have brewed up a wide array of functioning life forms, there are too many commonalities between the vast majority of these forms of life to ignore; gender being the single most prominent of the commonalities between almost every life form. In fact, it is so prominent and basic that it can be recognized anywhere in the world in the both plant and animal forms of life.

Logical observations reveal to us that things have a great tendency to follow this common gender pattern. Within the human realm, it is clear that the male is the offering gender and the female is the receiving gender. What actually causes this pattern? And does it affect any other aspect of our life?

From a naturalist standpoint, men have morphed into the form of the one that offers the seed, and women have morphed into the form of one that accepts the seed. This soulless point of view follows a very tight pattern of the give and take; or better stated—the offer and accept pattern that we always see in life.

There is a point in life when we need to look beyond the "naturalist" view and admit that the majority of the world believes there is a spirit or soul inside of each of us. Of course, this does not necessarily make that belief correct, but it is worthy of everyone's consideration. We can debate about who or what the soul may be from, or if it even exists, but worldwide it is prominently clear that the understanding or belief that our bodies contain a soul, spirit, or some sort of entity is widely held.

The notion that we morphed into humans from some other life form over a long period is somewhat of a minority belief. So in the spirit of appealing to the majority of the world, which is well in excess of five billion humans' assumption that we do have a soul, we should at least consider what the significance of a soul is and how it relates to sex and gender.

Your choices with regard to your beliefs about religion and a God, or gods, are your own choice, but to ignore the essence of spirit seems somewhat deliberately ignorant considering thousands of years of accounts, evidences, and opinions that are overwhelmingly in support of the concept of a human soul. Not to mention the multitude of humans who subscribe to that belief.

Assuming that a soul exists in every one of us leads us to have to wonder upon its purpose; just as the physical body itself leads us to wonder upon its purpose.

With a physical body it's simple to detect a great deal of its purpose. In the simplest sense, a man's purpose is to offer his seed of life to a woman. And the woman's purpose is to accept and receive that seed of life and then to bring forth a close combined replication of *he who offered* the seed and of *she who accepted* the seed—in their own image. The naturalist view stops short of this, and goes no further and has no purpose to go any further. But is there more to it? Is there more to us? Is sex something more than a morphed chance and chemical excitement?

With the soul, the offer and receive functionality is somewhat more ambiguous. Since we cannot detect a soul with our five senses, we have little to utilize in order to scientifically explain the soul. There is one "but" in all of this, and this is where people often differ and vehemently disagree.

That one contentious "but" is: But, there is a Creator who breathed the breath of life into man. Without this understanding, it is difficult to fully explain a *marriage*, its true function, and its true purpose. We are being ignorant when we refuse to fully consider this information. We must always remember to make decisions *after* we have carefully considered *all* of the available information.

If you do not believe in a singular Creator, and you still want to make your marriage better, then please continue reading with the understanding that there is a possibility that a Creator does exist. In the end, the decision is yours as to what you choose to believe. All of the cultures of the world are greatly affected by the belief of some sort of Creator, and these beliefs have a tremendous impact on our own understanding of our own relationships and on what we do.

Assuming that the bulk of the people in this world are correct, then we have a soul. If we have a soul, then it's from something, or from somewhere, or followed some order of design or creation. And as far as we can tell, souls have been around, at minimum, for all of recorded human history. In all of recorded human history, which is the last several thousand years, people were and are pretty much the same. For our purposes, we'll make the broad assumption that all the people from the past several thousand years had souls like we suspect we do today, and that their bodies looked much like ours.

If we have souls, then what is the purpose of those souls? If souls have purpose, then are there female and male souls?

Women Rejecting Men

Judging by the patterns displayed in the physical realm of life, including the animal kingdom and the human kingdom, it seems that it is the female who is typically the initial violator-of-expectation in a relationship. The subtleties of this are quite minute but have profound ramifications on any relationship.

When a boy and a girl are dating, it is common that almost every physical advance offered by one is accepted with great anticipation and enthusiasm by the other, thus making for a joyful and fulfilling early relationship.

As often occurs, the boy continues to make his offerings to the girl, but eventually she begins to reject his offerings. Being the hopeful creature that he is, the boy keeps his hopes high that at some point things will go back to the way they initially were when they first met. This hope is typically held out to the point of marriage, where the boy, who is now a man, finds that his wife's invitations and her interest in his offerings are becoming less frequent and less intense with each passing year.

Whether or not it is intended, this very common situation crushes the person who is being rejected. Being physically rejected is one of the deepest forms of rejection. In truth, the violation of the male's expectation is felt by him, deep inside, as betrayal, whether or not he realizes that fact. Again, remember that it could be the girl who is being rejected.

Most people respect the other person's right to say, "No." If we didn't respect that right, then we would force the offering which then turns the offering into something entirely different, and is referred to as rape. If a woman concedes to a request, without being forced or threatened, then it is not rape.

The single most precious thing to any man, whether he understands this or not, is to be accepted by the woman to whom he has directed all of his affection. This common pattern of rejection, which women often display towards their husbands, is a key reason many marriages experience problems.

This prominent rejection problem is increased due to the animosity towards men that was displayed by the women's movement of the late twentieth century. This is not about whether or not the women's movement had merit; but rather, at that time, it increased the instances of wives rejecting the advances that their husbands offered to them, and it increased the instances of the wives not offering physical and emotional invitation to their husbands.

When wives disregard what their husbands have to offer, it is very bad for the relationship. But remember, this goes both ways.

Not Only Women

The act of physical rejection is not exclusive to women. There are many cases where the reverse is true and the man rejects his wife's advances and invitations. Relationship issues are often difficult to resolve because there are so many variables. Discussions between spouses who are in a difficult marriage often break down because the trail to the source of the problem is littered with bad experiences. These bad experiences bring up strong emotions from years of reciprocal rejection, and are a large part of the tit-for-tat we mentioned earlier. Trying to get through the litter of bad experiences stops many couples from going down the trail because neither person wants to get hurt tripping over the shards of debris from their own past errors.

Men Rejecting Women

Besides the reverse of the preceding section, men also have their own common way of rejecting. Some men foolishly choose their friends, sports, or alcohol etc... over their wives. When rejection is not in the physical realm it becomes more difficult for us to detect.

The stereotypical rejection of women by their husbands is often in regard to feelings or emotions. Women, by-and-large, want to be understood, listened to, and cherished. For women, when their husband will not listen to them, they feel rejected. If you don't listen to someone, it will be difficult to ever understand them.

There are many men who do not listen well when their wives try to communicate to them, which typically worsens over time. As the husband's oblivion increases, his wife's frustration will increase proportionally. When a woman becomes frustrated, her husband might wrongly interpret her attempts at requesting her needs as nagging and complaining. This only serves to deepen the problems between them.

When women "nag" and complain, men typically withdraw even more. The withdrawal is felt, by the wife, as further rejection dealt to her by her husband. This creates a dangerous reciprocal cycle that is devastating to the relationship. Once again, it is tit-for-tat plaguing the marriage.

These examples are only the tip of the iceberg that we refer to as "rejection." There are many ways that we reject our spouses. If humanity could eliminate all feelings of rejection in every realm, then there would be no more wars or conflict.

Being rejected is not a pleasant experience no matter who you are. Men and women are either oblivious to reality, or simply are very cruel to their spouse with regard to friendships. In this particular case I am referring to opposite gender friends. If a husband has a so-called friend of the opposite gender that he hangs out with when his wife is not along, then there is a problem in the relationship. And similarly, if a wife has a so-called friend of the opposite gender that she hangs out with without her husband, then there is a problem in the relationship. Some people do not see it this way, but you have to either be very naive or very foolish to believe that this will not bother your spouse. This is true regardless of what your spouse says about the subject.

A Woman's Role and a Man's Role

In some ways, men and women are created equal and in other ways they are also created differently, but being created differently does not mean that one gender is lesser or greater than another.

Men and women are created different; therefore, we are thought of as not "equal" because we are not the same. If you derive or deduct that one or the other is of more value, because they aren't "equal," then you do not properly understand equal in this regard. This brings us to the question: What is it that we are measuring that is either equal or not equal?

From a physical perspective, there is simply no comparison between men and women. Worldwide, on average, men are about twenty-five to thirty-five percent heavier in weight than women are when neither gender is overweight. Further, women are born with a vagina and all of the female gendered reproductive organs, and women typically begin to grow breasts near to the age of thirteen. Where, men are born with a penis and all of the male gendered reproductive organs. If you see these completely different sets of attributes as not "equal" or that they can do the same thing, then you are have deliberately chosen to close your mind to the nature of this obvious design. While they are *different*, their value to one another *is equal*. This is because without both genders, and each of their corresponding contributions to mankind, all of humanity would cease to exist in a single generation. So in that respect, their value to one another is entirely equal, and that value is the perpetuation of humankind. Also, from a companionship perspective, men and women offer each other equally deep friendship when their relationships are good.

Since the wonderful and exciting gender differences between men and women are undeniably obvious, we will further scrutinize the purpose of those differences. Because the average size of women and men is a relative matter, we will not discuss the obvious size difference. However, there are a few glaring differences that all men and women come to realize upon seeing one another naked.

Those differences are that a man has a penis and a scrotum with sperm producing testicles and women have a vagina and typically noticeable protrusions on the chest that we call breasts. What is this very specialized equipment for? What does it mean? Did it morph into what it all is, or was the equipment made that way for a reason?

Because of the overwhelming evidence that there is more to humans than only our temporarily conscious live bodies, we'll approach this from the perspective that there is a soul that was somehow deliberately Created and is aware.

What is the purpose of gender? Since gender exists in the physical realm of our bodies, we should ask: does gender exist in our souls?

Now remember, this book is about making your marriage better; and since marriages seem to stagnate, and generation upon generation suffer the pains of marriage problems, we are going to come to understand the aspects that few people are aware of, care about, or are courageous enough to discuss or believe.

You are about to hear a uniquely true perspective that is seldom discussed. To be able to receive the information being offered to you here, you must be willing to consider the possibility that a singular Creator exists.

We'll take from a set of documents that are respected by at least half of the population of the world—the Bible. In the Bible it says that man is Created in the image of his Creator. It also says, shortly after his Creation, woman was Created by the Creator using a part of the Created man. Assuming that this is true, then what does "in the image of" actually mean?

It is unlikely that this brilliant Creator *arbitrarily* put a penis on the Created man. Logically thinking, the penis is a part of the image of the Creator. But what is its significance? Alternately, the woman was taken from the man and was Created to assist him as a companion. She was created with a vagina. Logically, this also is partly "in the image of" this Creator. So, what is the significance of this?

Interestingly, one gender cannot survive without the other as living breathing beings. Now, as our relatively long human history shows us, when a man inserts his penis into the woman's vagina and places his sperm or seed within her, she commonly becomes pregnant and creates a child in *their* image. Logically, then, this functionality is also Created in the image of the Creator.

To take this thought a bit further, after the woman becomes pregnant, she will, at some point, bring forth a child. The child will be uniquely Created in the image of its parents and share physical attributes of both parents. The strongest common attribute is that of gender, but others include skin tone, hair color, eye color, physical build, and other attributes.

Humans Create a child in their own image, just as their Creator created them in the image of the Creator. What does all of this mean? And who cares?

Having worked in various engineering fields most of my life, it is clear to me that: Where there is design—there is purpose; and where there is purpose—there is design. We don't have penises and vaginas "*just because*". There is clear reason, and that reason is for us to be able to Create as our Creator did—in the Creator's image. Further, since "practicing" to Create is generally enjoyed by both men and women, using this same logic we can also assume that the Creator also enjoyed Creating. All naturalist explanations fall short of adequately explaining the emergence of genders and the chemical changes that occur in anticipation of, and during, intercourse.

To get past the physical, we need to understand the purpose and what it was that the genders were "Created in the image of."

Since the Creator is "unseen", the Creator is not physical like our bodies are. So then, why did the Creator Create our physical bodies? What were they the image of? Since there were Created functions, what do those functions represent?

Keeping things as broad and simple as possible, to keep this book as short as possible, the function of man is to *offer*, and the function of woman is to *accept*. Or from a different perspective, a woman's function is to invite, and a man's function is to enter, or to accept the invitation to enter in. You will find this discussed in-depth in the book series *The Science of God*. These basic four functions are the foundation of a joyful marriage, but you will find surprising twists in the assumption you may now be making. Reserve your conclusions until after you hear the whole story.

Subtleties of Rejection

In understanding the four basic functions of Creation, which are: *offer, accept, invite,* and *enter,* we need to further evaluate rejection. Each of these four functions is critical and very dear to each and every one of us. This is especially so with regard to our marriages. Because these four core functions of a relationship are so dear to us, we are very protective of them. And this makes us very sensitive to any violation against any of the four functions.

Even the smallest violations against one of these four core functions send many people into a deep emotional display of frustration. This emotional display can show up in a multitude of ways such as anger, withdrawal, and fear. But besides the obvious anger, withdrawal, and fear there are a multitude of ways they might each be shown, thus, clouding our view even more. And the multitude of ways is limited only by the length of time mankind exists on this earth.

To understand just how subtle rejection can be, we must realize how finely these four functions are woven into every aspect of our lives. By tying expectation together with the functions: *offer, accept, invite,* and *enter,* and then all of those together with rejection we begin to see a clear picture of how easy it is for each of us to reject our mates.

Any violation of these four functions is ultimately felt as rejection by the other person in the exchange. This goes far beyond the physically intimate sexual aspects of marriage. Rejection is done through a look, a sound, a movement, direct words, the way words are arranged, where the emphasis is placed on a word, doing something, or not doing something, and many more very subtle actions.

Since violation of these basic functions is called "rejection", we will focus on that term. Taking note of the preceding brief list of some of the ways we reject each other, we can see how easy we quickly pile up a multitude of these violations against our own spouse.

"Midlife Crisis"

The mountain of *violations* that we each surmount is seen and/or felt by our spouse as a mountain of *rejections*. Since, based upon his Created nature, the primary role of a man is to offer, we can quickly see how it's somewhat easier for a woman to violate *his* functions' expectations. But this is only because it is a natural part of his function to be the first one to make a move. Getting into a blame game here does not help anyone. The goal is to get to the root of the problem and permanently rip it out.

The first act of the Creator, after creating the form of a man, was to breathe spirit into, or offer to man—the Creator made the first move. If man had rejected that, well... then we would not be here to discuss it.

Since the first woman was made in the image of the Creator, and was taken from the Created man, woman was Created to receive the man's spirit through his seed just as the man received the spirit of the Creator. He is a model of the Creator and she is a model of Creation, and together they can Create and are an even more complete model of the Creator and Creation.

Acceptance is the primary expectation that man has towards woman just like the Creator has toward man. When this expectation is violated, it heaps violation upon violation, and rejection upon rejection.

It is important to note that the "violations" that we are discussing are not necessarily intentional.

Consider violating the legal policy of a stop sign; you may honestly have not noticed that the sign was there, and, thus, proceeded right through the intersection without stopping or ever even noticing that it existed. However, if someone else is in the intersection at the same time, then it is no less injurious to both drivers—even if it is unintentional. When enough unintentional violations occur in this way, the other driver will eventually choose a route where they will not encounter you. Thus, we begin to seek acceptance from other venues where we will not be violated by someone crashing into us and breaking our hearts.

For a man, it is common to go to work daily to earn money to care for his wife and children. He offers this to his family because he cares for and loves them, and generally the offer is fully accepted. But when he does this, he sacrifices his life, not unto death, but he commits a portion of his life-existence in order to care for his family even though his work may be a job that he doesn't particularly want to do.

Generally, this system works well. But if his spouse and/or his family's violations have accrued to what he feels to be a great quantity of offenses, then, at some point, he might desire better acceptance from others outside of his family. This can be in the form of social acceptance, physical intimacy acceptance, or some other form of acceptance that makes him feel as accepted and as close to whole as possible.

When a man's capacity to endure the mountain of rejections of him is exceeded, then he will seek other venues of acceptance. This is commonly referred to as a "midlife crisis." It is very unfair when men are mocked by their family for having a so-called "mid-life crisis" after experiencing the typical long period of violations (in the form of a mountain of rejection) that his family built against him. Since the period of violations toward men is typically done throughout the twenty to thirty years before this occurs, it is surprising that he did not simply disappear when considering how a man in this type of situation is often treated by his wife and children.

If we go back to the six different versions of the story of *The Shopkeeper and the Woman*, we can more clearly understand a man's point of view when he is having a "midlife crisis". Version 3 of *The Shopkeeper and the Woman* is a good example of a man with a "midlife crisis". Anytime we disregard a human, we add to the mountain of violations against them. In the same way that you were probably glad that the shopkeeper found another lovely woman as his new favorite customer, and you likely thought that what he did was reasonable and well deserved, we can also connect this to a man's midlife crisis.

Because of our skewed perceptions of the way things are, men who have midlife crises are often seen as the initial violators. In fact, in having a midlife crisis, men often are rejecting or violating their family's expectations. But comparatively, what would we expect if the violations against him were vast? This is not always the case, but when it is, why would he not do what the shopkeeper did and seek acceptance from another lovely customer? A man who does not up-and-leave when rejected for so long must be very patient, special, or a foolish person. If you don't fulfill your spouse's fantasies it causes them to decide to look around, then they will see all that is available, and their fantasies might grow more out of your ability and/or willingness to fulfill them. Those fantasies won't necessarily include you. All of this makes it even more difficult to keep and satisfy your spouse. The fantasies are not necessarily always physically sexual in nature.

Women have midlife crises as well, but because their midlife crises usually don't include shiny new sports cars, they are not as prominent and easily noticed by everyone as much as men's midlife crises tend to be.

No No No!

This book is not focused on right and wrong, but rather on each person's *perception* of *right* and *wrong* (That is to say, each person's feeling of acceptance or rejection). It doesn't matter what we meant to say or what caused our action, because even if our intentions were purely kind and had zero intended malice, our action can still be felt by our spouse as a violation. From the perspective of the violated person—if it hurts, then it hurts!

Here are a couple of examples: When you try to help an injured animal, the animal typically does not have the foresight to understand your action. This causes them to see your action as an *attack* on them, even though you meant to *assist* them with their injury so that they would no longer have to suffer. To the injured animal, you're hurting them, so they often lash out at you as you try to help them. This is an extreme and simple example. So consider this next more common example that is more subtle, but better relates to human relationships.

When a spouse asks for a certain gift for the holidays for the traditional gift exchange, you graciously go out to get the gift to fulfill their request. You feel pretty darn good having been able to do that for your spouse—Your kindness is sure to be appreciated and rewarded! When the day to exchange gifts arrives, you open yours, and it is *exactly* what you wanted, and you are very pleased!

In your excitement, you hand your spouse the gift that you bought for your spouse. And when your spouse opens their gift the reaction is not filled with the excitement that you had expected. Why is this?

As you think about this, imagine the reactions in the above interaction as minimally noticeable and very subtle. In this scenario, your spouse asked for a *very specific* item, and you failed to fulfill that specific expectation completely and exactly as they imagined it. The item you offered was similar, but not *exactly* the same as *they* imagined. To you it appeared as the exact item, but it was not *exactly* what your spouse wanted. When their reaction was somewhat less than you expected, you felt the violation from them about your expectation of their reaction.

Our own feeling of rejection typically overrides our ability to see that it was ourselves who were the initial violators. Your spouse expected the precise item that they asked for. Your spouse specifically expected a certain color, brand, or other attribute of your gift to be *exactly* as they felt had been impressed upon you when they made the initial request. To them, the particular gift you bought, and the fact that you offered the wrong thing was a violation of their expectation.

To demonstrate how convoluted these situations can get, it is entirely possible that your spouse's description of what they wanted could have been told to you with errors. But that doesn't matter to the way they feel upon receiving the wrong gift that differed from what they had pictured in their own mind and anticipated getting. In their mind, they asked for it in the best way they knew how, and to them, that was sufficient. When the gift is in error, in their eyes, then it is perceived by them as a violation to them.

It is also entirely possible that they delivered the gift request to you with the precision of the item's actual stock number, the item's location in the store, and the store's address and phone number; yet, you didn't get that exact item for them. To you, any item that appeared close to the same was sufficient. You didn't get the wrong item on purpose; to you it simply was not a factor and you felt that you perfectly met the needs of your spouse's request. These violations go far beyond mere gift exchange. A very common area, and probably the most difficult area for couples to discuss is with regard to their physical intimacy.

Pay attention to the violations in this simple gift exchange: Your spouse requests (invites) a gift: You understand it wrong (Violation of expectation one). Next, you offer the gift you bought for your spouse and your spouse sees that it is not the precise item that they wanted (Violation of expectation two). Their reaction is less than enthusiastic and not what you expected (Violation of expectation three). Your spouse's mood is altered because of the broken expectation they had (Violation of expectation four). Your mood is altered because of the broken expectation of a happy occasion (Violation of expectation five). And this could have occurred in a matter of only a few seconds. So when doing things for your spouse, make sure that you take her to the ballet that *she* wants to see for Mother's day, and make sure to take him to the ballgame that *he* wants to see for Father's day. Pay close attention to your spouse's words and underlying desires, and you will find a whole new dimension to your relationship. All too often we are so focused on *our own* wants and desires, that we miss *our spouse's* wants and desires.

In many cases we detect dissatisfaction and will work to make it right. But in the previous example, we are simply looking at how many violations there were and how quickly it all happened. Some of the violations were mounted against you, and some were against your spouse. Often this back and forth exchange of violation-of-expectation continues, getting either less significant or even more significant. But neither is good in a relationship.

The less significant encounters are the very dangerous ones that quietly and slowly build the mountain of violations against each spouse. This mountain of violations-of-expectations is just waiting for the opportune moment to erupt!

If, instead of subtle quiet addition, the exchange suddenly gets even more significant, then it often escalates into a full-blown fight. A fight is a rapid exchange of intense violations-of-expectations. A fight is a flawed form of personal protection, which we will discuss shortly.

These violations are rejections of something expected. And as you can see, they can be very subtle actions. When we review our lives with the understanding of what has been discussed so far, we can see that we ourselves may also have caused a great deal of the trouble and violation in our own relationships. When the person making the offer is rejected, it is especially hurtful. Repeatedly rejecting offers, amounts to saying, "No, No, No!"

Chapter 7

Rejection in Marriage

Rejection has several levels, most of which go mostly unrealized but are felt nonetheless. When rejection is blatant it is meant for us to notice it. That sort of rejection is usually a deliberate form of tit-for-tat retaliation. What we are aiming to understand at this point is that the retaliatory rejection is launched due to the more subtle and far more dangerous forms of rejection.

If You Reject Long Enough, You Will Destroy Their Desire

Saying, "No" or rejecting too often destroys desire in most people in the long-run. When desire is destroyed, then that is also felt as a form of rejection. Let me explain: Looking back to our gift exchange example, let's assume that it was you who didn't buy the proper gift. In their natural human desire to not violate other people's expectations and spare you any hurt, your spouse would likely try to hide their true feelings about the *incorrect* gift that you kindly offered. This allows you to believe that you have *successfully* fulfilled your spouse's gift request, when you have actually *failed terribly*. When you learn to properly read your spouse's emotions and expressions you can easily see this.

When this approach is regularly practiced by either you or your spouse, it causes each of you to continue to fall short because you never become fully aware of the fact that you had been regularly violating each other's expectations by failing to deliver the expected response or action. When this is done long enough and repeated enough times, people become conditioned to expect the violations, and thus they lower their expectations in general. This form of self-protection is a sad testament to humanity, and it destroys the very essence of humanity, which is what desire is all about.

When we begin dating, we overflow with *excitement, enthusiasm, expectation, hope, desire,* and *passion!* Then, over time, these wonderful attributes often eventually vanish from our relationship. Part of this happens due to our own familiarity and complacency, and another part is from the constant violation of our expectations. Excess violation is the dominant problem with regard to loss of desire.

Our natural reflex of self-preservation causes us to stop expecting and hoping for something we had previously hoped for and anticipated. Our rationale is, if we choose to no longer want something, then no one can tell us "No", and therefore, we cannot get hurt. We are somewhat unaware how often we do so. This is a primary cause of the loss of desire. And its subtleties are many!

Self-protection, generally, is not done deliberately, rather, it is a natural response used as a false form of self-preservation. This is something we do without being aware that we are doing it. When we build these walls restricting our desire, then we no longer have as strong of a desire as we previously had and our reduced desire typically becomes a subtle violation to our spouse.

Since this particular aspect more notably happens to men, we can use that as a good example. In the early years of marriage men stereotypically are the ones who desire physical affection more often. When a man attempts to offer himself to his wife, he is often rejected. When rejected long enough, his desire for his wife eventually dissolves. The dissolution of his desire is seen as a violation by his wife, even though it was her repeated rejection that led to the dissolution of his desire for her to begin with. She will feel violated, because up until he lost his desire for her, his desire was always intensely for her. However, now that his desire of her has been crushed, he no longer pursues her in the same way that he previously did, and he might even be going elsewhere for his fulfillment whether or not it is seen as proper or moral.

She notices the fact that he seems to have lost interest in her, and so her expectations are violated. In this particular scenario, her feeling of violation is mostly her own fault and was caused due to her repeated violation of his expectations. The problem with this common tit-for-tat situation is that seldom do people catch on to exactly what is occurring. A spouse may behave badly for twenty years or more, and then decide to change their ways overnight but then expect their mate to *immediately* accept their apologies and be instantly excited about the change. This expectation is unfair because it takes time for the violated spouse to regain trust in their notoriously neglectful mate. Relationship trust takes time and *true effort.*

Fearing Rejection When Contemplating Confrontation

There are times when we are aware of the actual violation or rejection. In these more obvious times, it's easier for us to detect the problem. The more obvious occurrences are often deliberate rejections, though, at times, the rejections might not be deliberate but are still obvious.

These obvious instances are usually when people are able to see through the emotional confusion just enough to realize what it was that made them feel violated or hurt. This is the point in a violation situation when we often want to confront the person and speak out to tell them how we feel and "give them a piece of our mind!"

When we choose to confront our spouse, it often ends in failure with us delivering our feelings in a haphazard manner, typically initiating an unwanted argument. But even if we deliver our complaint of pain and violation in the most delicate manner, our confrontation and complaint will likely feel like a violation to our spouse regardless of our true intentions. This is because our spouse did not expect the confrontation—they expected nothing, but instead got an uncomfortable confrontation.

This problem places all of humanity in a very difficult situation. Can a relationship survive this? An extremely common situation with this sort of confrontation is that the person who is being confronted feels attacked. Depending upon their upbringing, your spouse may often respond by shutting down in various ways, like withdrawing, or more commonly, by displaying anger, or by using the "I'll show you" approach.

As it dives deep into how we interpret our personal environment, the cornerstone book *Hot Water* may be of additional help to you (Recall the meaning of "Hot Water" that was briefly outlined in Chapter 2 of this book.) Each method of dealing with confrontation is a form of our own personal self-preservation. In this case, the self-preservation is against a perceived attack. Self-preservation during an attack is different than the self-preservation we spoke of earlier where we respond a certain way to rejection in order to preserve ourselves and our feelings.

When your spouse sees you coming, not to offer good to them, but rather to reject them while using the "I'll show you" approach, for what they will take as an unprovoked attack against them, then their natural instinct to self-protect will be used and they will likely lash out at you. This lashing out is similar to our earlier example where the animal feels threatened and lashes out. It doesn't matter why someone feels threatened. It is that fact that they *feel* threatened that makes them lash out.

If you confront an injured animal to help them and the animal tries to harm you, then you may very well decide to walk away to preserve yourself. In the process, you let the animal suffer in their own fear, pain, and misery to fend for themselves. In this case, your self-preservation is from your fear or dislike of the thought of getting mauled or bit by the injured animal. And because you might get hurt worse than the animal, from the animal's violent response to your attempt at helping them, you choose to walk away and not help the animal at all.

The underlying function of your own self-preservation in your relationship is no different. If you confront your spouse, and they lash out at you, it is very likely that you will stop and retreat, or back down. If your spouse lashes out at nearly every confrontation in a way that you feel is too vicious and dangerous, then it's very likely that eventually you will completely retreat from any confrontation with them due to your fear of their repeated lashing out at you. This horrible situation fuels itself and only gets worse. When we allow our spouse to attack us in this way, then we set up a precedent of expectation with them and with ourselves. This precedent becomes more strongly cast and more difficult to cut through with each permitted instance of their *perceived* self-defense (that is to say, self-preservation).

Depending upon each of our own life experiences, we each handle our spouse's behavior slightly different than each other. One common result of this situation is that the confronter will become fearful of the confrontation, and thus, begin to withdraw from confrontation altogether and no longer confront. When we avoid confrontation, our purpose is usually to avoid the intense feeling of rejection that we receive whenever we attempt to confront our self-preserving spouse. Our fear of rejection in a confrontation is, in itself, also a part of our own self-preservation.

This presents a very critical problem: When a person is allowed to continue to lash out, unchallenged, then they increase the strength of the precedent being set. Every instance of non-confrontation builds upon their *familiar Hot Water* way, which deepens their stance. This makes the likelihood of their retaliatory lashing out a greater certainty when you eventually do choose to confront them. The sooner we deal with these things in a relationship, then the easier they are to correct in each of us.

Why Do Boxers Protect Their Face?

The confrontation scenario just mentioned describes the reason that we fear confrontation. It's about self-preservation. Fear is a natural instinct that we all seem to be born with as a protective measure, and it causes us to react quickly. However, not all self-preservation is rooted in fear.

I suppose any self-defense could be considered to be a reaction to the fear of being injured, so you react in protective mode. But we will separate that from real fear. Real fear is when you won't do something because of fear, but what we are going to discuss in this section is another perspective. In this case, it's not *fear*, but rather *courage* that drives the need for self-protection. It would be unfair to call a warrior fearful because he is wearing armor when he is courageously running into the face of battle. Wearing armor is simply the wise thing for him to do.

Take a look at a boxer in the ring: He knows that when he is in the boxing match he is likely to get hit in the face. He knows his opponent is going to attempt to hit his face, so he wisely protects his face with the hand that he is not throwing a punch with. While to some people, boxing is a brutal sport, the fact remains that he *must* have a protective method for stopping his opponent from hitting him in the face. Getting hit in the face too often leads to even further hits to his face and ultimately the loss of the boxing match—a victory for his opponent. Couples should not be in such a contentious situation to begin with.

As previously touched on, people lash out when they feel attacked. This lashing out can be both an attack, and a form of protection. In a verbal exchange, it's either done *offensively* or *defensively*. The exchanges between a husband and a wife should not be competitions like a boxing match is. But sadly, exchanges between spouses often are just that—competitions—and this is not good.

I feel it is imperative to remind you that this book is not about the right or wrong, but rather, it is about better understanding *why* we do and say what we do. This allows us to better understand ourselves. And more importantly, to help us better understand others. With that said, the truth is that spouses often compete in direct heated dialogue to be the victor in the end. When this is the case, a marriage cannot have sustainable joy and will be lackluster, miserable, or even end in divorce.

To connect the analogy of a boxer protecting his face in the ring: once heated dialogue begins in a verbal exchange, spouses often have something that they are holding for protection. This is something that will stop their spouse from being able to further hurt them.

These protective one-two knockout punches are usually something that only needs to be hinted at, and then the other spouse's verbal punches are not able to hit them squarely in the face. Often these same sensitive topics are used offensively as a method for landing the knockout punch. When these comments are thrown about, they typically bring tears or utter withdrawal. This might be things like bringing up a serious error that your spouse made but never fully rectified, and thus, it is used as a one-two knockout punch.

Married couples need to be made aware of this particular protective measure so that they do not use it. It is of the utmost importance to everyone's understanding, to realize that these things are often being harbored by both spouses. If you have something that you're hanging onto that you use as a verbal weapon, then it is something that needs to be discussed with your spouse and dealt with properly, completely, and promptly!

How Spouses Are Shut Out by Their Own Actions

There is a simple truth that for some reason has remained a secret. We will go into deeper detail about this in a later chapter. As you may recall, in the beginning of the book, I mentioned that if I write this apologetically, then I have to be dishonest and not explain things the way that they are and, in essence, lie, which I will not do. The problem is that some people won't listen because they get offended at what is being said. When they do so, then they won't ever hear the truth. In the first chapter it was stressed that you must *choose* that you want to be true, and with that understanding, you should have derived from it, that you made it to this point in the book because you want to hear it *all*—even if it hurts—therefore you are ready to hear it all.

In an earlier chapter, we discussed the Creator and the fact that we were Created in that likeness. This means that we can draw upon what was Created in order to understand ourselves and each other. Since, based upon a woman's physical design, we can see that women were Created to receive, what we need to understand is why were women Created to receive.

We could take the ignorant stand and say that women were Created only to carry the seed of a man. What is ignorant is not that women were Created to carry the seed of man, that is obvious. The ignorant part is the notion that women were "*only*" Created to carry the seed of man. That position is a naturalist view and it is very shortsighted, but even if only to carry the seed of man it is still a beautiful gift that women should wear with a great deal of pride (not arrogance).

The ability to replicate life with the beauty and precision embodied in a newborn child is truly an awesome event that should not be disregarded in any way. So then, looking at the Creation that is called woman, what can we derive from her design?

Women are Created to receive, nurture, to bring forth, and much more. These are primary natural expectations that man has of woman. When these primary natural expectations are violated it is an offense against the man. It doesn't matter whether or not any one agrees with this, it's true regardless. Man has expectations about woman because of the design each of them are Created with, and these particular primary natural expectations were Created in the man.

This section, "How Spouses Are Shut Out by Their Own Actions" is called so, because, in general, husbands want little more from their relationship than the devotion and love of their spouse, but women often violate their husband's expectations in that regard. This is not stating the right or wrong, but rather the "*why*".

When men are violated at the base level of what they are Created as, then they often retreat from the violations, thus shutting out their wives. When you listen to men where they gather, outside of the presence of women, if men choose to talk personal at all, it becomes quite evident that many men shut their wives out. Woman is an important purpose of man. Violating Man's Created expectations of woman removes a great deal of a man's purpose and causes much turmoil in his heart.

When people, both men and women, are stripped of their purpose, then withdrawal, depression, and disrespect typically are what result, but another result can be anger.

Check the Toilet Seat BEFORE You Sit Down

The petty debates between husband and wife that are usually addressed when it is too late are only the surface of what is really occurring in a relationship. Twentieth century Western culture has adopted indoor plumbing, which includes a toilet-seat-ring. When left in the "up" position an unsuspecting woman will sit in the cold porcelain toilet bowl and may actually have her backside set into the bowl and get wet. This is an unwelcome situation for any woman at 3 AM when she's half-asleep. This particular event has become the butt of many jokes, but it is also a serious issue. It's not the position of the toilet seat that is the problem, but rather, it's the thought towards one another that is problematic.

Women want men to put the seat down when the men finish using the toilet. Men do not want the seat down because they want a larger target when they use the toilet. When the seat is left up, it often results in a discouraging shriek from the washroom at 3 AM. This shriek is sometimes followed by a berating of the man. While it is understandable that her harsh response might result, the question is: is it justified for a woman to berate her husband for leaving the seat up? This has been commonly joked about in various forms of entertainment for many years.

Her expectation was violated, but we need to question: Was it the man's responsibility to place the seat in the down position? After all, the seat is an optional part of the toilet. The point in this ridiculous section is that, of our own accord, we are each responsible for these tiny tasks, and we should not attack others because of our own lack of care in any situation.

Men prefer the seat up, and women prefer the seat down. Neither husband nor wife should be attacked for leaving the seat in their favored position. But since it is often being moved by each person into their desired position anyway, would it not then be better and more thoughtful that men would leave it down for their wives and women would leave it up for their husbands? As a side note to men: If you're the type to leave the seat down while you stand before the toilet, then have the decency to clean the seat off when you're done so that she doesn't have to sit in your mess, which is a common and often silent complaint that women have about the topic.

This silly section is not about a woman's need to leave the toilet seat up for their husband or even wisely checking to make sure it is down every time before sitting down. This section is about all of the small things that we allow to irritate us that are a part of the tit-for-tat of a difficult marriage.

There is much in our culture that has been turned backwards. There's a saying that asks, "Why are you so offended?" We typically get offended by the *right* things, and we allow the *wrong* things to slide by without much notice, but underneath we are offended by those wrong things, thus, allowing them to build up in us. When people deliberately intend to harm us, we're often too reluctant to speak up, but when the small marginal events occur, we sometimes get all bent out of shape. Both men and women do this. But men are typically easier to please and, stereotypically, have less concern about such small matters, thus making women stand out more in this regard. No one deserves to be beat down for something that is an optional task. Berating anyone for anything is typically uncalled for.

Is Your Home Safe From Spousal Attacks?

While men often have a certain amount of complacency with regard to the small things, women typically do not. When this is the case, a husband will suffer at his wife's hand, or rather, at her words. Because of the high level of tolerance most men have, their wives can usually complain about the small things without challenge or penalty. Men typically say, "Yes dear" because they feel that it's not worth the struggle, and in some cases the battle, to stand up to her.

"Yes dear" is a terrible mistake and should be used *only* when you actually mean it. While, stereotypically, it is women who complain about the small things, they are not alone in this. Men also do so. Regardless of who is getting upset about the small things, the level of response to the small things should match the offense.

Something as insignificant as the toilet seat being left "up" should *never* be a reason for screaming at your spouse. Any small thing that sets a person off to attack their spouse is a sign that something deeper is going on and is undetected in the person's life and heart. But regardless, when you attack your spouse for petty issues, it causes them to always be on alert and in fear of your unreasonable and unprovoked attacks.

A man should feel safe in his own home, and a woman should too! If you or your spouse do not feel safe inside of your own home, then something is terribly wrong. There is enough trouble in this world to give every man, woman, and child several helpings of trouble, so why allow trouble in your own home?

Our home is intended to be a safe haven where we can feel loved and protected. If we attack our spouse, or they attack us, then that safety is violated. This is a worse evil than the ravages of war, and is far more dangerous. The lack of security that we feel within our own home is a sad testament to our relationship and to our humanity.

When the enemy becomes the person that you sleep with, it is a bad thing and it does not follow the pattern set forth at Creation. There is a tremendous need for strained marriages to come to an understanding that the security needed to make the marriage joyful is *trust* and *truth*!

The trust is broken when violation-of-expectation occurs. If a man approaches his wife for affection and she refuses his offering, then she violates his expectation. This deeply hurts him every time it is done to him. This is also a two-way street seen or felt during physical intimacy and at other times—men violate women's expectations too. With this understanding, ask yourself this question: Is it, then, good for a person who wants to be kind to their spouse—to comply with their spouse even if they do not **want to** want to do it?

What Would It Feel Like if She <u>Really</u> Meant It?

When a man approaches his wife and he offers her his physical intimacy, deep down he wants her to accept that offering with great enthusiasm! When she doesn't, it violates his hopes and expectations. When his expectations fade, due to her persistent violation in this regard, he may still hold out hope and continue to make his offerings to her due to his remaining hope. But if he is violated long enough, then his last hope will also fade.

At a base level, his *fading hope*, in some way, is felt by his wife, and in her compassion for him or sense of duty to him she may comply and accept his offering on occasion, often called "pity sex". If this occurs on rare occasion, couples will survive and both probably understand this to some extent. But if you've fallen out of romantic desire for your spouse, then you had better acquire a taste for your spouse and what your spouse likes, and it must be real! It's like pepperoni. If you don't like it you simply don't like it, but if your spouse happens to be pepperoni, *then that's a problem for you*. You had better do something about it and acquire a taste for pepperoni, since *you* chose to marry pepperoni to begin with.

When one spouse has no interest in something and they comply with the spouse who has interest, then there's often a mistaken feeling that the disinterested spouse has the upper hand because they have the power to accept or decline the offer. In essence, they feel that they are doing the other person *a favor* by agreeing to take part in the activities. When this happens in the situation of physical intimacy, it is a core issue and cuts to the very base of our humanness.

The common situation of a woman declining her husband's offer for physical intimacy has been the root of many marital problems. In fact, men often bring this issue up to their wives only to be met with mockery, condemnation, and ridicule. When men put up enough of a fight, then often their wives reluctantly comply and "lie down and spread her legs and then everything seems okay." While this meets the physical need for a man, it fails to fulfill his actual and underlying true desire.

To get a clearer understanding of this, let's make the full assumption that we are made in the image of the Creator. The husband is not the Creator, but he has been Created in that position within the family. Consider this example: We kneel in prayer and make a request of the Creator, and then the Creator makes an offering to us as a gesture. If we say, "Well, I *suppose* I will accept your offering," are we then to assume that the Creator is going to want to fulfill our request with great enthusiasm when we *reluctantly and begrudgingly* accept the offer? Or should we make the more logical assumption that the Creator will have the disposition of *maybe* filling our request reluctantly and maybe even disregarding us altogether? Can we reluctantly and begrudgingly accept an offering and then expect the person, whose offer we are accepting, to actually be pleased with us? What would it feel like if the offering was accepted with true excitement and passion? Perceive what the Creator desires you to do, and then do likewise to your spouse.

When we simply comply out of duty and agree to accept the offering that our spouse has made to us, it is passionless and downright insulting! But when our offering is accepted with passion and great enthusiasm, then it is a true gift to both spouses! Faking enthusiasm *does not work*. Eventually your lie will find you out and you will be exposed for your lie. We cannot hide the way we feel forever. Our feelings leak out, a little here, and a little there, until it's revealed that we are dissatisfied with our situation.

Clear refusal to accept an offering is instantly hurtful. Faking a joyful acceptance might work for a time, but each instance of the false impression of joy builds the resentment that is felt when the truth is finally realized by the spouse who made the offer. This resentment runs very deep. To them, you betrayed them and made a fool of them. They will lose faith in you and will have little trust for you with regard to anything dear to them.

So whose problem is this? Is physical intimacy that important? This problem is both spouses' problem, and physical intimacy is as important to the relationship as it is to the person who holds it most dear. Anyone who attempts to deny this truth is self-deceived. Remembering that either a husband or wife could be in this position, as an example we can use the man offering his intimacy, because it tends to be seen as more common.

Intimacy is an offering, no matter which of you makes the offer. If the offer is not met with the expected joy and enthusiasm hoped for, then it will be felt as a violation by the offeror. If it's not real joy and enthusiasm being shown in the acceptance, then it's even more hurtful; though, it does fulfill a physical need and desire.

There is one way, and only one way, to *properly* accept intimacy, and that is with authenticity and passion! This point of contention is an important issue that deserves a great amount of scrutiny.

If, in kindness, we reluctantly accept an offering, can we then expect our spouse to be thrilled with our reluctant acceptance?— Not likely! The real question in all of this is: What would it feel like if the receiver actually meant it? How do you feel when you do something for someone and it is accepted with great enthusiasm? The likely answer is that you feel good, and you typically will want to offer to do so for them even more so in the future. *Gratitude* of an offering is best shown by accepting something with true excitement. But this presents a problem when a spouse simply does not feel like it or is not in the mood. Recall how you felt while you were dating or first married when *all* of your advances were warmly welcomed and freely accepted by your mate.

Freedom to Love

Freedom to love others is an important factor in the joy of any human being—and is the point of it all! When this freedom is stripped from us, it is very painful and takes away a great deal of our purpose as a person. The only way that the freedom to love can be stripped from you is if another refuses to accept the love that you offer them. *Freedom to love* is a point of tremendous ambiguity for us, and we typically misunderstand our own feelings.

Some people have the belief that we can love anyway, but this is not totally accurate. A love transaction cannot be completed unless it is truly received by the person to whom it is offered. If one person does not accept the offered love from another person, then it strips away the freedom to give the gift of love from the person making the offer.

Does this mean that you must let someone love you? No, certainly not. Rejecting love is also a freedom that we each have. But we're not talking about just anyone here, we are talking about the person to whom you have committed your love—your spouse. It was you who made the agreement to "love them until death do us part." Stripping away your spouse's freedom to love you is a trap for them, and it is very unfair to them.

When we behave this way, it is as if we *lured* and *trapped* our spouse into a contract (the marriage agreement), and we did it in front of family, community, and the Creator. Then we turn and decline the love that they offer us; thus not allowing them the freedom to love us. This is a blatant and heinous breach of the marriage contract agreement, and when we do this, it will cost us dearly in the end.

Just because we're able to offer our love to a person, does not mean that we have loved them. It means that we have *tried* to love them. We did our part of the transaction, and now it's up to the other person to accept it. Just as it is with the Creator, so is it with mankind.

The Creator offers continuous love to mankind, but the Creator can only truly love us when we accept that love because full and true love is a two way action. The only reason to not allow love is due to the fear and hate we hold in our own hearts. There's a simple obviousness to this statement that we do not have room to discuss in this book, but you must realize that it is important. There is more information on this in the cornerstone book *Understanding Prayer - Why Our Prayers Don't Work.*

It's important to mention that something, such as rape, cannot be considered an offering because the person is *forcing* the act in that case. With rape they are in essence saying "You are going to accept me and love me *no matter what!*" The problem with this empty approach is that *true* love is *never* forced. We are blind and are in violation when we force any action on another person. For it to be True Love, it is never forced, and is always accepted. People commit to people and are meant to be given to one another by the Creator—to be bound as one in love. If someone rapes, then they are taking what was not offered to them, and they are guilty of stealing, coveting, violating expectation, and maybe even adultery, all at the same time.

The freedom to love includes the freedom to accept love. Accepting love is the other half of the transaction. Any reluctance or forcing destroys and violates what we call "love".

What Men Mean When They Say "She Should Take the Lead"

When discussing relationships, you sometimes hear men say they want her to "take the lead". This is often connected to physical intimacy, but it goes much deeper than that. Physical intimacy is often only the face of the truth of what is occurring in a relationship. We do what we are, and if we do not do what we are, then we are liars. This is to say that, what we do on the outside should be a reflection of what is felt on the inside. If you're doing something against your true desire, then you are not being genuine. This is no secret, it is an obvious fact. But realize that a true desire will not be something that is harmful to others and will not be evil.

Men often incorrectly think that life would be great if every time they walked into the bedroom their spouse would throw herself at him. If she agreed to do this, initially it would likely be a thrill for him, but eventually he would find that it is still missing something that he is seeking. Our problem is that we fail to connect with what is missing, and therefore we don't see it.

There is something very attractive about a spouse who is willing to take the lead. Please understand that "taking the lead" does not mean being demanding and asserting your ways on others. *Taking the lead* means knowing what you want and not being afraid to respectfully get or ask for it. When a man says this about his wife taking the lead, he wants his wife to have *him* be the subject of her quest while she takes the lead. In essence, she is inviting him and he wants her to invite him. It is a woman's way to offer. A woman can take the lead in many ways, such as by dressing in a way that pleases her husband, for her husband. And a husband can do the same for his wife. This means that they will wear, not what their spouse *asks* them to wear, but rather, what their spouse *wants to ask* them to wear, please make the distinction between those two perspectives.

The offering of taking the lead is best when something is done before, *in advance of* being asked to do so, then it is an offering. Wearing clothes that appeal to your spouse, rather than clothes that only appeal to you, is one way you can take the lead. There are many other aspects of life where both spouses can take the lead and make the kind and loving offering of actually listening to their spouse, and then doing things that the spouse would like *in advance* of them having to ask you to do it *with*, *for*, or *to* them.

Taking the lead is about—*in advance* of having to be asked—doing what is enjoyable and best for you both and disregarding your unjustified inhibitions that inhibit your marriage. It's when we think about our spouse, and our desire is to please them in our confidence without them having to ask, that we have "taken the lead". This is amongst the best gifts that wives and husbands can offer each other!

Who Should Take the Lead?

So who should take the lead in a marriage? For the most part, both of you should take the lead, but not necessarily at the same time unless you are going in the exact same direction. At times, one of you will want to go this way and the other will want to go that way, but you can't do that and still be together, so one of you will have to follow the other alternately.

Our problem is that we often fight what each other wants, which only causes more problems. We need to teach ourselves to share the lead and alternate leading, or we need to lead together. When we alternate leading and our spouse is taking the lead, then we need to do our part with true passion. If we don't, then we destroy their lead, and in turn, that will likely destroy our lead.

There is something that is better than you taking the lead or your spouse taking the lead, and that's when you are in harmony and you lead hand in hand by both of you having the same hopes, dreams, expectations, and goals. This is how we are meant to be—as one! Both leading together and being of one mind and one heart.

This rare blissful state is good for everyone who encounters a couple who has achieved this ultimate state of being that is free of selfishness and violation. There's nothing more important than the harmony created in your relationship via true support of your spouse's desires. If you cannot joyfully invite this into your heart, then you *will* have problems.

Invitations and Offerings

For a married couple, the lead should be shared. But there will be times when the "lead" is the immediate action. In the case of physical intimacy, when a woman takes the lead she is inviting. An invitation is the female equivalent of a man offering. It is her way of making an offering to her spouse.

A wife offers an invitation, and doing so is very appealing to her husband. Generally, men will joyously take their wives up on offers of such invitations, it is the most loving act wives can do when it is true. It's the way women love. Men redundantly offer their offering, where women, on the other hand, offer their invitation. It's when her invitation and his offering come together that a married couple achieves bliss if and when this is included in, and goes beyond, just the bedroom.

An important note for men with regard to a wife's invitations: Men should be sensitive to their wives' caution with regard to becoming pregnant if the two of you have decided that you have completed your family. This is an obvious reason for her to reject your offerings, or for her to not offer you her invitations unless proper precautions are carefully being taken *and respected*. Sometimes men approach intimacy with reckless abandon while in the heat of the moment, and then wonder why they got rejected. Be creative and avoid the need for such rejections.

The Way We See Things

Invitations and offerings are not exclusive to physical intimacy. In fact, they are heavily woven into every aspect of our relationships. If invitations and offerings were only in the intimate setting, then we could solve all marriage problems by getting people to understand that mutual intimacy would solve their problems. In many magazines articles that is indeed what you read; that physical intimacy solves relationship problems. While physical intimacy is problematic for some couples, it is the *everything-else-in-life* part that causes most problems in our marriages. And typically, we mistakenly assume it is intimacy issues causing the problem, which is why so many people do not understand what causes them to have troubled marriages.

An important portion of the everything-else-in-life part is the elusive itch that needs to be scratched that we spoke of earlier. Only this time, it's not about whether or not your spouse can hit the spot when scratching your itch. If a subject is not discussed, we generally assume everyone feels the same way that we feel about something. This is not something that we are aware of, yet this is our natural inclination. If you don't like to be touched and you never discussed the issue of touching with your spouse, then it is very likely that you will make the blind assumption that your spouse does not like to be touched either. You need only think upon this for a moment for it to become very obvious to you.

In general, from birth on, we rarely think of how others feel about something. We tend to become more sensitive to this as our own expectations are violated. Our sensitivity makes us privy to the fact that someone else has a different viewpoint than us. When this happens, we are better able to consider that others may or may not like something that we like.

A very troubling area with a married couple is—not being able to recognize that their spouse does not see things in the same way that they do. Since we started with scratching the itch, we will end with that. If someone does not like being scratched, then to them, it is unlikely that they will offer to scratch your itch. Even if you ask them to scratch your itch, they may respond to the request puzzled as to why you would even ask to be scratched. This is due to their dislike of being touched in that way.

It's important for all of us to realize that the offerings and invitations that we each make are easily violated. Also, realize that when you make your offerings and invitations, that your offerings and invitations should take into account what your mate actually likes. If you don't take your mate's likes and tastes into consideration, and you impose your offering on your mate, then you are asking them to like something that they do not like—and that is forced love, which is not love at all! We can begin to achieve true joy in the relationship when we each look into the heart of our spouse and truly work to understand what *they* desire, and we must have *authentic passion* to fulfill their desires.

Chapter 8

Being in Control versus Being Controlling

Life is short, and achieving joy throughout our lives can be a struggle. There are many people who want things to go their own way. This is fine when it's not at the expense of other people. Your life is *your* life, and you have to live it your own way, but your way should not adversely impact others. Always keep in mind that you have to live with whatever you create in your own life. If you create bad circumstances around you, then you will suffer at those circumstances. But if you create joy in your life, then you will enjoy the fruits of your efforts. This is true for relationships as well: If a person is trying to seek joy by controlling their spouse, it will not be pleasant for that person's spouse. But when you have trust and love in a relationship, then the relationship grows and becomes more robust!

With our inherent design, we have a tendency to understand things as: A man is supposed to control and a woman should submit. This wrong thinking is what the feminist movement of the twentieth century was born of. While some good points were made by that movement, in truth, it served to damage the true essence of many women more than almost everything before it ever did.

The feminist movement became the battle for control in women versus men. This should never be—it should never exist! There should never be a battle for who should control, especially within a couple. When this battle is in existence, it becomes about controlling, rather than about being in control of your own life. There is a world of difference between the two perspectives— *controlling* versus *being in control.*

For both men and women, there is nothing more attractive than someone who is *in control.* The question is: In control of what? The feminist movement rightly fought for women to not be controlled by men, but the movement forfeited its usefulness by instantly trying to control others via demanding compliance from men and the general populous for the feminist's extreme demands. This is why the mentalities leading it, and resulting from it, were such dismal failures, but it did serve to open the minds of some foolish men who wrongly held themselves superior over women. Generally, those who sing its praises are those who have come to be controlling of others, including men who fight for the superiority that the movement came to be fighting for and the men who are afraid of the women they are with. There were many respected women who were forceful but graceful leaders for centuries and millennia before the feminist movement ever came along. Many of these women possessed the secret that was sought, but missed, by the feminist movement.

Regardless of the purity of their intent, there is much wrong thinking in our society which is neither good nor Biblical that has been perpetrated on the citizens of our Earth by people bent on controlling others. Being *controlling* carries the meaning of controlling others, but being *in control* carries the meaning of knowing what you are doing and why you are doing it, and then confidently moving forward with the full freewill agreement of the others around you, while at the same time it being completely void of *any* coercion.

When we are bent on controlling others we declare our insecurity, and by trying to fill this void we have chosen to attempt to force others to submit to our will, thus giving us a feeling of superiority. This is not exclusive to the feminist movement. It often includes both male and female clergy, politicians, husbands, wives, and everyone else who has chosen to arrogantly try to control others through position or status. Those who do so, have the mistaken feeling that they actually control others as they force others to submit via coercion, force, and manipulation.

When we strive to control others, what we are not realizing is that most people only put up with us because of one or more of the following reasons: They are afraid. They are waiting for their oppressors to die. They are very patient. Or they are oblivious. *Fear* and *oblivion* are the two most prominent reasons, which is why we see so much fear talk, often referred to as fear mongering in government politics. When people fear something, then they can be easily controlled and manipulated through that fear.

The truth is that those who are trying to control others are the ones who are truly afraid. They have no oppressors but themselves, and there is no escape from themselves. This is perhaps the most tortuous existence imaginable for any person. The fear that they instill in others is not fear, as much as it is a desire for not being harmed and being left alone and not bothered by their irritating oppressors.

Manipulation Via Sex is About Control

Whether it is the man or the woman who is doing the manipulation, manipulation via sex is about control. It tends to be more common that women do this because they are the one who invites and that gives them a great deal of perceived power. When a person has something that others desperately want, then that person appears to hold all of the power and can command their price. When physical intimacy is used in this way, it is being abused, and the person who is doing the manipulation is trying to control their spouse. Doing so is not good.

Using intimacy to manipulatively get what you want amounts to prostitution, and it will fail in the long run. When someone is using physical intimacy as a form of coercion to get what they want, then they are essentially being a prostitute. Prostitutes by trade are after cash, because cash is what they want. At some point, the person who is bargaining to get sex from their spouse will come upon the realization that they can hire a prostitute at less emotional cost than a spouse is. This is because with a prostitute there is a perception that there is no emotional attachment with which to be emotionally injured and manipulated.

Being *in control* has the voice of command and authority. A person in control knows what to do and why they need to do it. They know the next logical move, and they do not hesitate to do so because they understand *what* they're doing and *why* they are correct. They gain the respect and trust of those around them because they are understanding the needs of the situation, and they are certain in their actions.

On the other hand, people who are *controlling* see this all wrongly. To them it appears that a person who is in control is forcing people to do things by demanding to have it their own way. Dictators are controlling. People who are controlling don't care whether something is right or wrong, they just want things to go their own way regardless of what harm it causes others. When a controlling person is faced with a person who is in control, then the *controlling* person's stubbornness to face the truth of the situation leads them to believe that the person who is *in control* is wrong.

Submitting to a controlling person and doing only as you are told can also have health risks that you will have to deal with as you age into your latter years.

Any controlling within a marriage is void of love and is utterly selfish. It cares nothing of the other person and only serves to benefit the controller. The difficult aspect of a relationship with a controlling spouse is that they likely grew up in a controlling atmosphere, so that is all that they know and understand. When we allow ourselves to be controlled by them it reinforces that behavior. They confuse *controlling* others with *being in control.*

Terrorists and Rapists Are the Same

Dictators are usually, ultimately, terrorists and they frequently obtain power by force as they overthrow everyone around them. They force their will on their subjects and impose their beliefs on them. They find weak people who fear them and then coerce those weak people to threaten others, usually with violence and death. We see this with any extremist group, both large and small. This happened all throughout recorded history and is still happening in our modern times. This will continue to happen until truth reigns supreme. No matter who or what the purpose, bullies, terrorists, and rapists are all the same in their underlying function and reasoning. Regardless of the age of the people being dominated, if someone is intent on having their way, despite what it means to your well-being from life as a youth all the way to old aged death, they are terrorists and have chosen to be evil of their own accord. They are free to choose otherwise anytime they desire. But sadly, few of them ever see the light well enough to save themselves from their own self-destruction.

This also happens within marriages and families. Often one or both of the parents impose martial-law on the family and rule their children with an iron-fist. These children almost always rebel or withdraw into permanent defeat. Then when they are adults, they typically emulate their parents' behavior. Those parents were either raised in this same way, or because of the way they misunderstood the world, they felt that they were raised in an iron-fisted family. Being an iron-fisted dictator quickly becomes terrorism when the person doing the demanding is not in power but *wants* to be in power and will do anything to obtain that power. This is true whether or not that power is rightfully theirs.

People who rule with an iron-fist demand control of others and view any attempt at resistance as an offensive attempt to control them. There is a tremendous difference between one person saying, "*I am going to control you.*" and another person saying, "*No, you are not going to control me.*" But a terrorist-type person does not see it that way. They always do what they think is best for themselves regardless of how many innocents are harmed or are killed in the process. In many cases, they try to justify their actions by painting a "poor me" picture of themselves to distract attention away from what is actually occurring, which is that they are hiding their errors and insecurities.

When someone resists a terrorist or bully, then that terrorist or bully sees that resistance as an attempt to control them. When we say to a bully, "Leave me alone," they feel that we are telling them what to do, which is something that bullies do not like. This type person sees this wrongly because their understanding of the world is very mono-centric. They see the world only from their personal perspective and fail to realize that others have the right to have a view of their own.

Having your own view is fine, even if it's wrong. The problem occurs when we try to *forcibly* and *belligerently* impose our view and demand that others accept our erred perspective. It's also a problem when we harm innocent people whenever it's more convenient for us to do so. This should not be confused with free sharing of good, true, and well-documented information. When people discuss topics in debate and lay down good, articulate, solid discourse that proposes different views, the terrorist's perspective sees such discourse as an imposition because they refuse to hear what might be true whenever it goes against their own desires.

We've seen this with religious matters: It's true that over the course of the centuries various religious beliefs were indeed forced upon the people in a terror-like manner. However, in recent times it has tilted to a different direction. Now those who do not agree with the religious perspectives scream and cry foul that "religion is being forced down their throats", but this is simply no longer true. In fact, it is nearly impossible to have discussion with this type of person because they refuse to hear any evidence that threatens their own non-provable points of view. This dangerous attitude is the basis of all terrorism, bullying, and dictatorial leadership.

The truth of the matter is that *anyone* who *unjustly* forces their will on another person, without proper discourse and willingness to hear and process the other person's perspective, is a terrorist or rapist. They are stealing from the other person, especially when it concerns an unsuspecting innocent third party.

Based on the previous section, someone could foolishly argue that forcing your own way is an *offer*, but that would clearly be wrong. When an offer is forced, then it is no longer an offer, and it becomes a conditional demand. This is often and easily confused with laying down final ultimatums. Final ultimatums generally have a person walking away in disgust; where on the other hand, a threat suggests aggressive and unjustified action for failure to comply.

A Culture of Women Wanting to Control

Closed minds get *angry* in frustration, but open minds *understand.* The difference between terrorism via controlling, and a final ultimatum, is a fine point that is easily missed by most of us unless we understand with our inherent ability to grasp what *truth* means. A terrorist can offer a final ultimatum and still be a terrorist, but someone who offers a final ultimatum is not necessarily a terrorist.

A final ultimatum is saying, "I will no longer tolerate your abuse of me", where a terrorist's final ultimatum will say, "If you don't do this, then I will harm you." The reason this is a fine-line point is that if you decide to offer a final ultimatum and no longer allow someone in your life, then in their eyes you're harming them by your withdrawal. Yet, you are doing nothing to them, and there is no malice or aggression in your actions. You are simply withdrawing. Where a controlling person, on the other hand, is specifically intending harm and malice as retaliation of what they perceive as an attack against *them*, from *you*, because of your resistance. Almost all controlling ultimately follows this fundamental pattern, and often a terrorist's final ultimatum will have been utterly unprovoked by you.

While we generally don't like to think of a controlling spouse as a "terrorist", they are still using those same tactics and, thus, behave in a controlling manner.

Those who choose to follow the naturalist's mantra do not want to hear that men are designed to guide their wives. If you believe in the naturalist philosophy, then a choice needs to be made by you at some point, as to which avenue you're going to take the rest of your life. Will you stay the same and suffer? Or will you change your ways at some point in order to achieve the joy you seek?

A man was Created first, and then was given a specific instruction that was intended to be shared with woman. He was not intended to demand her, but rather to guide her and teach her. Too often, for many men, *guiding* is mistaken for *dictating* a woman.

Dictating someone is simply wrong! Guiding, on the other hand, is a loving revelation of what is true. Because of our social culture and our upbringing, this often gets turned around and husbands are often in the dark. When this is the case, it is like "the blind leading the blind."

In many cases, the woman ends up guiding the husband because of the way they were raised. This is not wrong; in fact, anytime a person can bear the light of truth to another person it's a wonderful and good thing! But sometimes, when women attempt to "guide", it is mistakenly and unnecessarily done in a manner of controlling the other person as previously described.

True guidance can only be guidance to true things, and guidance will never force. But *controlling* someone will almost always force things. We must be diligent in keeping our best judgment at hand because someone might gently and unknowingly lead us down a wrong path as they kindly try to "guide" us to their erred belief.

Western culture is full of examples of "strong women" family traditions of controlling their husbands by using manipulation and terrorism to get an upper hand and have things their own way. This destructive behavior destroys families and devastates future generations, regardless of which spouse is doing it.

Forcing Your Mate to Be Compatible

When we control, we demand others to be and do what *we* want. The underlying goal of this can even be well intended; but in any case, change cannot occur without understanding on the part of the person who is being controlled.

If we look at child rearing, we can see that there are times when a parent must force a child to do certain things—Sort of like a mother bird forcing her chicks out of the nest in order for them to learn to fly. This becomes problematic when it is done for one's own self, rather than for the good of the other person. Making others do what *we* want is a dangerous double-edged sword.

Many relationships suffer because of fear. If one person's fear is focused on the failure that typically accompanies excelling in something, then having your spouse push you into trying something new may be a good thing. But if your spouse is doing it so that you become what *they* want you to be, then they are trying to force you to be compatible for them. This is never successful and it destroys freewill.

There's a great deal of misconception in relationships. The difficult part of misconception that must be addressed is the need to get those who are doing the misconceiving to begin to understand that they are, in fact, misconceiving. A good therapist will lead you to understanding, and you will see it for yourself. Then when you see it, it is you who had the realization. This is usually done by asking the person things like, "How did that make you feel?"

You should be getting a pretty good idea as to whether it's you or your spouse who is the cause of most of your problems. It may be that you're both more or less equally creating your relationship troubles. Regardless of what your situation is, immediately ceasing any actions that are an attempt at controlling one another is vital!

Can People Who Do Not Admire You, Respect or Learn From You?

A good goal to aim for in order to eliminate any controlling behavior in a relationship, is to earn admiration—not demand it. When someone admires you, they are more likely to respect and learn from what you have to offer them. It's important to know that if a person's familiar ways are such that they are mentally poor, then they may take your offering as an affront.

Your offering may be very well intended, but their *Hot Water* causes them to resist their respect and admiration for you because they were taught, by example, to not respect others. Thus, they cannot learn from you. This imbalance is not fair by any stretch of the imagination, but it happens nonetheless. The difficulty in this problem is that they do not understand what they're doing when they reject what you're offering them. It may hurt your feelings, but, in the long run, it costs them a great deal more. *They harm themselves* and they have rendered themselves un-teachable.

You could have a high prestigious degree in your field of expertise and could have invented widely used technology and have made billions, but if a person who needs your expertise does not respect you then they will disregard you and your information as if it is worthless. When they do this they render themselves unteachable. This means, specifically, that *you* are not able to teach *them*.

The sad fact is that this type of person often looks for the wrong things in life. They often see it in the wrong people and gravitate towards those people. And then these wrong people typically render the person's preexisting inability to *see clearly* even more clouded, ending in causing them even greater frustration than before.

A Person Who Demands Your Attention and Disregards Your Admiration is a Negative Draw on You

When people are in a state of mind that is clouded in a demanding but disregarding way, they will seldom understand that you don't admire them because they disregard you and what you think of them. In other words, they don't care what your impression of them is. Yet, they will still insist upon your attention and demand that you attend to them.

Their demands are usually not made by simply saying, "Hey, look at me." Their demands are often much more subtle. Their actions are self-serving and generally disregard any of your desires. This negative attitude can suck the energy out of you, especially when you're not specifically aware that it's occurring. They are parasites, but again, it's important to note that they might not understand that they do these things. Often their demeanor is cruel, but they are not necessarily being *intentionally* malicious even though they are behaving maliciously.

The pain that this kind of behavior causes is very intense for the spouse who is being controlled. By understanding this, you reduce the intensity of pain that is inflicted on you by them, and it gives you the ability to take back and regain from them, the control of your own life. Take great care in observing this so that you better understand what is occurring in your relationship. This will help you cope with a bad situation and allow you to better communicate your perspective to your spouse in the future.

Chapter 9

Givers and Takers

So far, all problems we discussed point to being caused by the improper *give* and *take* actions within a marriage.

What are givers and takers? To stay clear of semantics arguments and for the purposes of this book, it is not the words, but rather the specific concepts behind those words that we're trying to understand.

There are different kinds of takers: One kind could be compared to someone who *fraudulently* abuses the welfare system or the insurance companies and is illegally or dishonestly taking the financial benefits of those systems. This kind of taker is of little use to society because they do not increase the worth of the world, they are parasites. *Don't* be that type of a person. Another type of taker could be a boss, for instance, who demands excessive efforts from the employees and then contributes to the world but only for his or her own gain and at the expense of the employees. But in that case, usually the offering only benefits themselves, and is actually a net-loss to the world, just like fraudulently abusing the government or other companies is a net-loss to the world. If a boss takes joy away from the employees, and then only gives a little bit of happiness back to the world, then that boss is a thief and has robbed the world of a great deal of joy. The idea of "what goes around comes around" really does work its way through life, and in time it catches up with everyone for good or for bad.

This can happen in a marriage too. If one of the people in the couple is not contributing to the joy of the marriage, then they have become a *taker* from that marriage. When we take without permission and don't give back to the world or, in our case here, to the marriage, then we have a negative personal value to the world and/or to the marriage. There is nothing made by the hands of mankind in this world that would exist if most people did not increase the value of the world by giving more than they have worked for. There is nothing in this world that does not work on a checks-and-balance system in this way. When we are not building the world up to be a better place with our actions, then we are stealing from the world and we are tearing the world down and have become parasites. This is no different in a marriage.

Most people would say that when a woman accepts an offer that she is a taker. In fact, after she accepts, she does indeed take from the man. However, in the true sense of the word, taking is more of a controlling action. The difference being, that a mother can *offer* her children cookies and they will *accept* them, where on the other hand, *taking* is when the cookies were left on the table and the children just *took* them *without asking* permission, especially when they know that they were not supposed to take them without permission.

Alternately, givers can also be forcible givers. Generally, with this too, most of us would make the connection that a person offering something is a giver, and this is true, because when the offering is received, then the offering has been given. However, when we give something, it has not necessarily been offered.

An offering says, "I have this and I would love for you to have it", where giving can say, "Take this, or else!" leaving no option for the recipient to refuse. "Giving" in this way, is like the terrorist action spoken of in the last chapter. This unpopular approach is unwelcome and commonly used in politics and matters of government.

When comparing the terms *givers* and *takers* side by side, most of us look at takers as a more negative behavior and givers as kind and generous behavior. This is, by and large, true, yet we need to consider how and what is being given. The give and take examples just given offer you a clear picture of the *give* versus *take* behaviors without the biases we hold while analyzing our own relationships. The following list will clear up some of the confusion that we have about "givers" and "takers".

Offer: is to ask, "Do you want this?"
Give: is to transfer possession to someone
Accept: is to agree to receive
Take: is to obtain possession
Receive: is to allow into possession
Invite: is to request an offering
Reject: is to not comply with an action

Properly Understand Give and Take

You properly understanding the concepts in other people's minds that often lies behind these terms is critical to your understanding of a troubled relationship. An important part of a relationship is the *give* and *take*. When done properly, you both *offer* and *accept* with each completed give and take transaction.

When a person "offers" to you, and you willingly accept their *offer*, then you have completed a successful exchange with them. This is true whether it is a friend offering help, or a lover offering affection. When you refuse your lover's offer, your refusal will be taken as an insult unless it is done properly and fairly. Flat out rejecting an offer amounts to taking, and taking is always seen as a violation when there is no preceding offering because you robbed them of the ability to give.

If an offering does not allow an "out" for the person to whom it is offered, then the expectation is that the offering is going to be accepted. When that expectation is violated, then the person refusing has taken away the offeror's freedom to give. This gets a bit confusing if you go through it too quickly, so take good care in understanding this section.

The *intention* of these words that we are discussing centers around each spouse's perspective of the words.

We *invite* someone to *accept* our *offer*, so that they can *receive* what we want to *give* them. The following example details the instances of these concepts:

A husband offers to give: May I come in?

A wife invites the offer: Why yes, please do come in!

A husband accepts her invitation: Thank you!

A husband gives the offer (of presence): He steps inside.

A wife has opened the door and receives the gift: Please come in and make yourself comfortable.

Transaction complete!

There are at least ten instances of these concepts in the single transaction shown above, and each is an opportunity for transaction success, or transaction failure and personal violation. About the only thing that blows a perfect transaction is *rejection*.

These *give* and *take* issues we are discussing might seem petty to some people, but *all* problems are born out of this type of situation. In fact, *all* communication rotates around a relationship transaction. Master this and you master communication of all kinds!

Mastery of communication transactions does not guarantee success in every single transaction, but it greatly increases your success rate.

Transactions always have at least two sides. Properly doing your part cuts your chance of transaction failure in half. Doing any of this for purely selfish reasons breaks down the transaction and sabotages it, which will result in failure in the long run.

To *receive* and to *take* are similar, but when you *receive*, then your freewill reception allows me to place it in your hand. Whereas *taking* is your hand grasping it from my hand; and that is a world of difference.

Offer and *give* appear similar, but to offer is to hold it in my *open* hand, where give is to *place it in* someone's hand, which is also a world of difference.

Accept and *invite* are not similar in the direction of the action like *receive* and *take*, or like *offer* and *give* are. However, *accept* and *invite* are similar to each other in that they are uniquely dissimilar to other words, unlike the potential confusion between *receive* and *take*, and between *offer* and *give*. The concepts of *accept* and *invite* are not easily misunderstood or confused in meaning.

Then Must I Accept the Offer?

When a person offers to you, and you accept that offer, it was a successful exchange; but if you refuse the offer then it is an insult unless the refusal is done properly. There are times when it is not possible to accept an offer because of other pre-existing commitments or circumstances someone may have already had. There are also times when what is being offered does not appeal to you. So then, must you accept the offer so that you don't insult the other person? Of course not. That's where honesty, diplomacy, and gentleness come together. In an instance where you *do* want to accept, but are unable to, it's important to let the other person know that you are desirous of their offer, and that you desire to accept such an offer at a different time when circumstances allow you to do so.

When the offer is something offensive to your beliefs or likes, then much care must be used in rejecting the offer. It is a lie to say something is desirable when you believe that it is not. Finding the right words, and the order in which to use them, is critical to your future relationship with that person. If the differences are many, then you might not be compatible. Compatibility is not a make-or-break part of a relationship, but having similar beliefs and interests makes for a more comfortable, smoother operating, and more enjoyable relationship.

If you find yourself and your spouse frequently rejecting each other's offers, then you must come to understand that these rejections are possibly deeply rooted in your upbringings. Overcoming our own inaccurate interpretations of life is humanity's single most difficult obstacle. It is important to note that the offers we are referring to here are not offers that are meant to be malicious or harmful.

Kind, loving, and gentle communication when you are contemplating giving or receiving an offer is critical to a strong and joyous relationship. When this is not the case then the response is often malicious. *Rejecting an offer* in malice is equally as bad as *making an offer* in malice.

How do I know if Someone is a Taker? What to Look For

Offers that are born in malice are not offers at all! And offers rejected in malice are likewise. In truth, these rejections are violations and a type of taking—they are theft!

When we give something, then that gift is the tangible aspect of an offer, but offering something with any forcible action or intent of malice is an attempt to take freedom from the recipient. This violation is a hidden form of taking.

There is a more obvious form of *taking*. People who are *takers* seldom hold any regard for those around them, and the takers often see themselves as receivers. They jump in front of anyone to "get theirs". To spot takers, simply watch their intent. When you look for it you will quickly see the motives in their actions. This is like the cookie example used earlier where the cookies could be taken without asking, even if it's okay to do so.

Givers can be takers too. The root of the words "gift" and "give" are the same, so in truth it is inaccurate to say that a giver can be a taker. Let me explain what I mean: When someone gives to someone, if there is a specific expectancy or strings attached then they are not giving at all. They are, in fact, taking or stealing from the person. Putting reciprocal demands on a so-called gift removes the status of "gift" and turns it into a trap. You are, in a way, selling your soul to that person if you accept such a gift. Sometimes businesses have need of this, however, in a personal relationship that is supposed to be based upon love, and in this case it causes problems in the long run.

Alternately, someone who accepts a gift can also be a taker. If you offer something as a gift to someone and they accept that gift, but then they attach strings and have a conditional acceptance, then they have robbed you of the gift status that you offered and they have turned it into a manipulative acceptance. They have taken or stolen your generosity.

These seem to be strong words, but when we look at the problems caused by takers, which includes our own selves, we can quickly see how important it is to recognize these behaviors. We need to either depart from these people, or confront them with bold certainty when they attempt to violate us in this manner. If we don't, then they will continue to destroy their own life and the lives of everyone around them through their inconsiderate actions.

To understand how to spot this in people, and in yourself, you must grasp the difference between *receiving* something and *taking* something. It is the recognition of the difference between these two words that will give you the ability to spot taking when it happens to you. If you cannot detect the difference, then it is likely that you see takers as receivers, and you are likely often taking from others as well, and/or you are likely being violated in this way on a regular basis and are blind to it.

What are You Worth?
Your Time is Money

One area that greatly affects a marriage from the outside, where it is apparent that takers exist, is when it comes to money. There are many people who are covetous of your money. We often see where people will prey on the elderly in an attempt to take their money via phone scams and other such unscrupulous acts. There are so many different ways in which people want to take our money without proper exchange, that it would require a set of books just to explain them all.

When we take from someone, we become a consuming fire that destroys. This destructive behavior can turn billions worth of value into nothing—overnight! Interest or usury, the stock market, and many types of insurance are examples of taking with little or no return for many people. Some insurances and interest rob the majority of people of their time and stockpiles their money for the takers for no great purpose. This money often evaporates in economic turmoil, turning it into nothing every five to ten years.

Interest and insurance are not completely bad, but not understanding them and their purpose is bad. Interest allows many people to own homes and insurance helps many when they become injured or their home is destroyed, etc. When we misunderstand this, we allow the unscrupulous aspects of business to waste away our lives by taking the money that we spent so many of our days and hours earning.

The way we make money in this world, typically, is to work and/or think and create. When we put in our time or idea, then we get paid for a value that we agreed upon. The time we spend doing our work is converted into cash. This cash represents our time. We set our own value by accepting the offered wage.

If you work for a low wage you will need to work more hours just for your family to survive financially. This takes you away from your family and makes your money even more valuable to you because you have spent more of your time *per dollar* than a higher paid person does. A person with much more money will typically not value your money with the same time-spent index as you do. As far as our existence goes, no one person is of more value than another person, unless we have chosen to devalue our own self by believing lies. No person can have more value than being true.

Your money is a representation of your time, don't squander it, and don't allow takers to squander it. When we refer to squandering in this way, it is not meant that you must save every penny and become a miser; but rather, use your money wisely. If you die with your money, you have wasted the time that you spent earning the money that you died with.

Often, one or both of the two spouses in a couple squanders the money that they have spent so much of their time earning. Their excessive work-time leaves little time to enjoy each other's company. Additionally, they often spend money that they have not yet earned. This means that they already spent time that they have not yet put in, and they will need to pay that time back. The stress that results from this sort of time-debt often creates much difficulty in marriage and steals away your time together. When this happens, and the stress and tensions grow, then the husband and wife often come at odds with each other. Through their frustration and anger, they will either have reduced desire to be near each other, or their desire is altogether lost, which commonly ends in divorce.

When we are forced to work in order to cover our own or our spouse's debt, then we no longer are the masters of our own time and we must work to serve our new time-master. Thus, taking and stealing away the time we could or should be spending with our spouse and family.

Insurance, investing, and usury are not necessarily bad, but often the people behind them don't care about you or your time. They are only interested in your money. It is up to *you* and *your spouse* to be certain that you do not negotiate bad financial deals for your family. Out of necessity, businesses make their money by making deals that favor them, and it is your job to make deals that favor you and not to put you and your spouse at too great a financial or time risk.

When a couple buys a house, the mortgage for the house typically takes about twenty years to pay off. Often the payments amount to about a quarter to a half of the annual wage earned by the family. This means that ten about years of their full-time-work time is dedicated to paying for their house. Of course this changes with fluctuating interest rates.

If a family has their finances in order and has excess cash, then it is sometimes invested. When money sits idle it has a tendency to lose its value in the eyes of the person who earned it. When this money is invested or spent frivolously, it must be thought of as a representation of the time you spent working that separated you from your family during that time. The amount of money that you have is only about half of what you actually earned because close to half of people's pay goes towards the various taxes and getting to the job. Once you have that figure understood, you can double it to compensate for the expenses encountered during the time it takes to earn that much money. It's a good idea to calculate the hours needed to earn that amount of money; because doing this mathematical exercise changes many couples' perspective about squandering their money when they understand how long they have to work to replace it.

The same holds true for when you buy something on credit or borrow. You need to factor in all of the expenses and taxes and then divide by your hourly wage to see how many hours you need to work for that item. If we would always do this before making large purchases, and before nickel-and-diming ourselves into poverty, it would greatly alter our spending habits.

Your money represents your time; do not squander it! Financial stress on a marriage can be devastating. There are many takers lined up just waiting to take your hard-earned money that you sacrificed time with your spouse and family for. It's your own responsibility to get the proper perspective on this and then protect and wisely spend your money for the joy of your family and those around you. Please do not understand this as an attack on business. Most businesses are run by people like you, who have families and want to protect their own money for the joy of their own families.

Couples must be keenly aware of such money issues because the amount of stress finances place on many relationships is a catalyst for the destruction of those marriages. Understanding the driving force behind the taking of your family's hard-earned cash, gives you an advantage over the takers.

An Important Part of a Relationship

The *offering* and *accepting*, and the *giving* and *receiving* within in a marriage are the joy of a marriage! Without these key elements a proper marriage does not exist. If you're interacting without the key elements, you are then in a master/slave relationship where one spouse is servant to the other. In marriages where this is the case, neither spouse is able to experience the fullness of the joy of a smoothly functioning marriage.

In these joyless marriages one spouse is a taker, and their taking steals away the *offerings* or *givings* (gifts) of the other spouse. This sort of marital-taking often ends up positioning the perspective so that the innocent spouse either appears to be, or is accused of being, a taker, though it may not be thought of in those terms.

Takers steal. They are thieves! If you're a taker, then you can change your perspective and tactics immediately the moment you choose to, and join the realm of the living.

Become a receiver rather than a *taker*, and enjoy the fruits of *inviting, offering, giving, accepting*, and *receiving*. It's a wonderful way to live that gives you an unshakable confidence. You will no longer feel so afraid or be so desperate to protect yourself that you feel the need to control others.

The Dangers of "Taking"

I don't like to give words a bad or improper meaning like so many words today have wrongly taken on. It's difficult to even carry on a conversation without being giggled at by people for making a statement containing some word that has come to be associated with sex, a sex organ, or some derogatory remark. With this in consideration, all of what has been discussed so far, generally orbits around the concepts underlying a handful of words. It's not the words themselves, but rather the concepts of *invite, offer, accept, give, receive,* and *take* that must be understood.

When we label things, we're making a dangerous assumption that people will grasp what is meant by the label even if they are new to the label or have not taken the time to fully understand it. While labels often speak for themselves, the true meaning and essence becomes lost or overlooked by subsequent generations who are using the label, which presents a problem to future generations.

The word "take" in itself is not evil, but all evil takes. Evil does not invite, offer, accept, give, or receive. Evil destroys, it consumes. Anything or anyone who consumes without return or exchange degrades their own life and the lives of those around them. They are intent on destruction and generally do not know or understand that they are doing this.

This is why it's so important to teach your children to work for, and earn, what they get. Sadly, when children are taught, they are often taught not to earn, but instead they are taught to become servants—consumers.

When children are not taught to earn, they are often given everything without expectation of return. This causes them to be takers and they do not know or understand this. Teaching your children the value of—giving value—in exchange for money does not come easy to our society. This is because we ourselves have been taught to be servants or takers. This means that most of us do not notice exactly what we are doing to ourselves or to our children.

When we work, but do the minimum amount of work, and then spend everything that we have earned without giving back to society, then we are usually consuming more than we put into society. Most people do not understand that this is occurring because we believe that we earned the wage and can spend it as we see fit. This is true, but if our overall transactions amount to a negative contribution to society, then society will degrade. This applies to your relationship also, if you take more than you give then your marriage will degrade.

"*Taking*", in the manner that we are referring to it here, is a negative action, and it is destructive. Any effort to *invite, offer, accept, give,* or *receive* is destroyed by someone taking in the exchange. Often, the taker will try to turn the tables to make it appear as if the other person is the taker when they actually are not.

Try to grasp the underlying concepts behind *invite, offer, accept, give,* and *receive.* These fundamental concepts must exist for any relationship to be considered good, and certainly must exist within a relationship to be able to call it a "marriage" in the true sense of the word.

Everything discussed here centers around either the violation of, or the embracing of these concepts. Now that you are aware of the underlying meanings of these words with regard to marriage, if you were to reread the first eight chapters, you will most certainly see them with more clarity and understanding, than you did in your first read through.

We cannot make our errors of yesterday disappear. But the best part about life is that we can stop our errors from occurring tomorrow. And we can give value to our past mistakes by using them as lessons for tomorrow, thus, allowing our lives to become more joyful each day! Understanding and applying this to your marriage is vital for your marriage's survival. Takers are dangerous to you whether the taker is you, your spouse, or someone else who you interact with. Takers will affect your marriage in a negative way. Remove taking from your family and stop being a taker, and depart from the takers outside of your family and keep them out of your family. In doing so you will find that joy will flow back into your union to fill the void left from the now banished taking and takers.

Chapter 10

Why We Stray

By now you should be getting a pretty clear picture as to why so many marriages are troubled, especially when you consider the fact that these troubles are often *not* intentional. This happens because of our failure to realize that we're not understanding our mate properly, and because we often inadvertently reject them. To make matters worse, when we have feelings of low self-worth we are rejecting our own selves. When we reject ourselves we often reject others as well. After a long enough time of being around someone who does not care about themselves, it becomes increasingly difficult to love them in any special way, and eventually it is likely to put out any remaining flames of passion that one spouse has for their mate—It's never a good thing to extinguish the few remaining flames in a relationship. We also create deliberate and yes, foolish situations where we do things to irritate our spouses just to "get back at them". None of this does any good for a marriage.

When we hear the word "stray" in conjunction with marriage, most people's thought immediately goes to the *man* being "unfaithful". But we must remember that for every man cheating, there is a woman that he is going to, and many of those women are married as well—a fact that is often overlooked. Most of this applies to both men and women, though this chapter is aimed at what we *perceive* as the more dominant situation of the "unfaithful husband.

Alert for women: Pornographic or even racy media, including magazines, internet, video, pictures, etc. are abundant. For our discussion here it is very important that you consider some very key points if any of that happens to be an issue in your relationship.

Many, and maybe even most, women think of men as perverts, sick, or pigs if they ever view any pornography. This judgment is typically handed down by the viewing man's wife and by society. People often feel betrayed when their spouse partakes in viewing such material. We must first look at a few very important points before we judge people too harshly. This section does not speak to the socially or morally right or wrong nature of the act of viewing the material, but rather, is focused on what is expected.

Betrayal

Typically, it's women who are the ones who feel betrayed when it comes to pornography or any other such forms of infidelity. This is evident by the severe slant of printed material and entertainment venues that cater to men, versus the comparatively very small amount that cater to women in this regard. So we're going to go with the assumption that men are more often taking part in this, and then ask, "Why is this?" What do these sources of entertainment offer a man that his wife does not offer? Why would he look at pictures when the real thing is living and breathing right next to him in bed?

We are witness to a self-righteous female populous amongst many married couples, acting as if men are lowly perverts who are only interested in sex. In fact, many women tell their husbands just that "All you ever want is sex!" And then when husbands admit to that, or are caught taking part in any of those forms of entertainment, the men's wives get angry and/or feel betrayed. Wives judge their husbands as perverts, sick, or pigs, but seldom do we hear women questioning, "why would he want to view the material to begin with when *I* am right here, next to him in bed?"

Truth be told, there are some men who *are* "perverts, sick, or pigs". In most cases, women probably suspect why their husbands would do this, because in many cases, the women have allowed themselves to slip in physical appearance and/or perceive themselves to be out of shape, and, because of that, they deny their spouses of the joy of freely being with them. They themselves will admit to this, and yet, still be angry if their husbands entertain themselves to satisfaction through any other venues of satisfaction.

Please keep in mind that right now we are discussing *his* motives from *his* perspective, this does not mean that the husband is a picture of health himself; he could be in even worse shape than his wife is. But this has little to do with his actions. Sadly, when women make the assumption that "he is just a pig", then they have completely missed the point.

Could a poor physical appearance be a factor? Yes, it certainly could be. But is it? Typically, it is not.

Many people have been allowing themselves to get unhealthily overweight, including men. This can be a factor in infidelity, but in most cases, believing this to be the cause of infidelity only serves to veil the actual reasons for infidelity.

Going back to our various versions of *The Shopkeeper and the Woman*, it is clear that in Version 4 the woman disregarded the shopkeeper and he reluctantly tolerated the woman's presence, and so he would go into his secluded back room. What was he doing back there? The customer of his dreams had turned into a nightmare and he no longer wanted to be near her.

If he chose to do something else that was more pleasing to him, like going into the storage room to read the grocer's magazine to see all of the pictures of the lovely customers in other stores, rather than be near his actual customer, then is he a pig or is he doing something that gives him more pleasure than the real thing? Ask yourself, why would he want to do that? Consider a different version of the story of *The Shopkeeper and the Woman*—Version 3, where a second woman came in to the shop. Do you think that the shopkeeper is going to hide out in the back storage room reading the

Grocer's Magazine when the second attentive and lovely woman comes into his store? I assure you that he will not.

When a husband "betrays" his wife in this way, or by the company of another woman, it must be asked, "Why? Why would he do that when he has a wife right next to him in bed?"

The finger-pointing done by women has gone on long enough in this regard. Women need to take a look in the mirror and reflect upon their own thoughts and actions when this happens, instead of reading reinforcing articles that usually fail to address the true underlying problems in a relationship.

A great deal of money is being made off of women who are clueless about what men *really* desire. These articles, where too many women get their information from, are often written by people who are only trying to make money writing. Many of those freelance writers who write these articles are quite young and probably do not deeply care about this topic and have not studied it for any length of time worthy of mention. I can feel the outrage expressed by women who have misunderstood the point being made here believing that this is about having, or not having, a hot body. No spouse will complain about a "hot body" so it never hurts, but it is also *not* the underlying problem.

Often, such articles are obtained from entrepreneurial writers seeking work by submitting their proposals to magazines. When their proposal is interesting enough for an article then it is accepted by the magazine. At that point the eager writer proceeds to research and write the article that typically they know nothing about and can only offer their own opinions based only on brief research. This in itself is not wrong and is often entertaining, but using these articles as a guide *for your own relationship* is likely *not* your wisest course of action. Choose your guides carefully. Because so many women get information from such articles, it is important to know and understand that many articles are written by these freelance writers who are trying to make a quick buck. The fact that many young women use these articles as their relationship guides, and fail to look within, is often why they have relationship troubles.

Because men view pornography or seek other women and other entertainment, many wives have the misguided understanding that "All that men do is to think about sex." Some women accidentally succeed in doing the right thing when they compensate for this by means of added physical beauty-care, working in an effort to attract their husband back to them; but many others fail when doing so. Why is this? Why did the physical makeover work for one woman and then fail for the next woman? It is rare that women, or men, seek to truly understand what is being sought in entertaining themselves with visual stimuli or in the company of another person who they are attracted to. Some women accidentally get it right when they are visually and physically enhancing themselves to re-attract their husband. However, if the problem occurs again they typically do not know how to recreate the result, even though the woman may now be as stunningly beautiful as she was when they first met. Why is this?

Men certainly won't complain about their wives being beautiful, but the reason that women frequently fail at re-attracting their husbands is because women believe wrongly about what is actually occurring when they beautify themselves. This creates a difficult circumstance that can lead to what is thought of as an "addiction".

Addictions

Many wives who are encountering their husbands seeking satisfaction by other means often make an assumption that he is "addicted" to sex. It's possible that this has become his new addiction, but is this addiction *his* problem, or is it *hers*?

This problem is both of theirs. But it is the woman's problem more than it is the man's problem. Why? Because she is the one who has lost something, where he forfeited something on his own and chose a different route to an empty kind of satisfaction that he could not even achieve from his own living and breathing wife who lay next to him every night in their own bed.

The lucky ones find their husbands viewing questionable material. The un-lucky women find their husbands in the arms of another woman.

It's typically believed that addictions are bad, but are they? Is it not more about what all of us are addicted to that is bad or damaging to us? In accurate usage and definition, an "addiction" is something that we think about and *discuss* often as in "diction" to *say* or *speak*. Wives, please notice that there was a time when it was *you* who he was addicted to, but somehow this has changed and you are no longer the object of his addiction or obsession. Why is this? Why did your spouse obsess over you to the point of addiction? Was it good that he wanted to look good for you and the only thing that he could think about was you? Was it wrong or was it good, when you both felt good, and you both had joy when you were each other's obsession?

I ask you to re-evaluate your view on the term addiction, and instead look at the *subject* of the addiction as being the problem due to being the wrong subject. *You* should be your spouse's addiction. Husband or Wife, if you are not the focus of the addiction, then it is your job to find a way to make it so.

Obsessive Behavior Breakdown

Addiction is when someone obsesses about someone or something. Is this bad? What is "obsess"? In this case the "ob" prefix means *on* or *around* and the "sess" or "session" is to *sit* or *seat*. This should be understood as to be regularly *near*, *about*, or *around* something or someone. Of course there are limits to this where it could be considered invasive with regard to people, but the general idea is that we use reasonable behavior with regard to someone who is our focus and we also consider the fact that the person chose to be with us.

As with addiction it is not the addiction that is the problem, but rather it is what the person is addicting about. Similarly, an obsession is not the problem, but rather the problem is the subject of the obsession. Any woman who does not want her husband to obsess about her is a fool. Inversely, so it is with a man. Any man who does not want his wife to obsess about him is a fool.

This does not include them being a taker. If your spouse is a taker and is addicted to you, they will cause you a great deal of pain, because it is the *taking* that is the problem. In fact, if they are a taker, then you are not their obsession, but rather *they* are the subject of their own obsession and addiction.

When anything you do affects your life in a negative way, or impedes your life and progress or intrudes unfairly on any other people, then it is a personal problem with you, and it does not have to be an obsession or addiction. We often look at the wrong aspect of obsessive or addictive behavior, assuming that because someone focuses heavily on someone or something that the obsession is the thing that is causing a problem, but in truth, the problem is being caused by offensive and destructive actions, attitudes, and thinking of the offending person.

There are three things that a man should be addicted to and in this order: His Creator, his wife, and his children. There are three things that a woman should be addicted to and in this order: Her husband, her Creator, and her children. Why the bias? The order of Creation of course! But this *does not* make men superior—remember that *everyone*. Because of the order of Creation, society's expectation of men is different than it is of women. Men typically do not look to their wives for guidance, but often women do look to their husband's for guidance and are short-changed. If a husband is misguided then the wife must put her focus on his error and find a way to get him to see his own folly, without making him feel foolish and singled out. For men it is typically different, because much of their leading is done by the examples they set. If a man ignores the Creator then typically the rest of the family will do the same. But if he *properly* follows the Creator then the family will follow that example. There are many wonderful women who have overcome their husband's folly by putting them first in effort to redirect their husband's focus to the Creator.

At this point, we need to look to some ancient manuscripts for some guidance. The Creator had a particular group of people who were favored above the rest. The Creator promised to protect and care for these people, and referred to them possessively as "my people"; thus, making them special because of a certain kind of dedication and obsession that they originally had toward the Creator. But this was not to be the case for very long because the people consistently turned against their Creator and put their affection to other things and other peoples—they became obsessed with other gods. According to the documentation, all they had to do was to keep their affection set on their Creator and many good things, along with protection from disease and famine would have automatically been bestowed upon them.

Yet, they did not do this. In fact, they turned away and fervently defied their Creator, thus causing the Creator to lose respect and interest in them. In fact, the Creator even went so far as to withdraw all protection and allow other peoples to overpower them and nearly destroy them.

In retrospect, we often look at this account and wonder "What were they thinking?" Yet we see this every day in our own marriages, if you can call them "marriages". A woman's focal point should be her husband and her Creator. If this is the case then her children will be second nature and will be automatically very well cared for by her and her husband.

The husband was Created in the image of the Creator and the wife was Created of man and in the image of the Creator. We can take many clues from these ancient texts to better understand *why* things are the way they are.

Many people have the incorrect attitude that these ancient texts no longer matter and that they are not speaking about us, but I assure you that this is not at all true. What we are discussing applies to *all* people. When the people written about in the Bible had the Creator as their obsession, then all was well. But when they turned their obsession to other things, it did not go well for them. It was often the women who fell away first. They would be enticed by others to worship fancy idols, and then they would begin to serve those idols and eventually lure their husbands to do the same. This did not go well with the Creator who then chose to withdraw protection from them all.

In a marriage, the husband sits in the position of the Creator, and the wife sits in position of the Creator's people. She is his temple in respect to the relationship of the position of the Creator to the people. If we remain open to this line of thought, we can quickly see when the people turned against the Creator and put their focus elsewhere, then their Creator turned away affection from them and focused it elsewhere. Some people might wrongly take this to mean that women should bow to men and serve them, but this is not so. The often unrealized fact about men and women is that a man's deepest desire is to dwell *within* the temple of his wife.

Like it or not, this is exactly what happens in many marriages. Many wives put their trust in their husband's job or their own job. They also look to magazines or fortune tellers or other men for guidance and often do not agree in child rearing with their own husband. This type of behavior has been going on for thousands of years and has contaminated society so deeply, that it is difficult for us to discern exactly who is doing what.

A marriage is good when a wife wants to be and works to be, the obsession of her husband. Men are easy that way and want to be able to obsess about their wives, though I doubt that many men would describe it in those terms or admit to it directly. Most of this applies in both directions on the two-way street of marriage.

The Rut

Couples often get stuck in this marital rut and feel empty, insatiably seeking false love wherever they can find it. Alluring entertainment for men is similar to the false guidance women seek in some magazines, from talk-shows, from other men, and from fortune telling or astrology. Women are supposed to trust their husbands, but they seldom do. This is often the source of the problems in a troubled marriage. Sometimes the mistrust of husbands is well-deserved because the husbands have done nothing to create trust in the relationship. The lack of trust is not necessarily in regard to intimate infidelity. In fact it is typically *not* due to trust in that area. Intimate infidelity is usually a *result* of lack of trust elsewhere in the relationship.

Lack of trust becomes the normal way for many couples to operate, and then both spouses become very accustomed to it. This slowly tears the man down and often causes him to drift away and seek acceptance elsewhere. Men who do not want to have an actual affair with another woman will often gravitate towards alcohol, pornography, and material goods. These vices either numb their pain or give men an empty feeling of acceptance. The worst-case scenario, of finding another woman, is going to be far more to his satisfaction, but will harm him more with regard to family troubles and feelings of guilt.

Like it or not, this is how things often go. Many women do not want to hear this because it places much of the burden on their own shoulders in these situations. However, until women understand and accept the amount of control they have to alter circumstances, the problems will continue to get worse within their own marriage. Men also do not like to discuss this because it cuts to the core of the problem, and that is where men are very sensitive. Discussing it causes men have to admit how much they are hurting, which is something that society subtly tells men that they are *not* allowed to do. Women need to grab hold of the steering wheel because, in this particular part of the marriage, women are the drivers.

The seemingly ridiculous saying "If you don't know, then I am not going to tell you!" should not be disregarded. Often, this is associated with women using the phrase, but in truth, it better applies to men's behavior.

The last thing most men would ever say is "I need you to love me" thus, they remain quiet. Then the lackluster union continues to erode unto complacency, or worse—divorce! Eroding to complacency is "the rut", and it is something that many couples are stuck in and cannot see their way out of.

What causes this rut? Women usually do. Sometimes things are completely turned around and all things are opposite, and then it's the man who is causing the problem. But regardless of the *who*, the *what* remains the same. And it is the *what* part that is the cause of the problem which is redirecting the focus of the strayed spouse's attention.

Men Have Been Beaten Down

Culturally, men are frequently beaten down and disregarded as "foolish" by their controlling wives. These strong words are true. This is not new and it has been happening for thousands of years in marriages. You can observe most forms of entertainment and see this depicted regularly in relationships in such entertainment. In modern entertainment, they exaggerate these issues for entertainment-value.

In much the same way that people often mock the Creator, women are often taught to disrespect and have disregard for their husbands, demanding "do this and do that" always attempting to control. The result is the same as it is with the Creator. A husband will draw away and leave his wife to her own folly. Some women have embraced such disrespect, only to find a lonely emptiness during midlife and older ages.

There are certainly many men who disrespect their wives, and in some of those cases, it is the man who started and perpetuated all of the problems. But for many troubled relationships, it is the wife who is falling short of proper expectations. To women, this is obviously not going to be a popular viewpoint, and like it or not, it speaks volumes about why many marriages are in peril. We will discuss more on this later.

There's a more dangerous aspect of "the rut" problem, which is that often neither the husband nor the wife understands why they are in a rut to begin with. It is the "why" that a couple needs to pinpoint about the rut in their relationship; and without understanding the "why"—then in the rut you shall remain.

With regard to addictive vices or being in the arms of another person, when it is suspected that this is occurring, the job of correcting your marital problems just got a whole lot more difficult, and urgent! It doesn't matter what or why at this point because it has already occurred. Your spouse has had a taste of something that makes them feel better than when they are with you! Think about that for a moment, your spouse has had a taste of something that makes them feel better *than when they are with you.*

They have obtained a new addiction to be obsessed about, and that obsession is no longer you. Your only hope is that your spouse would prefer you to be their obsession. If this is the case, then your job is relatively easy. If it is not the case, then you have a great deal of effort ahead of you in order to get your spouse back. The problem is in your hands and it is up to you to first understand the situation, and then work to rectify it.

Many women reject the notion that this could possibly be of their own making because many women believe in their own minds that they "love" their husbands with all their heart. The problem is that men want to be mutually obsessed about like they were when you first met.

Boys are commonly the ones who drive around the block ten times just to get a glimpse of the "object of their obsession". Males are typically far more dedicated in this regard. Early in a relationship it's common that the obsession equalizes, and for many men that brief segment in time is often the only pure joy for the man throughout his entire life. As the years progress, men often continue their obsession for their wife, but the obsession is not reciprocated by their wife. This violates the first principle of acceptance-expectation and is a hidden point of tremendous contention in many marriages. It is seldom understood by either spouse exactly what is happening or that it is happening.

It's likely, that even though it has been repeated many times in this book, many readers, male and female alike, have missed the point and have connected this all to sexuality—this is wrong. Thinking along these lines will keep you where you have been, and you will not be able to escape the rut that you are trapped in. First and foremost, understand that it is typically *not* about physical intimacy, it is largely about acceptance and invitation. Grasping this is the beginning of the healing of your own marriage.

Chapter 11

Forgiveness, and Forgiveness Gone Too Far

Forgiveness is a funny thing that is seldom properly understood. A bitter person will hold a grudge even after a proper apology is received, and in many cases, carry the grudge to their grave.

Forgiveness is something done in advance of other people's stupidity and violations. The Creator forgave the people *ahead of time*—it is already done! You might wonder, "if the Creator has already forgiven the people, then why are they not accepted back during our modern times and protected as they were, in days long past, by the Creator, openly making the Creator's existence known to them with pillars of fire and parting waters, etc.?" It's because forgiveness is not for the Creator, forgiveness is for the people who have violated the Creator's hopes and expectations of them. It is *their* job to accept the forgiveness that was, and still is, offered. In the same way, when we violate our spouse's hopes and expectations, they have usually already forgiven us. So, why then do they refrain from coming close to us again if they have already forgiven us? It's because of our repeated and continued violations against them.

We must realize that when we forgive someone, or when they forgive us, the problem does not belong to the person who did the forgiving for having their reasonable expectations violated. The problem is in the hands of the offending violator. It is the violator who needs to make the next move by *actually changing*. Forgiveness is done *immediately* by the person who was violated, it is an offering and the offender must accept the forgiveness. There's a catch to this, and it is that the person who is violating cannot receive forgiveness while they are still violating. When your hands are full from taking what does not belong to you, then you will have no room for what is being offered to you. We must let go of violating others so that we can accept their forgiveness.

Often, the violator or offender accuses the forgiver of not forgiving them for the violator's ill deeds. This is because violators have an expectation that they are supposed to be loved "unconditionally" by the person that they have been regularly violating. But "unconditional love" is widely misunderstood.

People Want to be Forgiven
But They Keep Doing Wrong

It's common for people who are chronic violators to expect "forgiveness" regardless of what they are doing to others. They often will reference "unconditional love" vaguely referencing the Bible in that regard. This common tactic is saying, in essence, "Accept me as I am, and let me do whatever I want to do, to anyone I want to do it to, and then tolerate me while I *continue* to offend you." Violators would be very frightened to read the Bible, because it says nothing of the sort... at least not in the way that violators choose to understand the idea of "unconditional love".

In the Bible, the Creator consistently forgave the violators, and while the Creator's love is "unconditional," it is the violators that must seek the Creator. Every time they violated, they were already forgiven.

Let's simplify this a bit: Should the Creator go begging to a violator for love only to be the recipient of more of their violating ways? Just because someone is forgiven, that does not mean that they are going to be allowed to continue to violate the forgiver. In fact, if a violator is asked to forgive someone who violated them, they typically won't even consider forgiving them. They often hold a grudge about a violation of long ago, against a person who has not once since then violated them. Yet, they expect to be forgiven and allowed to continue in their own ill behavior as often as they desire. If you happen to be guilty of such behavior, then cease immediately and watch how quickly your life turns around and becomes pleasant, loving, and joyful. Always remember that *good* people *don't* destroy other people's lives.

Tolerance versus Intolerance

Violators are intolerant and often cry "Intolerance!" This, too, is one of the violator's most commonly abused words, especially with regard to "political correctness". When a violator misbehaves and violates others, then the person or people will often resist and comment back to the violator. To the violator, this resistance and the comments are seen as "intolerance". To the violator, this is unacceptable, and the violator will make it as if they themselves are righteous in their proclamation that their victim is being "intolerant".

Seldom will a violator allow anyone to review the violator's own behavior. And further, violators will never review their own behavior. In general, people are very tolerant of bad behavior and violation, which is both a good thing and a bad thing. It's good because it allows for quick forgiveness of minor violation, thus keeping the flow of life moving forward efficiently; but at the same time, it also allows violators to continue with their poor behavior. Allowing a pass on minor violations reinforces the violating behavior and allows the violator to deepen their violating ways. This makes it even more difficult for them to escape their self-imposed trouble and self-deceit.

Violators often accuse tolerant people of being intolerant whenever the violated people decide to finally speak out against the violator. The reality is that it is the accusers who are intolerant. These intolerant violating accusers seldom take responsibility for their own actions and violations, and often they try to put the blame on those who do not deserve any blame at all. Violators usually will not allow blame to be placed on themselves for what they themselves have done wrong in their violation of others. The intolerance that violators accuse others of is actually the people's intolerance of the violator's constant errors and violations.

If you find that you're guilty of any of this, *now* is the time to stop. In general, people are incredibly forgiving. And unless your spouse is equally as bad as you are, they have likely already forgiven you and they just want their torment to end, via *you* no longer violating them, and you likely want the same.

But, if you find that it is not you, and that your spouse is the one who is often violating, then discussing it is a good option, but often, discussion of their errors will not be readily accepted by them. It's difficult to explain to this type of personality that there is an issue that needs to be dealt with within their own behavior.

The truth of the matter is that your *in*tolerance for their violations is the best and most effective way of bringing the issue to their attention, but it will also feel like the most painful way to remedy the situation—even though it is not. It's often the person who has been violated who carries a good deal of responsibility for the problems because of their failure to call the violating person out properly on their constant violations. Continuing to put up with their relentless violation against you will be far more painful in the long run than promptly confronting them will be. You either deal with it now or put up with the violations for the rest of your life— The choice is yours.

While the violators' behavior is their own responsibility, a part of the responsibility of the problem is yours too. This is because we believe that we are being kind when we are tolerant of their bad behavior. This wrong thinking causes a serious problem with violators. And as mentioned a moment ago, tolerance reinforces a violator's bad behavior because there is no resistance to their horrid actions. Any lack of resistance allows them to continue *without consequence*, causing them to believe that their ways are okay and acceptable to us, when they actually are not.

Intolerance of bad behavior is the only good solution! When a person will no longer allow violations of themself it causes a great deal of conflict and becomes very confrontational. This is highly effective in quickly stopping the troubling behavior of a violator. The longer we have allowed someone to become accustomed to their ways, then the more difficult it is to alter their poor behavior toward us.

Standing firm and being intolerant of bad behavior brings about a potential risk that your spouse might decide they have had enough and then choose to leave you. If this happens to be the case, then you must realize that your marriage has long been in peril, and has likely been very painful for you, and for them as well. Continuing in a relationship with a person who will leave you if you challenge their horrid behavior is not going to be pleasant for you. If they decide to leave you then that is their choice to do so, and you must decide if that possibility is something that you are willing to risk. If you are not, then prepare to suffer a long and uncomfortable future.

Depending upon the nature of your spouse, there is also a risk of physical abuse. Much care should be used when deciding what actions to take in such situations. Consulting with authorities and/or seeking professional help is a wise course of action when you know that there is a real threat to your physical well-being.

If you happen to be the violator and you feel the resistance, now after reading this you know why you are experiencing resistance from your spouse and others. If you decide to continue violating while disregarding the resistance, then you should expect things to get worse in your marriage relationship and in your life. You should also understand that it is your own fault. This is easily solved by, first, simply stopping yourself when resistance comes along. And then evaluate the problem at hand with honest and true judgment. And finally, by rectifying the situation and apologizing for your own horrible behavior.

What is False Forgiveness?

False forgiveness is a concept that few people ever think about or even realize exists. Certainly, if someone claims that they have forgiven you, and you then cease your ill actions and they continue to hold your previous ill actions against you, then they have *not* truly "forgiven" you. But that is not really false forgiveness. In that case, they are just lying to you about actually having forgiven you in the first place. Yet, in general, this is how people would interpret the term "false-forgiveness".

The term "forgive", indicating that you are forgiven, means that foolish behavior is overlooked *in advance*, and you are allowed to proceed in a new direction even when taking your past violations in to account. This accurate description is generally not how we think of the concept of "forgive".

In general, people make an error and then ask for forgiveness; but that is not forgiveness at all. That technically would be post-giveness. The word **forgive** specifically is taken from Biblical accounts of the Creator overlooking the foolishness that the people repeatedly partook in, "**for**" meaning in advance of, as in *fore*.

False-forgiveness could possibly be considered as only releasing someone of their violation after they committed their offense; but that would also be somewhat misdirected word usage. After all, they are releasing the violator when being asked to. So for that part it is not false, or a lie, because it did actually occur, even though it's not technically accurate because it was not done in advance.

When we forgive someone it speaks of our love for them and the fact that we want them to no longer offend us or others. We must be as a guide to them to help them see their errors if we truly love them. If we allow someone to continue to live wrongly, without any opposition, then we become a part of their demise. We are paving the way in their own path to destruction.

This is easier to understand when thinking in terms of children. Parents who stop their children and discipline them for doing acts of an unkind nature will be rewarded with good children when those children are adults. However, when parents neglect to reprimand their children for bad behavior, then the children typically grow to be adults who are *not* model citizens and are then often disliked by many of their peers. Those children do not know any better because no one ever showed them the good way to live. Typically, parents who believe that they are being compassionate— by not disciplining their children—have problems with their children, and often their children don't have a clue due to the lack of discipline from their parents. They were not shown the right path while being raised.

Forgiveness is an act of unconditional love. But again, "unconditional" love is typically misunderstood. It's common for violators to say that they should be loved "unconditionally". To them, this means that others must allow the violator to do anything the violator wants to do, and the others then must still love the violator, similar to the tolerance versus intolerance issue. Unconditional love has little to do with tolerance. When you truly love others, at a minimum, you will try to get them to see their errors. The more you love someone, then the more you will try to get the person to see the better path. This is not something that violators approve of when you do it for them.

True forgiveness is built upon true love, and it will not allow offense without opposition. This basically means that you knew they might blow it, and instead of leaving them you're still willing to endure their violations in order to try to help them, but you won't tolerate their violating behavior any longer without opposition. As the violator moves forward in this regard, you will try to get them to choose a better path that is free of violating others. This is the only true forgiveness and the only way to display true unconditional love. Though at some point, patience will wear thin and eventually the incessant, repeated violations may cause the person who is being violated to depart and separate themselves from the violator when the violator won't see and correct the error of their ways.

Here is a different perspective on what false forgiveness is: False-forgiveness falls short of completing the mission. With false-forgiveness you have made the statement that all is forgiven, but you offer no resistance. This lack of resistance allows them to continue in their ill ways. Thus, they will never find a path free of their violating ways. This traps them in their errors and keeps them repeating their offenses indefinitely, often driving others into deeper resentment towards them.

Allowing anyone to continue offense without presenting opposition to their actions is not kind or loving by any stretch of the imagination. When we do that, we are ultimately cursing the person, and damning them by doing so.

False-forgiveness, or "I love you" type tolerance, can be defined as: Not following through with proper reprimand, thus, allowing continual violation without opposition. Doing this *will* weigh heavily on a marriage and cause many and increasing troubles in the long run.

People often have a difficult time separating disciplinary measures from freewill issues. While people have freewill to do as they please, they do not have the freedom to escape the *consequence* of their own actions. This is especially true within a marriage. You can continue to behave inappropriately as long as you want, but nowhere does it instruct your spouse to accept your violations against them without resistance. In fact, it is quite the opposite, and at times, very harshly so. In the Bible it urges parents to discipline their children so that when those children are grown they will choose a good path.

It is usually the violators who shout the loudest to demand their way. This is typically done by accusing others of interfering with their freewill, but their "freewill" has nothing to do with you allowing their offenses against you. We are not instructed to stop them, but we are instructed to protect ourselves and others and to try to teach the violators a better way. This seemingly contradictory information is not contradictory at all.

Understand that the laws of the lands are not there to stop violators. They are there for our protection and warning from—and of—the violators. The road signs at an intersection are a warning for you to proceed with caution because someone could violate. They are not there to stop the violator. How do you stop a person from running a stop sign? Sadly there are no actual stop signs in marriage that warn us of impending danger. However, there are emotional signs and actions by ourselves and our spouses that we can watch for. When you know that you are about to pass through an intersection, it is still your own personal responsibility, for your own well-being, to make sure that there's no cross traffic coming that might not stop for the stop sign. This is true even if, legally, you do not need to stop. Marriage is no different; there are things you can watch for that you know are dangerous. If we see cross-traffic approaching a stop sign at a high speed, then we will most likely stop even if we are not required to so that they don't hit us, yet we fail to acknowledge these high-speed warnings in our own marriages. False forgiveness will continually allow your spouse to run right over you without opposition, and allowing them to do so tells them that it is okay to do so. It's like deliberately and repeatedly entering the intersection when you know you will be hit by someone running the stop sign and then you accept the blame even though it was they who failed to stop and the fault was theirs.

We can teach people that they should not run stop signs by ticketing the person, but they actually might not see the stop sign and therefore they may accidentally run through it without stopping. Laws originally are put in place to give us recourse against violation and to learn not to do violations. They are not to stop violation. Not allowing violation turns ugly, as has been proven by many past civilizations, governments, and marriages. Each of us needs to clear the haze of false-forgiveness and understand the differences between not allowing violation, versus not allowing violation to go unopposed.

Consider martial law (military - not marital or marriage): it may seem good to kill any offender, but what happens when the people in authority consider something that is actually good to be an offense against them? Study the origins and results of communism and socialism and see how well imposing your own morality or beliefs onto others actually works. You will quickly find that trying to not allow violation against your morality or beliefs can go wrong very quickly! If we stop violators, then we remove their freewill. However, protecting ourselves does not affect their freewill, although it may interrupt their plan of action.

So as you can see, it is important for us to set limits and make those limits known when people violate us, this includes our spouses. We don't need to hate or harbor bad feelings, but setting limits of tolerance is vital if we ever hope to have our spouses see their own poor behavior for what it truly is. True forgiveness disciplines in this way, where false-forgiveness does not discipline.

Tolerance of bad behavior is false forgiveness. **In**tolerance of bad behavior *is required* of us all!

Joyful Confusion

Within the realm of false-forgiveness, unconditional love was mentioned earlier. Often, unconditional love is viewed as: love them and allow them to do *whatever* they want, *whenever* they want, and *as often* as they want. As was just explained, this is neither true nor good. We do not understand real love if we are unwilling to discipline. While we may have forgiven a person who repeatedly refuses to cease their ill behavior, we need only forgive them once for all time.

True forgiveness is done once for all time. However, it is up to them to accept that forgiveness. They have not accepted it when they continue in their ill ways. The person who has forgiven them does not need to be jumping for joy every time they see the person who continues to hurt them is coming their way. In fact, the forgiver may choose to stay clear of the violator all together so that the violator can no longer violate or hurt them. This is not un-forgiveness—it is wisdom! Allowing anyone to violate you harms both you and them. Instead, you can simply choose to turn away from them and depart from them if they fail to correct their abhorrent behavior.

No one can be expected to continually accept the bad behavior of others without resisting and/or leaving. We can be joyful and can have forgiven someone but at the same time be irritated with their continuing violations. This is what is to be expected, and further, it is also okay to increase the intensity of resistance with each of their subsequent violations.

Do not let violators steal your life's joy! Toss aside the confusion and forgive them, and then discipline them by resisting their ill behavior. The best method of having joy is to realize that *your* happiness does not depend upon them. You can be joyful whether or not they are there and whether or not they approve of your intolerance of their horrible behavior. In fact, it's important for you to have a firm grasp on the fact that—your intolerance of their bad behavior is a good thing; and your acceptance of this point alone will bring you much joy. This is mostly because you now understand that you can have forgiven someone even though you are irritated with their continuing violations against you. You can now free yourself of the guilt for feeling like you have been unforgiving when you actually have *not* been unforgiving.

Allowing others to consume your joy is simply wrong. It is bad for your body, bad for your soul, bad for your family, and very importantly, it is bad for your marriage. Keep your joy and protect it because it's yours!

Chapter 12

Jealousy and Competition and You

Jealousy and *competition* are never a good thing, at least not the way we think of them. Yet our culture thrives on competition and jealousy. Industries are built upon jealousy and competition and they drive and motivate the actions of large portions of the populations of our world.

To get a better grasp on the negative nature of our perception of these two words, we need to fully understand them. *What we think we see*, versus *what is*, are often at odds with each other. Continued misuse of a word forces a change in the lexicon and brings new meaning to the word. But when we look deeper we see the true essence of a word, and can then begin to understand why the erred change occurred.

Without properly understanding the underlying concepts of the words that we have been defining throughout this book, there is no hope to ever fully understand our own problems.

Competition is Bad, Especially in a Marriage

Competition is bad when considering the way we think of the idea of "competition". It's "defeat the competitor and kill the competition!" This is what is taught in our schools and on the playing fields all across the face of the globe. Why is this? Defeat the enemy, and then proclaim that you're the best! This is the motive of operation that is taken by many people. But is this good?

Society has come to know "crushing our enemy" as a good thing. When our enemy, or our violator, comes near to us, then we have a tendency to want to destroy them so that they can no longer violate us and cause us such great pain. We have a natural instinct for doing so. It's sort of a, good-versus-evil thing. Additionally, this has been ingrained into most cultures for thousands of years through the ravages of war—hurt the hurter!

Is "competition" really competition? Is it really what we think it is? Conceptually, the way we think of it in our minds may be somewhat accurate, but is this actually proper word usage? Or is there a word that better describes what we think of as a "competitor"?

Breaking the word *competitor* down, we can understand the word to be *compete* or *com-petition*. A "*petition*" is a request, and "*com*" means *co* or *with*. This means that the word competition has a true underlying meaning of *co-request*, which is actually the opposite of what we use it to be. The people on our own team are more true to the word's actual meaning.

So, what, then, would be a better word to use for the way in which we conceive the terms "competition" and "competitor"? *Enemy* or *rival*, of course. But "enemy" seems too harsh for friendly play in sports. The proper word to use is best defined within the heart of the person using the word because it is their intent that determines what the other person is to them. "Enemy" is specific in being opposition and means *not* and *friend* together; where *rival* means two people or two sides attempting a goal that can only be done one at a time in the same venue.

We need to rethink our understanding of what *competition* really is. A proper usage of the word *competition* is when two people are both trying to be excellent and are trying to encourage and increase one another at the same time, while not wanting either to falter, such as with team members cheering their teammates on.

Friends coming together to see who can do their own best while the others look on and cheer them on to success as each person takes their turn is "competition" in the true sense of the word.

Competition is often used in terms of removing others so that *we* remain the best because we are the only ones left. This defeatist method is born of evil. It is what was written of in the Bible where the Serpent deceived the woman, with the Serpent's intent being the destruction of mankind. And this is often how we incorrectly use the term "competition".

It's a sad day when a person is too lazy to make him- or herself better, so instead they attempt to destroy their rival in an effort to bring their rival to a lower value just so that they can feel better about themselves because they are too lazy to self-improve. This means that you are still a loser, but have only imaged to win because you no longer have anyone to be compared with. If you are rated with the lowest possible rating and everyone else is above you, and you then destroy everyone else, then you still remain at the lowest possible rating and are still a loser, but now, you are lonely in addition, and you no longer have any good people around you to learn from to become better yourself. This only serves to keep you in the self-imposed prison of losing.

Not a Competition

A marriage should never be a competition in a *rival* or *enemy* manner—ever! If a couple is in the—you are my enemy mode—then they are certain to face doom. So then, why do some marriages become this particular erred definition of competition?

We become rivals because of our violation, and our violations begin to invoke enemy status. Instinctively, anyone who tries to violate or harm us is our enemy. Our natural instinct to self-preserve instantly activates when we feel threatened in any way. What we do at that point is a part of what makes us different from animals. Will we destroy our spouse because they violated us? Or, will we forgive them and resist their violation by confronting them? Destroying your spouse will end in divorce and/or a great deal of misery for you both.

What is *"Proper" Jealousy?*

Are you jealous of your spouse? Are they better than you? Do they get paid more than you? Are they smarter than you? If you have any of these feelings about your spouse, then it is likely that you are jealous of them... Or are you? What does "jealous" actually mean?

When you feel small because of someone else's accomplishments, then it is *your* problem to deal with, not theirs. We often think that we are jealous of other people, and while in part this is true, it is also typically a misused term. *Envious* or *covetous* is more appropriate.

The word "jealous" is from the word *zeal*, which means to have eagerness towards something. So in the sense that you may have a desire for, or eagerness towards, someone else's belongings or life, we equate jealousy to a malicious manner. When people are "jealous", by today's understanding of the word, our attitude is: "If I can't have it, then neither can you; and even if I do have it, I don't want you to have it, too." This is not really a proper use of the term "jealous". This type of jealousy is more accurately described as *covetous, envious*, and *destructive*.

If we're jealous of our spouse in this way, then we are actually being covetous of what they have or what they are. This is very destructive to any marriage. So then, is what we think of as jealousy really jealousy as it is indicated in the word zeal, as in a zeal for something? Yes, it is when someone is trying to steal your belongings or your spouse.

You should have a zeal for your belongings and for your spouse, and you should get protective if someone is violating *your* possession of *your* belongings or *your* spouse. You must have a zeal and a passion for what is yours, especially your spouse and children. This is good jealousy, and it is true jealousy. The Creator is a "jealous Creator," and that description of having a zeal for your possessions is what is meant by that phrase.

In the Bible, when the people placed their affection towards other gods, the Creator was jealous for their affections. If you are not like the Creator in your marriage, you will have a lackluster marriage. If your affections are aimed somewhere other than your Creator, spouse, and children, then you already have problems—and more are on the way.

This does not mean that you should only be with your family and turn away from everything else in your life. No, it means that everything else that you do is for your Creator, spouse, and children. But we often do this backwards.

When "jealousy" is not *jealousy* or zeal but instead is *covetousness*, then that is when competition comes into play. This type of competition is not com-petition as described earlier; but rather, it is *evil*, it is *enemy*, and it is *destruction*. It becomes "Destroy the enemy!" And in our discussion here the enemy happens to be your spouse who was chosen by you.

Women's Liberation is a Forfeiture of a Woman's True Power and Strength

In reference to the way that people typically think of competition and jealousy, we can view women's liberation as embodying the horrible misconceptions of these words. Over the years, men certainly got a lot wrong with regard to women; and in many cases, men deserved the resistance to their violations against women's "rights". But women's liberation is a forfeiture of a woman's true power and strength. Most people have the view that the only choice is to be for women's liberation, or to be opposed to any freedom whatsoever for women, and we fail to see that there are other options and perspectives.

Regretfully, women's lib challenged some men's violations against the women who were around them by trying to be like men, or at times, trying to be as men are. Worldwide, women are smaller than men are, plus there are obvious physical and biological differences. Clearly, we are not the same. On average, men are larger and physically stronger, so men and women are not equal in that way. Trying to be something that you are not, will always result in long-term failure and disappointment.

Women's lib, as we know it today, was started by hostile women who were "competitive" and "jealous" or covetous enemies, and sometimes rightfully so. Most of these hostile women were being wrongfully violated, or they witnessed their mothers being wrongfully violated by men, usually their fathers. Women's lib was their manner of self-preservation and correction for an unjust situation. However, their handling of the matter may not have been the best possible route for society at large. The movement has since faded but recurs periodically and its underlying damage is lasting and may even outweigh its long-term benefits. There are many women who had wonderful lives before and they *were not* being violated but now have been violated through the women's liberation movement.

A woman has the ability to be beautiful and to have her spouse be desirous of her; this occurs to the extent that he will spend his life pleasing and protecting her; this is a woman's true power and strength. Turning against this is a foolish action and removes a woman's power as a living soul. You are Created as you are, and nothing can change that. Trying to utilize yourself for something other than what you are Created as steals away your power and strength, and hands it over to whoever you have decided to "compete" against, or better stated—who you are envious of. It also hands your power and strength over to those whom you follow.

When covetousness enters in, and the other party becomes the opposition or enemy, then you can be assured that there is hatred lurking somewhere in the mix. While there were some good reasons for women to confront the violations against them, meeting that with contempt was a grave error on their part. This contempt is now born into the hearts and culture of many people—both women and men. It doesn't matter how or why this came to be at this point, because the fact remains that this will steal away the power of those who hold these covetous values in their hearts. This will occur for all future generations as long as these distorted beliefs continue to be held in the hearts and minds of people.

Man and woman were not created to be enemies of one another. They were Created to be partners; co-petitioners! In the true sense of the words, they are competitors, meaning that they would be zealous or jealous for—not of—each other and also for their Creator. And they would co-petition the Creator for their needs and for love.

Women of this world, do not forfeit your power and strength for the lie of dominion over men—it will not succeed. Women and men cannot survive without each other. We are equal partners on this earth and can defeat any evil that comes our way, provided that we stand together in competition as one.

While women are not physically able to do everything that men can do, and men are not physically able to do everything that women can do, in the realm of intellect, there appears to be no readily discernable difference with regard to ability. Though, it does seem that there are certain stereotypical predispositions of compassion levels and certain types of mental skills that each gender naturally tends to gravitate towards. It seems to be a violation of nature to specifically suppress that gravity in ourselves or in our children.

Don't Challenge My Beliefs!

Why all of the emphasis on the proper definition and usage of these and other words? Because when we do not use words properly, then we're blind to what is really happening and to what is really meant when using those words. Our blindness about the true meanings hides the true intention. For example, calling something competition sounds friendly, but often our true intent is to destroy our opponent.

There are many words that we use in a completely opposite manner, such as those just discussed. This misuse of words hides their true concept in our fog of confusion, thus making our actions appear not as harmful as what they truly are.

When we find the words whose definitions truly match our concept of what is actually meant in our mind, then our actions are revealed and we can better see our errors. This is why it is of the utmost importance for you to understand the underlying meanings of these words. If you don't understand these concepts, then you certainly will not be able to properly convey your issues with your spouse, to your spouse, especially because your spouse likely does not know about the inaccurate perceptions of some words either. Many men and women have their beliefs challenged because they believe wrongly about things. And they believe wrongly because they have not been taught the underlying meanings of many of the most basic words and principles. You will see life much more beautifully and robustly than you previously had, once you begin to grasp the underlying meanings of the words that you use when communicating with your spouse.

People often become angry and lose out when their beliefs are challenged, and they cannot offer good explanations as to why something is as the way they believe it to be. Or better stated, why they believe what they believe—and therein are the dangers of blind faith.

People do not want their beliefs challenged when they don't understand their own beliefs. Challenging our beliefs forces us to have to consider why we believe what we believe. When we put our whole heart into a certain belief for all or most of our lives, then we have a tremendous emotional investment in that particular belief. Everything that we do is built upon our beliefs. When a belief is challenged, it is seen as a violation against the believer. This is why the fight against and amongst religions is so passionate.

Blind-faith is faith that says, "Believe it because I said so!" This is asking people to believe something without proof. Many people have been defying this and demanding proof, but in doing so they have come to believe a new religion requiring the same sort of blind faith. This occurs within the tiniest of details within your marriage as well: you and/or your spouse may have an idea of something that is *believed* to be right in your marriage, but it might not actually be right. Whether it is your words or your thoughts, it's all the same. When we believe that our way is right, we must be willing to check or challenge our own reasoning to make sure that we are correct in our thinking. If we are wrong or unfair, then *we* are part of the problem.

When we conduct ourselves in a "don't challenge me" manner, we don't take kindly to any opposition of our belief structure, and typically we become angry or mock our challenger. This is our natural response to what we perceive as a violation. This is done for our own survival. But in truth, this will ultimately destroy us and our marriages, and it will be done at our own hand.

If you fear to have your beliefs and actions challenged, then you have no basis for your belief structure and your beliefs or actions are likely false, in error, dangerous, or at best, weak.

We should welcome challenges to our beliefs so that we can prove to ourselves and to others what is actually true. "Blind faith" is the most dangerous thing of all, and it ultimately leads to evil. Strong words? Yes, truth often hurts when we live in lies and deception.

Consider this: You believe what you believe because that is what you were taught. But what about others who do not agree? They have the same blind faith, but with a different approach and beliefs. This is also a part of what all wars are born from, including the wars we create within our marriages.

As long as you happen to believe what is true, then your blind faith will be fine. But if you do not understand what you believe and why you believe it, then you can very likely be convinced to believe other things that are actually wrong about marriage and life in general.

"Faith" is misunderstood. Being faithful means to be true; which is to say, what actually *is*. Most people have blind faith. I say this with much confidence because few people can truly say why they believe what they believe and have what they say be based on a foundation of understanding. When asked why they believe what they believe, the question will often be met with hostility. This behavior is suspect of the frustration of their own not understanding their own beliefs.

The Bible says, "Unless you have faith as a child you will not enter the kingdom." I ask you to examine that statement carefully. It was not *what* the little children were told that matters. It is *the way* in which the children believe what they were told that matters. It might sound to us as if blind faith is a good thing. The faith part is faith and it is true and good, but the blindness is not faith and is bad. Believing things wrongly is bad for everyone around you, including your spouse, yourself, and your children. This is especially true with regard to marriage. Understanding words and their bearing on your relationship greatly aids in building a better and stronger marriage. Blindly following information without understanding your blind faith is bound to fail at some point because you are essentially guessing and following blind information. Provided that the information is good and true, you're okay. However, if you are receiving bad information, then your blind faith will cause you a great deal of trouble because you are then believing a lie. This is a very common problem.

When you and your spouse choose to understand the underlying concepts or ideas of your words and actions, then you will find your marriage to quickly strengthen. It is more difficult to excuse away your own bad behavior when you actually understand it.

I Can't Overcome Problems Because of "The Man"

The stress of life puts a great deal of stress on many marriages. Much of this stress is from the pressures of life that are often attributed to "The Man".

"The Man!" Who is this dastardly fellow who holds us down and stops us from becoming successful and joyful? We may be more familiar with this man under the alias of "Blind Faith". There are certainly people who will oppress other people by means of greed. An oppressor's own fear leads them to their destructive covetous habits of making everyone their enemy and being envious of others. In order to feel fulfilled, the oppressors want to destroy others. This empty, vain activity that oppressors do is fueled by those who have blind faith.

Blind faith does not question—it blindly submits. We are not supposed to submit just because someone said so. When we believe the lies told to us, then we hold ourselves in bondage and are subject to our oppressor's lies. When we do this, the oppressor can control us. This brings us back to the tolerance versus intolerance issue regarding the violator or oppressor. When we permit repeated violation without confronting or resisting them, then *we* become "The Man". In our marriages, we often point to our spouse or the troubles in life that plague us, but in truth it is each our own responsibility to deal with "The Man".

Societally, we often want to blame the oppressor and accuse them of being "The Man". After all, they are the oppressive violator. However, when we allow this without holding them accountable, it then becomes *our own* problem. We are then the ones responsible for our own torment; this is especially true in marriage.

We must stand for what is true and stand by that truth. We must not stand for something that is not true, and we must not stand for something that we were told to believe just because *they* said so. Investigate for yourself and understand! Strengthen your marriage through love and full understanding. Do not do only what some counselor says. Instead, understand your marriage and your spouse, and then you won't need a counselor. This is done through true, full, and open communication.

When we blame our spouse for their violations it may be accurate; but that does not help us unless we understand and confront those violations and resist them properly. Resistance will be unpopular with the violator, but it is necessary!

This chapter addresses the mean-spiritedness that often dwells within marriages. It is important to note that *not* resisting violations, even minor ones, will go unnoticed and subtly erode your marriage. This will occur until far bigger issues are born and erupt out of the mountain of hidden violations that we have allowed to accrue in the relationship.

We humans are "The Man" when we fail to resist violation, and this includes violation within our marriage relationships. We would like to think of "The Man" as the other person—the violator—that is to say, our spouse, but in truth, *we* are "The Man" when we do not resist the violations of people, and this includes our resisting violations from our spouse.

When we fail to resist the errors of the person who is violating us, then we are held in a self-imposed prison. Remember, they have freewill to attempt to do as they please, but we have a duty to ourselves and we have the freewill to protect ourselves. We fulfill this duty by *not* allowing others to violate us, which is done via confronting them and by standing firm in kindness, love, and truth.

People are Competitive and Territorial

When we have blind faith and believe what we are told, as opposed to what is actually true, then we are susceptible to a great deal of fear. We can truly understand things when we have actually seen the truth with our own eyes, due to all of the evidence. For instance, believing that you are somehow better than others just because you have the initials of a college degree behind or in front of your name is a very arrogant belief.

Most people who take much pride in their degree get hostile when their ideas are challenged in a fair manner. This is not exclusive to those who have completed higher education. It touches all walks of life. Fear drives us when we perceive life in this arrogant way. This is because we have blind faith in our education and other things that cause us to behave arrogantly. As explained in the cornerstone book *Hot Water*, we wrongly believe that *beliefs*, *status*, or *things* are what make us valuable. When we do this we become protective of our belief because we have made *it* to be all that we have.

When someone treads on our territory of "expertise" and questions our belief structure, then we attack what we see as a violation against us even if we are actually incorrect. Being territorial appears similar to being jealous or full of zeal because we deeply believe in our only information and are willing to fight for it. We feel violated when our belief in that information is questioned or challenged regardless of the validity of the information.

When our blind faith is questioned, the result is often the lashing out we spoke of in an earlier chapter. This territorial behavior is very similar to what we discussed in those earlier chapters. But territory is more closely associated to areas of expertise than it is with the what-you-do part of life. Having this type of competitive nature between spouses causes you to work against each other. This is not good and will always end poorly for both of you.

This, too, can be difficult to understand. When a couple has an argument, the debate usually comes down to who is right; or more appropriately, who is less to blame. Spouses will often hold their ground and stand strong by fending off what they *feel* is a violation.

Let's imagine that one of you is actually correct, and one of you is actually wrong, but we are not sure who is correct and who is wrong. So how do we solve this problem? Taking a stand so strongly in attempt to keep those violations at bay can cause marital gridlock, thus not allowing *any* progress in a resolution. So what's the problem then if they are both standing strong for their position against what they perceive to be a violator's violation? What is the problem? The problem is being territorial. Arguments would never even occur if both spouses would be totally honest and would both seek the truth. But alas, seldom is this the case! Truth is usually ignored and is obscured by our own personal arrogance.

In our example, one spouse is wrong and one spouse is correct. Demanding that you are *right* does not make you *correct*. Additionally, you can be correct and still be territorial and be behaving poorly. So how do we come to know who is correct and how do we come to know who is territorial?

The way to know who is territorial is simple: Just see who is willing to have their ideas or thoughts tested. See who will admit, in a kind manner, that their position was right, or that it was wrong. Regardless of who is correct, it should always be done with dignity when the truth finally arrives.

If a person actually happens to have the information correct, but will not allow testing of their information, then they are territorial. Also, if they just happen to be correct and are a sore winner then they are also territorial, but at least we now know who is correct; problem solved—mostly! But what about the person who is wrong *and* territorial?

We Render Ourselves Un-helpable

When we are both wrong and territorial we have caught ourselves in a self-imposed hell from which there is no escape. This will torment us and those around us. It offers no hope or chance of reconciliation as long as the behavior continues.

Those who are both territorial and wrong are a bit more ignorant but are equally as foolish as the territorial person who is actually correct. A person who properly does their research will often be correct. However, when they will not allow scrutiny or testing of their ideas or conclusions, then they, too, are trapped in their own arrogance.

At some point, a well-researched territorial person will eventually be wrong and will not allow scrutiny. If they do not allow scrutiny, then they are at risk of never knowing the truth about their error.

Those who are often wrong *and* territorial render themselves utterly un-helpable!

The reason the two are different is because the type of person who is often correct, at least has the desire to learn and do research. Thus, on their own, they may encounter the truth at some point and then adjust their wrongness. But the person who is frequently wrong and refuses any testing of their ideas or beliefs cannot be helped—ever. They are un-teachable or non-teachable and they must somehow awaken on their own.

When we are territorial and are frequently wrong, and we are questioned, then typically we will viciously attack in an unfair manner, or we conquer by volume of voice or by use of tears. Some people will withdraw in shame only to repeat the same behavior again at a later point, which is what caused their shame to begin with.

If you won't invite testing of your ideas, then *you* are the problem. However, even if you do allow testing of your ideas, but then berate the other person when you are correct, or even when they correct you, then *you* are still the problem.

If you look around, you'll begin to notice much wisdom in those who embrace testing of all ideas and are eager to correct their own thinking. They do this so that they are in accord with what actually is true, rather than always being wrong.

Graph of Societal Sway

When our life is falling apart, we often look at all of the bad in the world and think that everything is getting worse; and at times, this is true. Often, from our youth forward, most generations can see an erosion of good within their lifetime; but to what extent?

If every generation was worse than the previous, then today we would be in serious peril of the "fire and brimstone" level. Think about the dark ages or about Sodom and Gomorrah. Those were not good times; robbing, raping, and plundering. We are relatively far from that in most of the world as this is being written. So, why do we feel as if it is always getting worse?

If life were a graph and was measured left or right (bad or good), then in the middle it would also go bad or good but to a far lesser degree.

Fire and Brimstone	Minor Rebellion	Contentment And Order	Paradise

Generally we sway between *Minor Rebellion* and *Contentment and Order*. This sway generally varies in the length of time from only months to many decades. But when it passes *Minor Rebellion*, it quickly rushes toward *fire and brimstone*. Though, as a society, it seems we have not yet, at any point in time, figured out how to achieve paradise.

The erosion that we feel in our lifetime is generally relatively small. It seems that we quickly go towards Contentment and Order and then slowly fall towards Minor Rebellion. Then another catastrophe or international earth-moving event occurs, and we quickly go back to Contentment and Order again. Then, once again, we slowly erode to Minor Rebellion. It seems that we have been repeating this cycle since the arrival of mankind on Earth, and during that period, a handful of times we have managed to erode to the Fire and Brimstone extreme.

This type of graph also applies to the historical big picture about the statistics of marriages and the divorce of those marriages. It can also be applied within each marriage, where the Fire and Brimstone would be replaced with divorce.

Only each our own willingness to have our thoughts, ideas, and beliefs tested can stop this erosion in a relationship. It is when we refuse to rationally discuss and admit to our problems that we become trapped by ourselves. Open, honest evaluation will instantly stop the strife in our lives and in our marriages.

Chapter 13

Cherish Me My Dear

A common feeling amongst women is that they want to be cherished and respected. There is good reason for this: it is a natural desire that has been built into us to want to be loved. Women are not alone in this; men want the same thing. Though I don't know that men would use the term "cherish" in describing their feelings.

Let Them Love You

In an earlier chapter, we talked a bit about loving people in *our* own way, and loving them in *their* way. Either is good, but a combination of the two is the best. Don't be afraid to love, and don't be afraid to let someone love you.

The conflicts that arise between spouses are all from violations, whether those violations were intended or accidental. In most relationships, the conflicts start accidentally and then slowly become more and more intentional as the tit-for-tat erosion progresses. Often, this can be very one-sided, where one spouse is much more of the problem than the other spouse is.

In a one-sided relationship, the spouse doing the violating will frequently, and repeatedly, violate their mate. Then, just at a time when their violated spouse begins to heal and forget, then the other spouse will once again violate their mate's expectations and hopes. This destructive pattern is seldom known to the violator, and often, the other spouse also does not quite see the problem clearly enough to deal with it properly.

When the violated spouse is ready to offer their love again, then the other spouse crushes that expectation and hope, and then pushes them away through more violations—repeatedly.

You must allow your spouse to love you in their own way if you ever want them to love you in your way. When you keep violating someone, you are stopping them from offering their love to you, and it keeps you in your own chains of misery. And it will also likely keep them in your chains of misery as well—until they have had enough and they leave you.

Whether it is one spouse who is crushing the expectations and hopes of the other spouse, or the husband and wife are both doing the same destructive behavior to each other, the bottom line is the same: If you do not let them love you, then you can never be happy and joyful. This problem is far more likely to end in divorce when both spouses are repeat-violators who are *also* territorial.

When only one spouse is the major violator, and they repeat this behavior for many years, then they must realize that their mate is either extremely patient, or in extreme torment—and possibly both. When the violated mate is a dedicated person who has been enduring years of violation, then the violator is stealing away their spouse's life and their joy.

The worst kind of pain is to not be able to give love. This is because you truly cannot be loved if you are not allowed to give love. Love is a two-ended transaction. When we push people away by violating them, then we are rejecting their love, and thus, we are not allowing them to love us. Also, when we push them away, we cannot truly be said to "love" them, because we are rejecting them through our violations against them.

The Creator is said to have "unconditional love" for us, yet, we suffer at the hand of our own foolishness in that regard. If this Creator is so loving, then why does our suffering continue?

Our suffering continues because we reject that love and repeatedly violate the Creator's hopes for us. It is only when we receive the love that the Creator is able to actually complete the love transaction. Without our acceptance of the gift, the Creator's love is *only* offered. This same thing is true within a marriage. When we reject our spouse's love, then we are not allowing them to love us. If they can only offer their love to us and are never allowed to deliver that love, then we unfairly hold them in the bondage of a loveless prison.

Being Cherished is a Privilege

Starting this chapter, I commented that women want to be cherished; and in truth, men do too. If a woman expects to be cherished by her husband, she has some hurdles to overcome in order for that to occur. There's this notion that we should all be "cherished" regardless of our behavior. This is just like the misapplied "unconditional love" assumption.

Our society has come to misunderstand what a "right" is, as in "the *right* to free speech". It seems that we have also forgotten what the term "privilege" means, or maybe that it even exists. Your "right" to free speech does not mean that the rest of us have to listen to you. It means that we should not stop you from talking. But it also means that others have the right to walk away while you talk, and that others have a right to talk too. These two points are entirely different aspects of the concept of a "right".

You can say what you want on the radio, but I can turn you off. In the free world, we are supposed to understand this as our voice cannot be stopped or quieted by the government, and also that we cannot force others to have to hear or listen to us.

And so it is the same with being cherished. You have a *right* to be cherished, this is true, but this does not mean that someone must cherish you. The only way others can take away your right to be cherished is if someone wants to cherish you and the others will not allow that person to outwardly cherish you. Only that could possibly take away your right to be cherished. But even then, for their part, the person can still cherish you within their own heart.

A right to be cherished is not referring to you being cherished, or even that someone wants to cherish you. A "right" refers to the fact that someone must not stop others from cherishing you.

Inversely, we do not have the right to cherish others. That is each their own decision. The Creator wants to cherish us, but when we turn away, then we are not allowing that to occur; and in doing so, we are violating our own right to be cherished. This same scenario also happens in marriages. In many cases, the spouse who is most frequently violated still does desire to cherish their mate, but their mate's violations are a rejection of that cherishment.

A "right," in this case, means that someone can, or is allowed to, cherish you. Your part of the right is only as seen from your perspective, and someone can only cherish you if you allow them to.

Being cherished is a *privilege*, not a *right*! It is a privilege to have someone cherish you. If your spouse is trying to cherish you and you repeatedly violate their expectations, then it is you who is rejecting their offering of cherishing you. This all may seem contrary to many people's understanding, but think upon the following scenario for a moment and judge for yourself about *rights* versus *privileges* in regard to being cherished.

In the beginning, the Creator Creates man and then woman and they are frolicking happily in their garden. They are the showpieces of the Creator's handy work. They are cherished! Then, they choose to follow the lead of a different master and are thrown out of their home that was a gift from the Creator—they are cast out of paradise! Having no choice, they trod the ground and forage for their survival. The Creator wants to cherish them, but must wait until they choose to receive the gift of cherishment.

I want you to consider this: If they say, "Hey Creator, I'm mad at you, because you threw us out, and we don't like you any longer. Go away and leave us alone! All you ever want is for us to be perfect and do everything you say." If they were to actually say or think this, then can we expect the Creator to continue to cherish them?

What if, in response, the Creator says, "Okay, I am sorry, I love you." Then, the outcast couple is content for some time, when, eventually, another problem occurs; let's say the cold of winter is coming. Then the couple berates the Creator again, "We're cold. Why did you make it so cold here? We're freezing! You're so lazy, make it warm! You won't even warm things up for us." Then should the Creator cherish them?

So then the Creator kindly chooses to give them fire and clothing and gently says, "I'm sorry. Here, keep yourself warm." Then the couple says, "We have pain in our bellies. Give us food to eat! We are hungry. You never feed us! Feed us now!" Should the Creator cherish them then?

Now the Creator makes it rain so that the plants can grow to produce food for them. Again, the couple complains that the fire went out from the cold rain, and they say, "What are you doing? Your stupid rain put out our fire!" Then should the Creator cherish them?

Some people might find this to be a ridiculous example, but this is typically how it works with couples. Often, those who violate other people's expectations and hopes expect to be cherished and respected regardless of their own poor behavior and attitude. And while their spouse is continually doing good things for them, they still violate their spouse and reject the very same cherishment that they believe that they deserve.

Can we really expect someone to cherish and respect us when we constantly violate their reasonable expectations and hopes? On top of that aspect, the violator feels violated when they are no longer cherished by those whom they have so often violated. Is this correct behavior and thinking? Do they have a right that people *must* cherish them?

An interesting point in this is that, often, the other person wants to cherish the person who is violating them, but the person who wants to be cherished cannot be cherished because of their own rejecting of the offered cherishment by means of the violations that they continually commit against their spouse.

Being cherished is a privilege and must be earned by being cherish-able. If we are not able to be cherished, then how can we expect someone to cherish us? Being cherished needs to be earned.

Should our spouse simply cherish us if we are complaining at them and/or unfairly criticizing them all the time? When we do this, we reject their ability to cherish us. If you want to be desired and cherished, make it easy for your spouse by being desirable and accessible—be easily accessible—but not easy. Be cherishable!

Many wives want to be, or expect to be, treated as a queen because, in their own heart, they act as a queen. The question then comes down to, what type of queen is she behaving like? Is she a demanding queen who ruthlessly controls her peasant subjects? Or will she act like a beautiful dignified queen who is well loved by all of those around her because she is sweet, loving, kind, generous, confident, understanding, caring, and *cherishable*?

The People Who You Look Up to Will Affect Your Future

What is "cherish" anyway? Cherish means *dear*, *love*, and *friend*. Relationships and love are both a type of transaction between two people. You must *cherish* to be *cherished*.

Realize that when you cherish someone, you admire and respect them, you look up to them! Who you choose to admire or look up to, will affect your life, your future, and your marriage.

Violations are disrespect, and might be more easily understood as disregard for someone or their thoughts. When we make the decision to violate someone through our actions, whether it be unintended or intended, it is still our own decision.

We are responsible for the way we treat others, and no one gets a pass on this. In the end, we all will get paid for our efforts in life. Treating our spouses poorly can appear to gain you much for the immediate time, but it will end in self-destruction while those who we have violated watch in horror as we destroy our own lives and try to take the onlookers along with us.

When we turn people away with all of our violations, we affect our own future. Every person who you have the opportunity to connect with can change your life in a very profound manner. And every person who you are currently connected with has already changed your life more than you might imagine.

We must each decide who we will have in our lives. Will we allow destroyers, the violators, to continue to steal away our life and destroy it along with themselves? In some types of relationships, the answer is clearly, "No, depart from them", but in a marriage relationship, sticking to it is often a good route to take. The problem is: How do you address the problem when the problem is your spouse?

When we ourselves are the problem it's simple, just wake up and smell the roses. We need to open our eyes to see what we are throwing away, and then come to understand how we have been cheating ourselves out of a joyful life, but even that can be selfish.

How about we also take a look at what *we* have done to our spouse? How about thinking about how they have felt, having to endure *our* violations against them and about how *we* have cheated them out of their joy for so long? When we cheat our spouse in this way, then in many ways, we would have been more kind to have sent them away with a bill of divorce and allowed them to find someone else who would accept the abundant love that they are trying to offer us.

But even if we did send them away and freed them from our prison, then that becomes a major violation against them. The best action to take is to change, and to do it now! Apologies are useless and can even be considered violations, unless change accompanies those apologies.

What should we do when the violator is our own spouse? Patience is our best option, while at the same time, trying to get them to *understand* by confronting them about how badly they are hurting you. What is the best thing to do? Not to violate them, and at the same time to be honest. But this is the challenge of challenges! It's not easy to confront a violator without having them feel violated.

When we confront people, even if we are correct and are in utter honesty, they may still perceive the confrontation as an attack on them—as a violation against them. Gentleness and loving-kindness are about the only options of approach that we are left with. Sometimes, parental-style verbal discipline might work with a spouse, but if that is what is required then there are also other deeper issues with the spouse that promptly, but carefully, need to be addressed before you will be able to properly take care of the issues that are apparent on the surface.

Do They Demand That You Understand Them or Does Your Spouse Want to Understand You?

How do you know when you are cherished? In general, you will feel loved. You will feel joy! You might wonder, "Why don't they respond? After all, I do all that's mentioned here." This may be true, but we have to remember that relationships, love, and being cherished, are all two-way streets or doors that swing both ways—they are two-way transactions. You cannot complete the transaction if *they* do not receive it. You can only do your part.

Recall here, the concepts of *invite, offer, accept, give,* and *receive.* If the first four happen and the last one does not, then the transaction is *not* completed. A spouse who demands to be cherished cannot be cherished—ever—until they realize that *it is they who must receive* the cherishment.

There's a problem that often occurs in marriages, where one spouse is a repeat violator and the other spouse patiently tolerates those violations and eventually becomes weary of trying to work with their violating spouse. When the violated spouse ceases trying, then their mate will begin to notice, and only then start to see the light.

A violator's delay in realizing their own errors presents a problem, because by the time the spouse who was doing the violating decides to change, their mate may have already lost interest in the relationship and may have moved on in their own mind. If this is your situation and you have violated your spouse to this extent and they are now turned off by you, your only chance is to not violate them any longer and spend the rest of your life actually understanding your discouraged spouse—they will likely come around—eventually—even after all of the pain that they experienced at *your* hand.

If you're a violator then it is likely that, without realizing it, you have spent your days demanding that your spouse know and understand you, and at the same time you refused to let them do it. You also likely refuse to know and understand them. But, when you truly cherish someone, then you are going to get beyond yourself and you are going to seek your mate.

Get to know your spouse and watch your problems vanish! If you do this only to get your way, then you're not understanding the points being made here, and it is you who is the problem and your troubles have only just begun.

How Do They React to You?

Touching on the last chapter discussing jealousy, consider how your spouse reacts to your counsel, achievements, concerns, offerings, and gifts. Does your spouse rejoice in your triumphs? Do they invite your counsel? Do they consider your concerns? Do they accept your offerings and gifts? An answer of "No" to any of these questions brings up another important question—should they?

First, ask yourself the following questions: Do you want to *share* your *triumphs* with them? Do you offer *wise* counsel to them? Do you offer your concerns with care and love? Are your offerings and gifts pure, unselfish, and worthy?

An answer of "No" to any of those questions places the root of the problem in your own hands. Correct your own approach first. This should be reliably done until it becomes your normal habit. It must be your customary way of communicating with your spouse. Only after you have dealt with *your* own shortcomings are you worthy to examine *their* shortcomings. This falls into the category of the Biblical phrase, "pull the board out of your own eye before you try to remove the speck from your brother's eye."

When you're certain that you have no error, then you can realistically begin to question your spouse's behavior. If you have asked yourself how they react to you, and if you have found their reaction to fall short of your expectations, then ask yourself: are my own expectations realistic? Are my expectations true? If you answer this honestly and you are realistic and true but find that your spouse still falls short, it's likely that your spouse is blind and nearly un-teachable in their current state—they are still asleep.

The method for waking people up is something that even the Creator has not been able to reliably do with regard to humanity.

So how do we get someone to understand that there is so much more to life that they are missing because of their self-focus? Often, we want people to know how we feel and that we're angry or sad. While this self-focus is important and okay, it is far less important than facing what is true.

Depending upon who is doing the violating, their self-focus often torments us, or our self-focus often torments them. Our only hope of reconciliation for the violations is persistence, patience, longsuffering, and prayers that their eyes be opened. As explained in the cornerstone book *Understanding Prayer - The Prayer How-To Manual*, when you pray for a person who behaves badly, you do not need to ask that blessings pour down upon them. What you should pray for is that their eyes are opened and that they are able to see the errors of their own ways. Sometimes this is a very difficult thing to watch when those prayers are truly answered.

Finding ways to get our spouse to understand us is a monumental task. This is not easy, and sometimes it is going to be a long and painful process for both people. If it is you who is the violator, then understand that everyone has a breaking point. And at some point there will be a breakdown in the relationship if nothing changes.

Misery, divorce, a cold torturous relationship, or utter withdrawal are the only byproducts of a blind spouse. To achieve joy, both spouses must awaken and see! If it is you, then the power is in your hands to decide, in an instant, that you will change. If it is them, then your task is to find a way to kindly help them to awaken from their blind-slumber and find a way to teach them to see.

What Are You, to Your Spouse?
Are You Someone They can Confide in and Pray With,
or are You only a Shoulder to Cry on?

Another method of detecting if you have a one-sided relationship is to look at how your spouse interacts with you. Do they trust you and tell you their deepest thoughts? Can you pray openly with your spouse? Or do you have to constantly clean up their mistakes as if you are babysitting them? Do they only come to you when they have problems, so that they can cry on your shoulder and have you make things better for them? Or do they offer themselves to you?

I am not saying that when your spouse comes to you with a mistake or a problem and they are crying about it, that it is a bad thing. But, you can gauge the slant in a relationship when you look at whether or not they *also* come to you with the good things, like their trust, love, and prayers.

When we *confide* in someone, we are not only offering to share our problems with them, but we also receive their input, and we desire their advice and counsel. This doesn't mean that we will, or must, follow that advice, but it does mean that we will process their advice in our hearts and minds. We will consider it, think about it, and partly make our decisions based upon its validity.

Even if we are wrong, we get frustrated or irritated with people when they do not understand what we are trying to tell them. When we get frustrated because our spouse does not understand us, then we violate them and often place the blame on them for not understanding us. But in truth, they cannot possibly understand us, because what we are trying to get them to understand is wrong. We can understand that something is wrong, but it is *not* possible to understand a thing or subject when it is wrong. There's nothing to understand in an error, and if you think that you can understand the error then you are an irrational thinker. Understanding that an error exists and how it occurs is different than understanding an error.

If a person misunderstands something and believes their erred thinking is true and then tries to convey what they *think* they understand, it is not their fault even though we feel this as—them violating us when they try to impress their misguided views upon us. When we misunderstand in this way, we are being irrational and we do not understand that we're doing so. Our frustration is because of the blindness of our own misunderstanding, but it is also because of our inability to communicate to others that we believe we "know" something. This is a blind-faith issue and it is technically impossible to properly communicate something as if it is truth when it is actually in error.

This irrational inconsistency and error-filled way is the destroyer of many relationships. When people are angry or frustrated, it is a clear sign that someone is not understanding or seeing something clearly, whether it be our error or our truth that is being attempted to be conveyed.

The same is true of ourselves. Because much of the solution to our problem is bound in our frustration, when we begin to feel frustrated or angry we must stop and ask ourselves why we feel this way. If we would all ask "Why?" and investigate it, then there would be very few problems in our marriages and in the world. We could all then move on to bigger and better things.

Are Men More Passionate than Women?

A stereotypical perspective that we often tend to have is that women are more passionate than men. This can certainly be true, but often women's moodiness is taken as more "passionate" because women's emotions tend to dictate their words, thoughts, and actions more so than men's do. And when emotions run wild, actions often appear to others as passionately heartfelt and are often also felt so by the woman herself. This does not mean that she is "passionate" or *more* passionate than her husband.

Passion and *patience* have the same root, which is to suffer. That is why patients are called patients and why patience is called patience. It is because we must suffer something or bear something until our wait is completed. When we put up with a spouse's poor attitudes and behavior, it is *we* who suffer, and it is us who has the passion for them in our enduring of our suffering from their poor actions and so-called "passionate" moodiness.

If you are longsuffering and have been putting up with your spouse's poor behaviors, then you are likely the more "passionate" one, and potentially the more creative one. People who are more creative are typically less afraid to reveal themselves. They are often more open and willing to figure out what is real and true, which is the reason they are creative. I'm not referring to attention-seeking-artist-types here, but rather, people who truly have something wonderful to offer to the world

Whether it is a song, a painting, a poem, or even as simple as the way we keep our house, *creativity* is a way of sharing. It is a way of dividing up what you have to offer and allowing others a portion of it. Singing your "song" allows others to enjoy it!

Passion is not getting all worked up about something, though that can happen when you are truly passionate. No, *passion* is enduring love. It is desiring to love someone so deeply that you are willing to wait out their ignorant blindness and injury against you until they awaken.

When someone is passionate about something, they may speak with much enthusiasm, but that is not what makes them passionate. What makes them passionate is their willingness to endure persecution for what they believe in. Many people who believe in their dreams will pursue those dreams, even though the naysayers around them condemn them *daily* for what the person who pursues their dream is trying to accomplish.

What naysayers seldom realize is that, it is these passionate ones who make the world good by finding cures for disease, inventing furnaces to heat our homes, and telephones to communicate with, etc. Most people would be crushed by the adversity that was endured by the inventors of these and many other wonderful inventions that we all enjoy today. Yet, all of the mockery and trouble they endured were foreseen by most of them, but they didn't care much about that because they understood that everyone would someday come to enjoy their contributions to the world—now that is passion!

So ask yourself, who is more passionate in a marriage: The one who gets "passionately" and emotionally upset, demanding that *they* be allowed to viciously share their emotions? Or is it the one who endures the scorn and ridicule of those vicious emotional outbursts because they passionately believe that something can be better and more joyful with their spouse?

Chapter 14

Wives Hold The Keys
to a Joy-Filled Marriage

While we are stereotyping women and men here, the reality is that *people are people*. This means that both genders do almost all of the behaviors that we have been discussing. But stereotyping doesn't exist because it's never true. No, rather, these stereotypes are there because they are often true, and they are usually true far more times than not.

Most stereotypes exist because of the way we people generally are. Stereotypes are reflections of our human nature. This then, forces the discussion back to asking: What were we Created as? What was our order in Creation? It is in this where we can find the formula for most troubled marriages to be quickly healed. And it is the wives who typically hold the keys to a joy filled marriage. This *does not* mean that problems are the fault of the wife. No, rather, it means that it is the wife who typically has the luxury to more readily correct the problems in a damaged marriage.

Women Have the Power
to Make Their Marriage Relationships Great

Recalling the last chapter, we touched on the Biblical "chosen people" and their Creator, and how the Creator wants to cherish the people but cannot do so until the people complete the transaction by accepting the offered cherishment. This acceptance can only be done one way, which is to say, by no longer rejecting the cherishment through our violations—it really is that simple!

Wives: you truly do hold the keys; but since men are human, and are not the actual Creator, women have an additional task, and the task is to try to connect to their husband even if *he* is the violator.

Unlike the Creator, who does not violate, many husbands violate their wives' expectations. If you think back through many of the questions that you should have asked yourself through the previous chapters, it should now be clear to you that it is easiest for women to initiate a great marriage. This is not to say that a man who reads this is allowed to sit idly by while his wife does all of the effort in the relationship. In fact, since the man is the primary guide in the family, *he* is the foundation that the family will be built upon. If he refuses to put in his part of the effort, then he is casting a faulty foundation that the wife sits upon and the relationship will only be as good as his foundation.

It may be unfair, but *initiating* repairs is always up to the person who is hurting and has come to the realization that something needs to be changed. The *violated* spouse holds the responsibility to get the other person to awaken from their oblivious error-filled slumber. Having read this book up to this point has put *you* in the situation of having the responsibility to *initiate* the changes in your marriage relationship.

It is possible that not everyone can be awakened to a life free of violating others, but it is also true that most people can be awakened to a full, wonder-filled, and robust marriage. It is your task to guide your spouse to that end.

Men typically want nothing but love from their wives and children. And typically women want little more than security and love from their husbands. How can we test this theory? By simply taking a look at the industry of media and what draws men's attention and what draws women's attention. Our attraction to things in the world of media drives their existence. If we were not interested, they would not persist.

Look at the articles in magazines and the contents of television shows and internet sites: just who are all of these venues aimed at? It becomes very clear when you question the content of any given medium just who the particular content is aimed at. This stereotype exists for a reason—it is because it is largely true and consistent as a stereotype. Drawing upon the information that we can gain from this, we now have the opportunity to generically see ourselves through the eyes of society, allowing us to see what we actually desire in each our collective gender.

The simple fundamental needs of each spouse are as follows. Women want security and cherishment. Men want to offer love and support and to have that love and support joyfully received.

When these two inherent aspects of human nature are met for each of the respective genders, then most problems vanish on their own. The initiation to satisfy these is more easily done by the wife than by the husband. This might seem unfair, but it is based upon the nature and the design of our physical forms.

When a woman trusts her husband, she offers him the best gift that she can possibly offer him in trusting him. Men will almost always rise to that challenge and take delight in pleasing their wives *when they are allowed to do so*, and then the transaction is complete and most everything else will fall in place automatically. However, if a wife does not trust her husband to care for her, and she places her trust in other people, money, or her or his job, then she steals from him his ability to love and cherish her. Men display love and cherishment with their support and undying admiration for their wives.

If you happen to be someone who has, with honesty, read the entire Bible from cover to cover in your adult lifetime, then you will likely recall how often the people turned away from the Creator and placed their trust in other peoples or even in carved images that were idols. They requested favors and sustenance from these people and idols. This was a violation of the Creator's expectations of the chosen people. The Creator wants to care for the people and the people essentially said, "We don't want *your* support!"

Eventually the Creator turned from the people and basically said "Fine, then do it on your own!" Is a husband expected to react any differently? Husbands around the world supply the needs of the family in care and protection, and their wives generally receive that. This is what makes our world a beautiful place to live in. It is the order that we all desire, and it is a part of the way we are designed.

When a wife supports her husband through her trust in him, her trust is the single most important gift she can offer him. If she does not trust her husband in the outside world, then she is not likely to trust him anywhere else, including in her heart and/or in their bed. When a husband has been doing his part, then it is the wife's obligation to find it within herself to fully trust her husband.

How do I Satisfy Expectation?

A wife's trust towards her husband cannot be only mere lip service. She must stand beside him in his passion. If she finds that his "passion" is of an ill nature, then she must be there together with him to reason it through so that they can arrive at the proper direction together. If she is condescending towards her husband, then she is implying to him that he is of little or no value to her and that she does not trust him.

There are also men who are utterly selfish and little can be done to change their unfavorable ways, but the remaining men which is most of them, will respond quickly to their wives when their wives trust the husbands without fail. That is a man's expectation and hope—trust is how a woman cherishes a man.

What if a man is not trustworthy? Provided that it was not his wife that caused the problem in him to begin with, then it is still up to the wife to gain his trust and help him. "What?" you say "She, should gain his trust?" Yes, exactly.

We gain other people's trust by trusting them. Yes, there are occasionally people who just can't ever seem to be trusted, but *most* people can when given the chance. If a man does not trust his wife, it is probably because she does not trust him. (Or it could also be that in the past he was violated by women other than his wife. The reverse situation is also true for women.) This is a two-way street. Why is trust such a big and hidden problem?

Men expect to be trusted by their wives. That is a man's expectation and hope. Of course, if his direction is wrong it is going to be more difficult to trust him, but his wife should trust that he will redirect when they work together *as a team* to find what is correct so that he will no longer be wrong. When this issue is violated, then men eventually lose trust in their wives. This terrible cycle has been the fall of many a marriage.

Trusting does not mean that if a husband says two plus two equals five that his wife should believe it. No, not at all. In fact, that is the sort of attitude that brought about the destructive aspects of the women's movement. When a wife clearly sees error in her husband's judgment she should have already been a part of his thinking. If she had been a fully bound part of this thinking and had trusted him, then the error in judgment would likely not have happened to begin with because their decision would have been as one, and she would have guided him from his foolish errors.

A husband's Created task is to guide his family *together with* his wife, but since he is a human, and not the Creator, he is susceptible to error. Working together as a couple brings about a much more robust unity. This is typically the expectation of a man, and when this is violated, there will be a divide in family direction. A divide in family direction is never a good thing for the family of the marriage!

This does not mean that you must do everything together or that you must always like all of the same things, but it does mean that the two of you should think as one and be of a single mind.

A couple that is married could be likened to a car. The husband is driving and he steers the driver's side tire and his wife steers passenger's side tire while the kids are safely tucked away in the back seat—or are they? What happens when those two front tires begin to go in two different directions? Sometimes a car will hit a curb or a strong bump, which can cause the two companion front tires to be knocked out of alignment or agreement from each other.

Even though the car is generally heading in the right direction, it is no longer as stable as it once was when the two front tires, which are supposed to guide the family safely through the streets of life, are no longer in agreement of exactly which direction to go. This slight misalignment causes undue wear on the marriage-tires and will cause the need for much more tire maintenance. If the misaligned tires continue long enough in this way, the tires will prematurely wear and eventually burst, causing a crash, thus, putting the safety of the entire family in danger.

How do we stop this disagreement in the direction of the marriage-tires? This is corrected by bringing the car in for a re-alignment or adjustment of the front tires. The adjustment will bring the front tires back into a trusted alignment so that they are once again rolling along in truly perfect unity and accurate harmony to a common goal.

Marriage is no different. If husband and wife are going in even the slightest different direction, it causes unneeded friction in the relationship and that *will* cause undesired wear on the marriage. When this is allowed to go on long enough, it unavoidably and negatively affects the children. And children will be injured when a marriage heads in two, or even slightly, different directions.

This disorder or lack of harmony within a marriage might not seem like much to us, but that's often because this is something that we also grew up with all around us, and so we don't recognize it as bad within our own marriages. Some marriages may even consider this divergence in direction to be good, but while people can often have "financial success" while heading in two different directions, it is unlikely that their family life will be left unharmed when this is the case.

Women Hold the Power and the Keys

This destructive marital misalignment typically is mostly in the wives' control. Not that she caused it, but she typically has better position to address the situation. A powerful ability to be in control is often perceived by women, but seldom is it properly understood by women. A husband's desire—for his wife to receive his expectations and hopes—is often abused; but how so?

Husbands are smitten with the woman of their affection—his wife is his obsession. His tolerance level for violation from his wife runs high because his passion is high for his obsession. His wife can easily doubt him and not put her trust in him or their Creator. This type of violation often continues for many years. The control she feels that she has over her husband is a self-deception on her part. In truth, the problems are usually set off by a tiny spark of tit-for-tat that eventually grows into this difficult problem.

When this is the case, it is he who is tolerating her and allowing her poor behavior to persist while she sees herself as the controller of the relationship. When a wife takes this position, she must realize that she has stepped from being a cherishable wife who is desirable, into a role that will quickly make her, her husband's worst nightmare that he must endure for the rest of his days.

Women: the power and keys to a wonderful marriage are almost always mostly in your hands. This certainly does not mean that women are always the cause of the problems, but it does mean that they can more readily make adjustments in the marital realignment. Men are typically longsuffering and desire only to have the trust of their wives. When the trust is lost or is unobtainable, then the husbands no longer have reason to please their wives and may have even lost the desire to love their wives. Then a husband will likely withdraw and find trust and acceptance in another way—maybe in the arms of another woman, alcohol, or some other mind numbing way—but something *will* replace the wife because she has replaced her trust in him with trust in others or other things. It is important to mention that some people, husband or wife, choose to not be trustworthy no matter what we do on our part.

The keys to your joy are in your own hands. What will you do with those keys? Will you choose to use them as a manipulative device to demand your own way? Or will you unlock the joy and happiness that has not yet been achieved through manipulation by either person? Strong words?

When You Give Yourself to Him You Are Accepted

Everything in life is a choice—even when we are being forced—and everything has a consequence whether it is good or bad. If we are being "forced" against our will, in reality we are not being forced. It may not be a fair arrangement, but we can always defy something that we don't like. However, then we must accept that our choice may have consequences, even if those consequences are unfair.

No matter what, the choice is still ours to either comply with or deny someone's demands even if those demands are wrong or unjustified. Freewill always exists for each of us when we realize this simple truth.

Using the passion any person has towards you for your own advantage is a foolish error that will cost a great deal in the long run. People who are willing to manipulate in this way are less likely to fully understand this next thought without seeing it as an advantage for themselves: When you give yourself to the person who has a passion for you, and you place your trust in them for what they are to you, then you will gain much favor with them for yourself, and they will offer much more generosity towards you.

Most people, especially women, do not want people to *not* like them, so they try to be people pleasers. (This is especially true with young women just entering the dating age.) This, in many ways, is the complete opposite situation. Instead of allowing the love and assistance of a husband, the wife will reject that and look to other means of stability in which to place her trust. With this "opposite" problem she will serve the other people in attempt to gain their trust and love. Often, but not always, when one of these situations is happening, the other is also happening.

Trying to please unpleasant people is simply unpleasant! In attempting to do so, you quickly get nowhere because an unpleasant person is much the same as the person trying to please them. When we do this we are focusing on the wrong kinds of people.

Wives: give your trust to your husband and to the Creator and you will see your lives quickly change! You cannot do this only once in a while—it is an *all-in* task. If you're going to do it, then do it!

Give yourself to your husband, and when you do, you then are accepted. Sex is certainly a part of this, but we are not speaking of sex in this section.

If you have been the violator, it may take some effort and time to regain his trust. But without your effort, it will never happen because you hold the keys to your own joy-filled marriage. You must take those keys and make sure that you are in alignment with your husband in trusting his sustenance and love. Watering your relationship in this way will help it to grow into a harmonious garden overflowing with joy!

In a physical way, giving yourself to your mate is something that is done more by body language and voice intonation than it is by anything else. Men are attracted to a woman's invitation, which is why flirting is so appealing with both men and women. When men feel fulfilled they generally don't seek such invitations from other sources. The way a wife communicates with her husband is her key. Learn how to effectively use that key!

Some women are led to believe that their key to a better marriage is a better physical appearance. Certainly most men want their wives to be fit and well-kept, and women also want this of their husbands. But if this was the only thing that mattered in marriages, then there would be many people whose spouse would have long ago left them for a more fit and well-kept mate. Understanding this is important because, all too often, women think that it will make their marriage better if they get fit. Doing so typically won't hurt, but if there are other underlying problems it will seldom help your situation.

When you're communicating with your spouse, look at his invitation with sweet, loving, flirty acceptance as you did when you were dating. Getting into this habit will draw his attention to you, and it will pull him away from other sources of this type of acceptance. This is the most important physical action that a woman can take in preserving her marriage. The fact that the spouses in a marriage fail to do this is the primary problem that most marriages face.

A feeling of acceptance is what other women, prostitutes, and the like offer to men. Men understand that prostitutes and pictures are not real in this way, but it often feels better to them than what they get from their very own wives. This is a sad testament to those wives. A wife can complain about this all she wants, but her complaining will not take away from these truths of human nature. In general, *men want to feel wanted by the object of their affection.* It is the wife's mission to make sure that *she* is the object of his affection and that she wants her husband.

A wife might think, "What if I do all of this, and then someone more beautiful comes along?" As stated earlier, if that were what husbands *really* wanted, then many wives would have been out of the picture long ago. You must realize that this world is filled with many well-kept stunningly beautiful *single* women who are searching for a devoted and capable mate. Here is an additional thought to consider about this subject: What about all of those supposed "beautiful women"? How many of them have been divorced? If a wife does get perfectly fit and is very attractive and keeps herself well, and then someone else comes along and steals her husband away, then it is obvious that the husband is looking at something *other than* her looks.

The fact that beautiful women get divorced should make the picture very clear, that it is the wife who is the object of the husband's affection, and *not* the wife's body; though, the body is a part of the overall picture. When you fail to make yourself beautiful in his eyes you are risking your investment in your relationship. Physical beauty is pleasing and desired, but true inner beauty is what husbands, and wives, really desire in their mates. We show this desire by accepting our spouses and by revealing our true selves to them. Inner beauty and the way you think about yourself are often reflected on the outside by your appearance and by your actions, especially those actions that happen in your bedroom.

What's beautiful in his eyes? Does it include looks? You bet it does! But it includes *your* looks, not other women's looks provided that you are attentive to your husband in your interaction. What does this mean? It means the way you take care of yourself is all part of *one big picture.* Men don't expect their wives to be in a push-up bra, wearing a skirt, heels, and makeup all the time, though many would not mind that. Men expect their wives to care about themselves as much as he himself cares about her. It's that simple— Love yourselves! *He* expects *her* to look at him with trust and adoration.

Adoration cannot be faked. Deep down, we humans are all very aware of the deeper feeling that others have towards us, even though we try to hide this knowledge in an effort to feel loved. Trying to fake desire for your spouse, will only bring temporary satisfaction for your spouse and for yourself. That sort of false love can be bought from a prostitute, and it is far less expensive and less emotionally involved in the open market of sex, but it will never satisfy his true desire. Don't let fake adoration happen in your marriage, because your spouse may find something that better fulfills those expectations, and you may find yourself all alone.

You Got What You Deserve!

Is there a difference between the phrases "You got what you deserved" and "You get what you work for"? In the end, no; they are the same. However, depending upon your own attitude, you may see these as negative or positive statements. "You got what you deserved."

Let's consider what this actually means:
You get what you work for
You get what you deserve
You get what you planted

For everything that you do, there is a reaction from the world around you. If you work a lot and invest your efforts in something lasting, then, in general, it will pay long-term dividends back to you. Everything seems to follow this pattern, whether what you invest in is something lasting, or some short-sighted goal; and whether good or bad, it simply does not seem to matter. In the end, you will get (paid) what you have earned.

Often this frightens people, and for good reason. If you have not lived the most giving life, you will then have an inner fear that your selfish behavior will eventually come back to you—which it will.

Most cultures have terms for this balance. In western culture a common phrase is, "What goes around comes around." In the Bible it repeatedly indicates that, in the end you will all be "rewarded according to your deeds" even if the "rewards" come after death with Heaven or hell. As a matter of fact, our entire world system functions on this principle. We can pin the blame for our problems on evil leadership, but in truth, it is us who have failed to speak out for righteousness and goodness; and thus, we have allowed those corrupt and misguided leaders to come to power. While it may seem unfair that we are held at a disadvantage, in many ways this is our own fault. However if something is not our own fault, then we should expect that at some point everything will be made right and proper when we stand in firm direction and work to take action to remedy the situation.

If we have a job at a place of work and we repeatedly fail at our job, then we generally expect to be let go or fired. Yet, when we treat others poorly, we often expect them to repeatedly tolerate our bad behavior. Is this a reasonable way to think? What should we really expect? Many marriages fall short in this area because there is often much expectation cast upon our spouse to accept us just as we are. It is a ridiculous notion that we should be able to behave poorly towards others, and then assume that others will simply back down and be delighted with our horrid behavior. The best way to state this is: what do you expect!

Women are often allowed to get away with a great deal of poor behavior because men are generally very patient, or too lazy, or afraid regarding confronting the situation. Excuses such as PMS are used to berate and belittle husbands with unjustified attacks at the whim of a premenstrual wife. Or "I had a bad day at work" is often used as a pass for rude and unacceptable behavior by men and women against their spouses. Additionally, in general, people want to believe whatever they want to believe, even if it's not true. This means that many of us try to justify the erroneous behaviors of ourselves and others so that we can keep up our false hope and keep our current lifestyles of arrogance and self-deception.

To be treated well, we must first treat others well. When we have done this, then we can and should become *intolerant* of other people's poor behavior and stand for what is good and right. And through this, we can make our marriages and the world much better places to exist. There are no excuses for unjustified bad behavior, because bad behavior is simply not justifiable.

Chapter 15

What is "True Beauty"?

What is true beauty? To answer this question we must understand what is attractive. True beauty is attractive! But why? Why is *true beauty* attractive?

It's difficult to understand why true beauty is attractive without first understanding what true beauty is. Additionally, and inversely, it is difficult to understand what true beauty is without understanding why it is attractive. This seemingly impossible catch can be better approached when trying to see both aspects at the same time. So, we will discuss the two views alongside each other.

The two questions could be said to be one and the same thing because true beauty is what is attractive. So, exactly what is it that we are attracted to? Since the consistency of natural human behavioral differences between men and women are so utterly thorough, we are going to approach this from the understanding that we were actually Created *for a reason.*

If there's no purpose in our Creation, then life is truly without meaning and everyone can do whatever they want with no regard for anyone else but themselves. However, most people in the world understand that this line of thinking is utter nonsense.

Whether cultures believe in the one Creator, or many gods, most believe that some sort of deliberate Creation occurred. All creation has purpose. Even art that appears valueless to most people had a purpose of gaining the attention of those who would, at some point, regrettably view it. People may not agree as to what the value of the created art is, but even something that many assume to be junk, has a created purpose, even if that purpose is only the artist's vain glory.

It is said that we are Created in the image of the Creator, so what is that image? And why did the Creator Create mankind? When we answer these questions we can begin to understand what true beauty is.

What Men Think is Attractive

When listening to men talk amongst themselves they are typically attracted to: Face, hair, breasts, neck, high cheek bones, small waist, cute butt, legs, and little things like the crease under women's butt cheeks; and maybe, the particular way a woman smiles, particular breast sizes, hair color, eye color, and including just about *every other* imaginable physical aspect of a woman that you can dream up. These are only some of the items on the long list of what men find physically beautiful about women.

It appears that if a woman could fulfill all of these that she is an automatic winner! But, alas, most women have all of these! That makes you all winners in the eyes of the men that want to love you. So, what is it then? What do men really think is attractive? And, what is true beauty?

Let's go back to the Creator subject and ask: What does the Creator think is attractive? Repeatedly in the Bible, the Creator told the people that their offerings where empty and vain. So then, why did the Creator request that the people make these offerings to begin with?

The Bible explains that when some people made offerings it pleased the Creator, but others would offer the same or even better, yet their offering would be rejected? Why is this? Should it not be that the offering that is even more valuable be more desirable to the Creator?

There's a Bible story about a woman who gave her last two bits as an offering. And the Christ said that she gave more value than anyone else who was there. Why was *her* money so much more valued than the money of the others who gave more?

Her two bits had the same world-value as any of the other people's two bits did. Now, understanding that her money had the same world-value as the money of the other people's offerings, we can conclude that it never really mattered what physical item was being offered or how much world-value was being offered.

So, what was the purpose of the Creator requesting the offerings to begin with?

An offering is an outward symbol of underlying intent. This outward symbol could be completely different for two different people, or it could be of the same monetary value, but for two different levels of wealth.

Would it affect a multi-millionaire to give up ten-thousand dollars? Not likely. But, what about the person who has next to nothing? Would giving only a few dollars affect a poor person? It's very likely that even a hundred dollars would devastate a poor person if they gave it away. So, who then, gave more? The person with much, or the person with little? Many people would still debate on the side of the wealthy person because they gave the larger amount.

Based upon the Creator's criteria, it seems that money has little to do with your offering, and much more to do with your passion and the actual intent of your offering. How do we measure intent level? The people were all instructed to give, to the temple, one tenth of their harvest's take for their year's work. Yet, even this did not equalize them in the sight of the Creator. What was so attractive about the woman who gave her last two bits that made her offering so valued?

It was her true intent in offering all that she had, and it was her complete trust in being cared for. She trusted the Creator so much that she offered all that remained of what little she had. So how do we show this kind of devotion? It's not so much that she gave all she had; rather, it is where her heart was when she gave it. She put her heart in a state of full trust and placed that trust in the hands of the Creator. This is the primary element that is anticipated in a marriage, but is often disregarded. Since we were Created in the "Image Of", it's fair to reason that humans would desire the same passion of devotion from their spouses as the Creator desires from humans.

What Men Really Like

Husbands don't want money from their wives. If they do want money from their wives, then they have been taught in a very uncommon manner. Men want much the same from their wives as the Creator wants from the people—their trust!

This brings us to the next logical question: How do we show trust? We can allow others to make our decisions and trust that they will do well in choosing, and thus, we will then benefit from their choices; but that is not what the Creator desires of the people. The Creator did not want the people to abandon their hopes and dreams and lay all decisions on the Creator. That would actually be opposite of the Creator's intention and desire.

The Creator's intention was for the people to do everything to please the Creator, *while* still being their own person and being creative themselves. The Creator wanted the people to want to please the Creator. The Creator wanted their desire!

So, what do men really like? Men's real passion is trust, and through the action of trust, men also want the desire of their wife directed *at them*. And it must be true, real, and robust. We can only love as much as we are allowed to give love. Since love is a freewill action, women cannot be forced to accept the love that is offered to them by their husbands.

If a woman pretends to "love" her husband by only physically giving herself to her husband, she risks being a liar, and her offering is therefore worthless. Our actions should always be true.

Giving yourself to your husband when you are actually not enjoying it is a lie and is like an offering that is not pure of heart. It is near to harlotry when doing it for any manipulative or loveless transactional purpose, and it is, then, without meaning or connection. Learning to overcome our own selfish ways and come to once again fully love our spouse can be a very difficult task, because when we are not feeling it, then we are simply not feeling it.

How to "Seduce" Your Husband

So how can a wife seduce her husband? The word "seduce" means: to be, to lead away (-duce means to lead). A wife needs to be so attractive to her husband that he is drawn to *her*. But, if she draws him away from the Creator she has done herself a disservice. What she should be leading him away from is *other women*.

Taking from the hard lessons learned by the people in the Bible, being pure of heart is critical! "Pure of heart" means to be true, to be real, to be honest in what you are doing—to actually mean what you intend and then show it outwardly. The underlying theme of this entire book revolves around this one simple principle. But this simple principle is one of the most difficult things for any of us to grasp when we are blind to it.

We are taught that the real value of life is in what we have— our things or goods. But this could not be more wrong. It's sad that many people don't realize, until after they are on their death beds, that all that they worked to earn, including their status, has no worthwhile value. It is often realized only at the point of death that they have wasted their *entire* life chasing that lie. This does not make having *things* bad or wrong unless you're sacrificing what is real and good to get your worldly wealth. If you are sacrificing the true and good in exchange for the lie, then it is the lie that you are serving.

Failing to have true beauty in the eyes of your spouse will cause your spouse's obsession to be something other than you. Invite your husband into you spiritually, emotionally, mentally, and physically. By inviting him only physically, you leave your husband feeling empty and that his expectations were violated. This causes him to lose interest in you, and it also causes him to look elsewhere for his fulfillment. Desire him, accept him, receive him, and trust him, and then everything else will fall in place in your marriage.

While your *true* beauty is your husband's primary desire, physical intimacy does also matter, and failing to address those needs will violate a husband's physical marriage expectations, resulting in negative long-term ramifications in your relationship. True seduction is complete, and it includes heart, mind, body, and soul. Surrender yourself completely!

How to Seduce Your Wife

Women want strength, guidance, and control in their lives, and your children will want the same. When you take care of your family in this way, it is very attractive to your wife. Be *in control* of things, but do not be *controlling* other people. We discussed that critically important difference in Chapter 8—make sure you understand the difference!

Women do not want to be ordered around by an iron fisted jerk of a dictator like some vile warlord leading his country into certain destruction. Women want certainty, and the only way that you can offer certainty to a woman is to actually be certain *and true* in all of your thinking and actions. Being certain is not the pretend thing that the arrogant typically do. Being certain is *knowing* because you follow *only* what is true. When you have achieved this, then you will be confident and will proceed to guide your family to a good way. There is no guarantee that this will satisfy your wife, but it is certain that without this type of stability you will never truly obtain the adoration that you desire from your wife.

We live in a world that has placed its focus on money. This is nothing new and it has been going on for thousands of years. Women, and men, have been trained to believe that money equals security. Yet, about every five to fifteen years there is a major economic adjustment that crushes the finances of many people. And this sometimes sends marriages in a dangerous spiraling plummet, often ending in divorce.

If money brought security and happiness, then divorce would not happen when people have money. Rich people also have problems with relationships and get divorced just like other people do. Money can certainly make life more comfortable, but it is not what makes a great marriage. Only being certain and true is lasting. How can you be certain and true? This we will address in a later chapter.

While much of this book goes beyond the physical, our physical acceptance of one another *does* still matter. Men: your wives often want to feel secure and comforted in your certainty and truth, and also by being close by cuddling, holding hands, walking side by side, and talking. When a husband fails to accommodate the basic female desires of his wife, he violates her reasonable expectations of the relationship. And this will likely have negative long-term ramifications on your relationship. And of course, let's not forget about staying in good physical shape for her because she deserves to have a healthy mate just the same as you do. Seduction has little to do with sexuality and is far more about your truth. The sexuality part is an indicator of that truth.

Self-Image

When someone has a poor self-image, it is seldom attractive to men or to women. But a good self-image is always attractive to both men and women. The problem that we humans run into with self-image is that we often misunderstand what a truly good self-image actually is.

Far too many women fall for arrogant, foolish men who continuously disappoint them. Because these men's arrogance makes them appear to be more than they actually are, they appear to have a good self-image, and it makes them false, or maybe it is better stated as—liars. Being false is not at all attractive to women once the women become aware and see through the falseness. But often, women fall into the snare of such men, and then end up feeling badly about themselves because men who lie in this way, generally, will treat their mates very poorly, and often, they treat the children poorly too.

It seems to be more so with women, but men also have very distorted self-images. But with women in particular, somehow, from somewhere, women often adopt an—I don't look good enough—self-image that is very damaging to their marriages. Then there is another group who does the exact opposite and will be quite un-fit and yet flaunt themselves as if they are supermodels. The problem with the second case is not that they show themselves off, rather, it is that they act as if they are better than others who are in far better physical condition. But even when people are somewhat arrogant about their own bodies, at least, then, they are not afraid to show themselves to their mates. The real problem comes in when no matter how often you tell someone that they look great and that they are beautiful, or handsome, they, for some reason, cannot accept that they are worthy.

A woman's poor self-image has a similar effect on men and it is not attractive. A poor self-image translates to, and appears as, humility as perceived by some of us. A poor self-image is the opposite of arrogance: Arrogance is acting as if you are more than what you actually are. Where feeling lowly about yourself is making yourself out to be less than you actually are. If anyone questions whether or not many women have poor self-images, just watch them struggle to lose weight and consider how much of the weigh-loss industry is fueled by making women feel badly about themselves. Though, if we feel bad about being overweight we must not blame our feelings on the weight-loss industry. Instead, we must realize that we feel badly because we know that we're overweight and we don't like that about ourselves.

The pharmaceutical industry has been taking advantage of our self-image and has come up with medications that are supposed to solve our problems. Sexual dysfunction is one such area that they have been profiting on. Outside of complications from serious injury to the involved parts of the body, sexual dysfunction is mostly a mind issue. Not that we are mentally incapable, but rather we have been mentally conditioned and trained through many experiences to turn ourselves off. These parasitic companies prey on our poor self-images, and then they feed that by getting us to believe that our body has failed us. When in truth it is society and our gullibility in believing things that are not true that has failed us and caused our troubles.

Don't get drawn into these lies, you are capable of sexuality greater than you can imagine! Believing that you have a physical dysfunction is not going to make your life any better. If this so-called "sexual dysfunction" is something that you're dealing with, then it's time for you to force yourself to think about sex and *deliberately* allow yourself to entertain *good* thoughts of sexuality with your spouse. Doing so will help you to feel better about yourself and allow you to see yourself as whole when the gift of your passion and "sex drive" towards your spouse return to you.

Self-image is driven by the world around us, and we allow it to alter our mental and physical state of being. It's our own responsibility to overcome this with proper thinking and actions. The way you see yourself shows up in all of your actions and can be a very dangerous thing for you when you do not see yourself properly as you were designed. Pretending to be more than, or less than, what you actually are does not do anyone any good.

These two views—*arrogance* and *lowliness*—are not exclusive to either gender, but dominantly lie with women having a lowly self-image and men having an arrogant self-image. Both of these are cheap imitations of what is truly being sought by any one of us or our spouses.

Women want men to be in control (not controlling) and, in that, women feel safe. Men want women to look to them, and desire them. Not because the woman is lowly, but rather because she admires him and sees him as a valued and worthy partner. Then, together, the married couple should walk in confidence that they are of one mind.

Both men and women are attracted to a humble mate who is in control of their own life. A true and confident sense of direction is very attractive to all people. But still, envious and covetous people will try to crush that. True beauty is true confidence and certainty—these are things that cannot be obtained when you are wrong, deceitful, or when you are outright lying.

There are real problems with self-image when it comes to our physical condition. This is especially true for women. And sometimes the more physically attractive a woman is then the lower her self-image is. This isn't good, and there's no reason that a woman should feel badly about herself if she is well kept due to taking good care of her body, unless she fails to take care of her own heart, mind, and soul.

Perceptions
Fat-Thin People and Marriage

Often women will be very self-conscious about "cellulite" even when they are very fit and at a healthy weight. This self-consciousness often causes them to hide themselves because many women associate cellulite with being overweight. But there are limits with regard to "cellulite" and its removal. It is especially important for women to understand that most pictures that we see of "perfect bodies" have been smoothed using photo editing programs. And while, societally, we believe that we would like to appear as the pictures appear, the reality is that those pictures are often not realistic.

This is not implying that pictures seen in magazines are not mostly accurate; there are many women whose form and fitness is very good. But even many of those women will have had someone photo-edit out the imperfections for the magazine cover. We must think of it like a pimple; if you had your face on the cover of a magazine and had a pimple on your nose would you want it edited out or should it be left to be? Similarly, if you were wearing a skimpy swimsuit in a photo for a magazine cover would you want *every* imperfection scrutinized by what is sometimes a very harsh world of armchair critics? Thus we must realize that even minor imperfections will be edited out when pictures of people are used for commercial purposes, and so what we see is typically not actually achievable regarding *zero* "cellulite" for nearly everyone who has ever lived. Ask any photographer and they will tell you that it is all about lighting angles, and what lighting cannot hide photo editing will. Do not be too self-conscious because it is unfair to your spouse and to yourself.

Does your physical appearance matter in true beauty? Yes and no. You look the way you look: hair color, height, eye color, skin color, and general build. Your spouse picked you for who you were when you met, just as you picked your spouse. But keeping yourself well-maintained for your mate *does* have an effect when it is an honest reflection of what you are inside. Be careful everyone, because this door swings both ways. Our self-image is important to each of us, and when it is a poor self-image we will typically withdraw from our spouse.

It is said that being plump was thought to be attractive during the renaissance period, and that being plump was a sign of wealth. If that's true, then we have to admit to ourselves that it was not the fact that they were plump that was attractive, but rather, it was their money that was being sought. Seeing this any other way is choosing to be ignorant of what was likely true.

If we choose to lie to ourselves about issues of weight, then we will be stuck in our own deceit and will continue to be unfit. If the women of the Renaissance had chosen to control their eating, then it is likely that thin would have been in. And the women would have likely been even more sought after if they had money *and* were well-fit. But let us not confuse this with starvation.

People who are truly starving are often very thin and fragile in appearance, and you can very much see the form of their skeleton. At various times over the centuries, there were these two polar opposites—*plump* versus *skeletal* (often referred to as anorexic in more modern times). Perceptions are perceptions, but let's not deceive ourselves, we all understand what *overweight* is and what *dangerously thin* is. As is typical, neither is particularly sought after and the in-between is where people are meant to be with regard to what is obviously healthy and good for the body. If a man was going to choose between the two options of *overweight and rich*, or *underweight and poor*, then there would likely be an obvious gravitation towards the money of the plump. But is this really love? Let us also take note that the wealthy people of the Renaissance were the only ones who could afford to have their portraits painted, thus, leaving the majority of the people with healthy, properly kept bodies out of the historic eye. The art of that era skews our perspective of what the reality of that era was and what the bulk of the people actually desired and looked like.

Since weight and self-image issues are such influential factors in marriages with regard to offering ourselves to each other, we must briefly address this issue. This most notably occurs with women, where the wife will withdraw from her husband because she feels that she is unattractive due to her weight gain. But, what is even worse is when a woman is not "overweight" but is overly self-conscious of some attribute of her body, such as the much-overblown "cellulite" that so many women unjustifiably fear. Again, it is important to point out that when a woman withholds herself from her husband for this reason, she is hurting him a great deal, and, over time, doing so does much damage to the relationship. Cellulite is an overblown topic, but we will briefly address it here, so that you understand it in order to minimize it as best as possible if you so choose.

As discussed in the cornerstone book *Dream Thin*, if you're overweight, it is likely that your weight reflects something about you on a deeper level. Fixing the inside usually makes the outside part automatic. Grabbing a hold of your life and dealing with the problem is the only thing that will make you feel better about yourself. This includes the weight loss issue, and it applies to men as well as to women.

There are so many people who want to lose weight, but cannot seem to change their habits. This has been affecting marriages for a long time, and has gotten much worse since the end of the twentieth century. Why are we discussing weight and physical appearance in a book about marriage? Because many, many marriages suffer from the easily solved poor self-image problem that often plagues one or both spouses.

Stereotypically, it's the wife who dons the flannel armor and snuffs the lights at bedtime or during romantic interludes. However, many men act similarly as well. This sort of hiding one's self does not do any good for the relationship. So how do we overcome this? We do it with understanding, wisdom, and knowledge regarding this topic. We want to *not* feel this way so we continue to hide our self-appointed shame. You may be good in most other aspects of life, but then feel ashamed because you believe you're somewhat overweight. While our weight problems typically reflect our inner problems, it may be that you have already dealt with your inner problems, but have been unable to get back into shape.

We are afraid to admit when we are fat. And we scream and shout to avoid discussing anything about us being overweight. We will attack others and berate them and tell them that, "Big is beautiful". This is fine, if *you* are truly good with being overweight yourself. But, if you are really not being totally honest, then you are lying to yourself and to those around you. And doing so will affect them and you in the long run.

It is the lying to yourself part that destroys you and serves to add even more to your weight, and troubles to your marriage. Consider this: We will accept a compliment of observation when we are told that we look good, but then viciously reject it when we are told that we have gained too much weight. We do this because we're ashamed of ourselves and are attempting to hide our obvious unhealthy error of weight gain. If being overweight was good then we would take it as a compliment.

Here are a few facts to invite into your understanding: Being overweight is not genetic. Believing that it is genetic only keeps you overweight. With our all-too-common sedentary lifestyles that most of us live, the "recommended" daily calorie consumption is far too much for most men, and especially for most women, who are generally smaller and shorter than most men. Most people are too sedentary and/or too small to consume what is thought of as the "recommended daily calories". We need to change what and how we eat. Most overweight people eat far more than two thousand calories per day. Often the food that we eat is food that is meant to be a "treat" rather than our main course. People take their dog for a walk, but not themselves. Why do you walk your dog? People need this too—we need *some* exercise. If you want to learn more about weight loss, look for the book *Dream Thin—The Weightloss Repair Manual - Lose Weight While Sleeping*. But what about when you don't need to lose weight, yet you still have cellulite that you are overly self-conscious about?

Many women have a dislike of cellulite on their bodies which usually shows up below the waist, and they feel extremely self-conscious about it even though they shouldn't. Even women who appear thin sometimes have this. Why is this? Mostly, it is because of lack of understanding.

Just because you don't look as if you are overweight does not mean that you are lean and fit. Thin people who have cellulite do not need to lose weight; they need to gain muscle if they want the cellulite to go away as much as is reasonably possible. Nothing else will do the job. And even then, due to our nutrition consumption, sometimes that's just the way we are with our low muscle mass.

Cellulite is nothing more than bunched up fat cells. And in many cases it is a very thin layer of fat. If you already appear thin and still have cellulite, then losing more weight will typically make you look too thin and possibly appear undesirable to people. The way to correct this is to exercise and increase your protein building sources and general food quality in order to help you build more muscle. People who are "fat-thin" do not need to lose weight, they need to gain muscle if they need to do anything at all, and then the rest will take care of itself.

Understand yourself and your body and be honest with and about yourself, and then most of your problems in life will vanish. Too many people do not understand the fat versus weight issue. We are more concerned about *weight* than our fat level and thus we deprive ourselves of great nutrition. Muscle is firm and specific, whereas fat has no ability to be specifically directed and sculpted, thus muscle makes you heavier on the scale but makes you look thinner; where fat has a tendency to look somewhat saggy giving us an appearance of being overweight even when we are not. This means that two people of a similar frame size can be the exact same weight and one will look very fit and the other will look plump or saggy. Or the same person can look as if they are overweight but then workout for a year without losing any weight and at the end of the workout year they might look far thinner.

But even when you do all of this you still might have some cellulite. Learn to accept it because it's a part of life, and even the most beautiful people in this world have it to some extent. It's just that most people do not obsess over it, and it is deceptively painted away in most printed advertisements or they are very careful about what light they are seen in.

Accepting these few basic truths about your weight and appearance will eliminate all of the needless nonsense that torments the self-images of so many people and aids in plaguing and destroying so many marriages. Accepting the honesty of this information will reduce the tension that this issue causes in your home, marriage, and life.

Because of this hidden "fat-thin" problem, which is typically not allowed to be discussed, many women foolishly withhold themselves from their husbands because they have an unjustified poor self-image, which is due to their incorrect perception of their own weight and/or muscle tone. But it is mostly due to the photo-touched world of media. And as mentioned earlier, no matter how often you tell people that they look great, many still cannot overcome their poor self-image. What's worse is that we refuse to allow discussion about it because we feel ashamed about being overweight and out of shape even if we look really good. It's all about how *we* perceive the way *we* look. These self-imposed lies must end. We must unconditionally invite and welcome assistance from our spouses if the problem is ever going to be corrected. This holds true with women as well as with men. A person who is hiding their self-imposed shame is far less likely to be able to effectively deal with the problem on their own that they believe is the cause of their own shame.

Allowing yourself to be seen by your mate and discussing the reason for the shameful self-feelings can be of immense value and relief to a relationship. Stepping beyond these needless inhibitions allows more satisfaction to both of you. And it will lend to the conquering of issues and to the effort needed regarding physical appearance. Remove these excuses of a bad relationship by taking good care of your mind, your heart, your thoughts, your body, and yourself.

It is our—not understanding—these few aspects of our health that causes too many of us to always regain any lost weight thus further stressing our relationships. Take care of yourself, for yourself, and for your spouse. It's more desirable and healthier for both of you. Neither of you need health to be the cause of a troubled spot in your marriage. I have never heard anyone speak about anything bad regarding their properly done exercise and weight loss. Married couples are usually happier with each other and save money on food, doctor visits, medicine, and much more when they get enough exercise and eat properly. Doing so is a win-win situation!

It's not fair to your spouse if you gain weight after marriage and then expect them to accept your appearance and be happy about it. Yet, most men typically want to see their wives' bodies regardless and vice versa. Letting yourself get out of shape cheats your spouse and violates their long-term expectations. If you were overweight when you first met, your spouse would still probably like you to be physically fit. It is a selfish and lazy attitude for anyone who is overweight, man or woman, to expect their spouse to be happy about their appearance if they are gaining weight. The sooner we dismiss such selfish and lazy thinking, then the sooner we can be in control of our own lives, health, and weight.

True beauty is not found in weight loss; but our visible outer condition and our outward mental attitude is typically a clear reflection of our inner condition. We see true beauty in people, but we do not quite recognize it as true beauty. This is because many people who have true beauty throughout are also in good physical shape, and so we equate the wrong thing to the true beauty. It's not what is outside that is beautiful, rather it is when our inner attitude is true and beautifully attractive that it is commonly reflected physically on our outside as a natural effect of our thinking. It is that inner beauty that is true and it is what we all desire of our spouses.

Chapter 16

White Room Rediscovery

When we allow pointless worries to distract us, then we become unable to focus on what is truly important in our relationship. We also lose our ability to see what the cause of our trouble is. Let's start from the beginning and strip away all of the unnecessary and meaningless troubles that we allow to distract us in our marriages, while, at the same time, realizing that the beginning of your relationship actually started long before you ever met your spouse.

Imagine yourself alone in an empty enormous all white room: You just became aware that you exist! You don't know anything other than that you are thinking. You can't see yourself because there are no mirrors, and you're the same color as the room. You are, for all practical purposes, invisible in this perfectly and completely lighted room where the room is so big that you can never find the walls. What would you be thinking? Likely, not what you are thinking right now.

All you would be able to do is wonder because you would have no other experiences and you are only now just awakening.

Now, imagine walking and walking. You would not be able to detect if you are walking straight, or north, south, east, or west. In fact, you would not even know that those directions exist because you have only just become aware.

Out of wonder, you continue to walk, and as you are walking you see two dots in the distance. Because you wonder about these two dots, you move towards them. When you are close enough, you can tell that there is another presence near you. You reach out and attempt to touch, and begin to compare yourself to the other presence.

You notice only minor differences. And as you touch the other one you begin to feel and sense shape and form. You then touch yourself to compare as you feel the size and shape differences of various parts of you both. This other presence does the same thing to you, the two of you notice these differences together; yet, you also notice that you are somehow the same.

Because you have little ability to see one another, you both have a natural curiosity about each other. And through and because of that curiosity, you both stay near to each other. Since only your eyes are visible to each other, because everything else is pure white, everything else you see or feel is compared to the eyes that you see. Other than yourselves and the floor, there is nothing to feel. Yours and the other one's physical form and eyes are what you will compare everything to.

Because you are not familiar with being with another, you bump into the other and make a noise, both of you hear this sound and now you compare other sounds to that sound. You are learning together. You wander for a great deal of time, trying to find something more, but the only thing you have been able to detect is each other and the brightness of the room.

After exhaustively wandering and finding that you are the only two existing in the brightness, you turn your attention back towards each other.

Assuming that this imaginary body has the same sensations that your actual bodies do when you touch each other, you experience the feelings caused by the rush of chemicals created by and released throughout your bodies. This excitement leads you to further exploration. What is happening?

You do not understand the concepts of concern or worry, so you continue touching and exploring, uninhibited and without distraction. The bright light is what gives you your energy, so you have no need for food or eating. You look into each other's eyes with intrigue and wonder, each wanting the other one to reach and touch, so that you can experience the sensations from the chemical rush once again.

Because you have nothing else to look at, you both become accustomed to the look in each other's eyes. While you have already done a great deal of exploration, you have truly only just begun. You hesitate, and the other one reaches out and takes your hand and places your hand on themself, and this gives them a great deal of pleasure. In your intrigue, you accept this invitation to touch them where your hand was placed by them. When you do this the other one expresses satisfaction with their eyes. You like this and desire to repeat offering this same pleasure to them.

You also want to experience this type of pleasure for yourself, so you reach out and grasp the other one's hand and place it where it causes you to have similar feelings. The other one offers their hand to you and does as you invited them to do. The other one sees the delight in your eyes, and also wants to repeat offering this in order to please you.

With your feelings of pleasure, you both make sounds at the times when the rush of chemicals flow through each of your bodies. These various sounds become associated with the pleasure you now feel. And because you both now understand the sounds as pleasurable, you associate the sounds with what you feel when you yourself make the sounds.

After periodically doing this, you both become aware of the look in the eyes of the other and know when the other wants to offer you that pleasure. This look alone is enough to cause a small chemical release that makes you feel good. When you look at the other presence, their look has changed and is now inviting you to offer them pleasure.

You can imagine yourself and your spouse in this situation, alone, just becoming aware, only you two. There are no clothes or things, only two bodies in a saturating, warm, and bright white light. You have nothing else but each other and the light that gives you your energy allowing you to see.

You can see in this example that you have created a language of the eyes. You likely imagined those looks while reading about it. You were also beginning to develop another language of vocal satisfaction. Since no corruption has come into your all white room, you have no particular reason to know any other type of communication. All of it is of a good manner, and is pleasing to both beings.

You both instinctively understand that you are sustained because of the brightness of the light, and you are pleased to be there with one another. You continue to please each other and communicate your desire for one another with your eyes and sounds. You have no hesitation and are satisfied just being together as you are.

Sometime later, while walking in the expanse of this room, you *don't* see something far off. It is very clear to you, and it appears as an absence of the warm saturating light. It is as if a part of your room is gone.

You go near to the curious black spot and can feel a peculiar consuming warmth when you are near to it, but because of the brightness of the room it only appears as black to you. As you wonder about this difference that you both see, you notice that this dark heat seems to be consuming the whiteness of your room.

The expanding black spot makes you both begin to wonder about everything that you have become accustomed to through your exploration of the room and each other. Because you have never seen such darkness as this before, you move nearer to it in order to wonder at it even more. When you do, the consuming heat of it burns you both, and you both quickly pull away.

For the first time, you have experienced a displeasing sensation. You see the pain in each other's eyes and discover a new range of feeling that, up until now, you did not understand.

While musing at this harmful darkness, you look invitingly at the other, and reach to grasp and draw their hand near to you in order to place it on yourself. But this time the other pulls back their hand because of their intrigue with the consuming darkness. The feeling that you experience from the other being pulling away is similar to what you felt when you were too near to the consuming darkness and felt the pain of its consuming heat.

For the first time, one of you has experienced rejection. When the other one has finished musing at the darkness, they approach you with a look of offering. But you still feel the burn of the pain of their rejection from them favoring the darkness over you just a short time ago. When they reached out to grasp your hand to place it on them, you pull back because of the pain you still feel from their rejection. So now, they too, have experienced this pain of rejection.

Now you both have just learned how to hurt one another. You now know that you can create pleasure for the other, or you can cause pain for the other.

As you think about the white room, allow this to continue in your imagination and see where *you* end up with it. It can give you an indication of the way you currently feel or would like to truly feel or behave with regard to your spouse.

Marriages are not a whole lot different than this. When we begin courting, we are largely in a state of innocence and have not experienced pain within the relationship. But, not long after, when we become more comfortable with each other, we begin to hurt each other in subtle ways that are often entirely missed or overlooked by one another.

In regard to the one we "love," few people escape being guilty of deliberately withdrawing from their mate for the purpose of deliberately inflicting pain on them—often called "the silent treatment" or "the cold shoulder". We seldom admit that we do this, but it becomes very apparent when you're looking for it in observing any relationship. In some cases, it is rare and minute, but in other relationships it dominates the interaction between spouses. With some couples, it's only one spouse doing it, and in other couples both spouses behave in this way. If any of this is too familiar to you in your own relationship, now is the time to make the changes to stop it.

Anything that you can do in order to strip away the distractions in your mind in an effort to help you more clearly see the root-cause of the problems in your life will be of tremendous benefit to you. Going through this white-room mental exercise is bound to bring up some unanticipated emotions that have long ago been hidden by the distractions of life. Bear through it, and immerse yourself in this mental exercise and see what you discover.

Let the exercise go where it will in your mind, and you will likely find that your feelings about your spouse—or your perception of your spouse—will be stripped bare, revealing what is truly bothering you.

Once you find out what it is that's bothering you, then you will need to evaluate your own actions towards your spouse. Often we are the cause of our spouse's bad behavior. Bad behavior is usually caused by frustration. And frustration is usually caused by not being able to communicate our true desires to a person, either because they won't listen, or because we fail to properly articulate our message to them. Our frustration comes from them not understanding us regardless of whether we are right or wrong, and regardless of us delivering the message poorly or them misunderstanding the message.

All frustration that we feel is due to our expectations being violated. It does not matter if the frustration involves another person, or if it is situational while dealing with an object. In the end, it comes down to the fact that we have a desire, and an expectation in our mind of the way something will occur. Whether right or wrong, when it does not proceed as anticipated, or cannot be brought into submission, then we become frustrated and angry because it is not occurring as we had hoped or intended.

When this happens while dealing with an object that won't comply with our goal it is of little consequence to us. But, when it is a person's desire to be loved, then it feels as if the entire world is falling apart around us—realize this when trying to understand yourself. And just as importantly, realize it when trying to understand your spouse. Strip away all of the petty nonsense in life, and see each other at the most base level, and then reveal your true self to your spouse.

Chapter 17

Removing Stress in a Marriage

The burn of the consuming darkness that exists in marriages is often felt or known as stress. Stress is one of the worst destroyers of marriage, or any other relationship for that matter. The word "stress" is a short version of the word distress, which means to take something as a means to satisfy a claim or obligation.

In understanding "stress", relate yourself to which side of the distress transaction you are on. Are you the one who has had something taken from you, or are you the one doing the taking? If you are experiencing stress, then you are having something taken from you. When others take from you, it is causes much tension in your marriage and life.

The taker can be your spouse or it can be the bank, a creditor, some other lender, utilities, or anyone or anything that demands your attention. Sometimes, it can be your own self that takes from you. Backing up a bit, we discussed expectation and hope, and how when expectation and hope are violated, that it causes a feeling of hurt. This "hurt" is a form of stress. An occasional small bit of stress does not present much trouble for us because we overlook it and quickly move on. It's when these violations continually repeat that the stress builds up in us.

We're not speaking of the stress being caused by violations of a spouse in this section. While that exists and is certainly a factor in troubled relationships, a spouse's violations are often fueled by *outside* stress, and the outside stress is sometimes ignited or reignited by inside stress. This is a terrible cycle for anyone, or any couple, to be trapped in.

When we have internal marriage conflicts causing stress in our relationship, then we tend to have an incorrect gravitation to compensate by doing things that have no true value to us. We have a tendency to feel that if we had a better car, a better home, or could get away on a vacation that it would make our situation better. But when we go into debt to obtain these empty desires, it causes extra unwanted financial stress. Then, when it is all said and done, we are no more satisfied than we were before our purchase and subsequent financial commitment. For a short time, we feel good about it, but then we have to spend the next several years or decades slaving away to pay for something that does not give us any true joy. Later, when money falls short, we begin to stress about the money and often place the children in daycare and choose to take a second job just so that we can pay our debt. This only serves to increase the stress that started the nasty cycle to begin with.

Remove Stress

If your marriage is filled with this sort of stress, then getting control of the outside distress that attacks your marriage is vital.

Many marriages are attacked for reasons too numerous to list. Often these stress inducing attacks are from others who are forcing their opinions on the troubled couple. However, the input from others is not necessarily going to be about the couple's problems. It's often criticism in general that causes the stress on a couple. In fact, the couple may not even know their attackers personally. If a couple is doing something that they enjoy and then they see or hear something that unfairly condemns what they do, it typically puts stress on the couple to some extent. For instance, if the couple wants to dress a certain way together, or more importantly, do certain things in their bedroom together, and they are indirectly mocked and/or shamed for it, then they often feel that they should not do it. These seemingly insignificant situations occur constantly in our lives, but we don't realize or acknowledge that this is going on. And it may be happening to only one spouse. Besides the fact that we typically do not specifically recognize that this happens, we also have a very difficult time conveying this sort of frustration to our spouse *if* we actually realize that it occurred at all. When we do succeed in stating our feelings, then sometimes even our spouse will add to our frustration by supporting the unwelcome opinions of the original source of violation.

Stress is not always going to come from the outside from other people. But it often is, because you might owe them something, such as owing the bank for a home loan, or owing for credit card debt. It could also be that you work for a stressful company. Removing this stress is often easier said than done.

Consolidate your debt and get your payments arranged to an affordable level and make those payments as reliably as is possible. Be firm and resolute in getting rid of the parasite of debt-stress from your family and marriage. Debt is also a consuming black hole that never benefits as it promises, and it will burn you when you get too near it or when its fire gets too big and out of control.

Overcoming debt is also easier said than done. Often, people get everything in alignment and are paying down their debt only to lose their job before paying off all of their debt. It is a troublesome test of your fortitude to be able to stand against stress in your marriage, and it is a test of the two of you together to be able to stand together as one in doing so.

If you are, or have been, in a situation that gets worse every time you make an adjustment to accommodate the stresses, then you know how difficult this can be. The two groups that most prominently experience this are small business owners and people who lose their jobs. There is little joy to be had when you are unable to meet the financial obligations that you signed on for. There may come times in your life when there is nothing that you can do but to hang on tight and wait it out. While hanging in there, you must cut your expenses to the bare minimum, but even that cannot always solve the problem. You cannot save more than is being spent. At some point you need to earn money to live, and it is these testing times that create an enormous amount of stress for many married couples. Much stress can be released and removed from our lives when we understand how to pray properly as discussed in the cornerstone book *Understanding Prayer*.

Whether you have zero income, or you are just falling short a little bit every month, it still hurts and can cause tremendous stress in your life and relationship. Remove the stresses by paying away debt as soon as is possible, and remove stressful people from your life as well.

When all is done, the most important place to remove stress is between you and your spouse. Welcoming each other and allowing each other to share each other's ups and downs and lending an ear with kind and helpful thoughts is a good way to start. Do not allow internal stress in your relationship. Keep it far from you.

Do not violate each other's expectations and hopes. Comfort one another. Confide in one another. Trust one another enough to allow suggestions, help, and true and open communications without attack and judgment. Allow each other to share each of your hopes and dreams, both the grand ones and the intimate ones. Many couples end up needing counseling because one, or both, of them are too selfish and cannot get over themselves enough to fully open up to their spouse to *rationally* discuss their concerns, hurts, problems, wants, needs, desires, and life in general. Couples should never need a counselor, but all too often they do because of their stubborn nature of withholding themselves from each other, which only serves to increase internal stress. This is a *trust* issue, and if you fail to properly place that part of your trust in your spouse, then no amount of counseling in the world will be able to help you or your marriage. If your spouse has proven trustworthy, then you have no reason to withhold your trust from them.

As a couple, keep away from internal stress and trust each other and be as one! You will find that when you become as one with your spouse, all of the external stresses become meaningless and fade away even though the problems may still exist. Never panic about external stress. Panic will only draw that external stress internally into your marriage and continue to erode your joy. It is not the world that controls this, you control this stress within yourself, and only you can make the choice to overcome.

Relaxation is Important, But...

The excessive busy-ness of the last third of the twentieth century has brought about a desire to relieve the unwanted stress caused by the busy-ness of life. Many people of the time sought relief from stress by means of meditation with various relaxation techniques in order to release themselves from the distractions of life. Some of this involved vocalizing a distractive hum in order to bring the mind to a clearer state, thus thinking only of the hum. And also by doing stretching exercises and holding position, then repositioning and holding position again. For a few people, these and other methods of releasing stress appear to have proved successful, but most other people find that they need to do this every time they are stressed.

There is an inherent problem when you need to continue to do these exercises in order to relax. This does not mean that someone should not do such exercises more than once. If it's really a joy for you to do it, then enjoy yourself during the activity. But if this is the *only* way for you to relax and if you need to do these exercises whenever you are stressed in order to release the stress, then there are deeper problems in your life that you are not dealing with, and your relaxation techniques are only a superficial bandage for the real problems.

As discussed in the cornerstone book *Understanding Prayer-Why Our Prayers Don't Work*, feelings of stress are actually somewhat of a gift. "How is that?" you may be asking. When you feel stressed, it is a sign that something in your life is not quite right. When you learn to recognize stress as the sign that it is meant to be, then the sign becomes a gift to you. Think of stress like the warning lights on your car's instrument panel. When the oil light goes on, you had better check your oil or you are likely to experience serious problems with your car's engine. Stress is the same, when your stress warning comes on, you had better check your life or you will likely be headed for serious trouble in the long run. *Repeatedly* having to use any meditation stress relief techniques, tells you that something else in your life or thinking needs to be corrected.

No amount of relaxation techniques will solve your underlying problems. Biblically speaking, the people were supposed to place their trust in their Creator, thus relieving themselves of all stress. If a wife trusts in her husband, and together they correct their problems and then place their trust in their Creator, they will build an unshakable foundation that no distress can touch.

It is not the stress that we must release, but rather, we must release what it is that we are stressing about. If the initiating source of your stress is so important to you that you're unwilling to release it, then it is unlikely that the stress will ever really go away from your life.

If a source of stress is tremendous and that source happens to be your spouse, then you might need to adopt the attitude that you can live without them and that they are an option to you. Accepting that you can survive without your spouse frees you from their bondage. This does *not* mean that you walk out on them and leave them. It means that you greet their violations with enthusiasm, unafraid of them, not fearing if you violate their violating ways by *justifiably* confronting their poor behavior.

Stand firm against stress and distress. Don't try to relax it away so that you can ignore it. And don't "release" the stress, rather, release or remove *that which is causing* the stress. If you are in pain and bleeding because you have a thorn in your foot, then placing a bandage over the thorn might stop the visible bleeding, but it will not remove the pain.

If you remove debt and keep it gone, then debt stress will vanish from your life. If you meditate until you are calm and your stress is gone and then you go right back to the same stress-causing financial problems, then you have gained little if anything. Meditation might have a value, in that when you release the stress momentarily, sometimes you're able to think clearly enough to see the root source of the problem, which in doing so may assist you in eradicating the root of the problem. But other than that it is merely a bandage.

Whether it's money or people, the cause of stress must be released and removed from your life. If you do not remove a problem, then it will keep coming back over and over and over... If you're going to meditate, then do it in a state of prayer and ask for guidance and understanding about the *source* of your stress. You are likely to get your answer in the form of a realization of what to do or what not to do in order to solve your problem and remove its root.

Stress Notifications

Stress or stress hormones lead to things such as constriction of blood vessels and a thousand other physical effects. Our bodies are incredible machines that are designed for a specific purpose. The naturalist view falls short in so many ways of realizing the magnificence of this amazing device we call the human body, and it fails to explain most of the body's functional purposes.

With a naturalist view of life, the body's *design* is not allowed because "design" shows preexisting intelligence or intent. Design is believed to defy the idea that progressive changes occurred to get us to our current form that we see today. A naturalist view typically examines either one small part, or a small group of parts as if it is one whole part, but their view never simultaneously tries to understand *all* individual parts and *all* aspects of each of those parts together at the same time, or *how* and *why* they work in complete union and harmony. When we look at it all together with each component and all of the subparts and the sub-sub-parts of those parts, it is more undeniably designed with each more intricate level that we seek. All of which are affected by what you do and *think*.

We can decide that we will follow the naturalist's understanding of the *theoretical* progression of mankind, but then we are forced to discard much of the understanding that we already have about ourselves. (For more insight on the Creation versus evolution topic, the books *The Science of God* and *Bending the Ruler* are full of answers to questions like: are we alone in the cosmos? and other interesting points that have gone mostly unnoticed.) In taking a naturalist approach we blame everything on genetics, and frequently think and/or say, "Mother or Father had this disease, so I will, too." This irrational thinking can only be born out of the naturalist belief system about the progression of life, which is to say "evolution".

The naturalist way says that, "you can't help it, your parents were stressed, and therefore you will have the stress gene also." While this often appears to be the case, it is important to note that if it were progressive genetics, then the problem would be far worse and the stress or other problems would be inescapable in much the same way that being born with arms and legs is mostly inescapable. However, when it comes to stress, this is not the case. Anyone can shut stress off in a moment's notice if they simply deal with the root source of the stress, and in doing so they get some relief in the marriage.

It is somewhat shortsighted to accept any belief that is less than your body having been designed as an incredible machine. Our bodies have abilities that most people won't ever even begin to utilize or realize. We don't need to look deep into the physics of the body in order to see that there is more intent in a single cell than the amount of intent that any person can produce in an entire lifetime.

Why is this all so important to your marriage? You coming to the realization that your body is *designed* with *purpose*, makes correcting any problems in your body *and* life far easier. If a mechanic does not understand how a car works, then their ability to repair it is greatly impaired. If the driver of the car does not understand the purpose of the car, then the likelihood of using it in an improper manner is greatly increased—just go ahead ask any mechanic about improper use of a car and you will quickly find how damaging it is to improperly use something. Our bodies are not any different with regard to their design and care.

Purpose is *purpose*, design is *design*, and intent is *intent*. If something has purpose, then it has been designed. And if something has been designed, then it has intent.

Accepting the fact that your body is an incredible and intricately *designed* mechanism with built-in warning systems will fast-track you towards seeing and understanding the many physical problems we encounter throughout our lives, thus allowing us to avoid those problems.

Stress is one of the most notorious and corrosive signs your body will ever encounter. The destructive forces of stress on your body are incredibly strong and will cause it to deteriorate rapidly— along with your marriage. We need not look far to see the outside physical signs of stress on people.

Besides the obvious distressed look that many of us walk around with most days, and the particular wrinkles and lines that result, there are also other damaging effects that are believed to be caused by stress: things such as hair loss, torso fat, poor skin appearance, etc. Internally, stress is believed to alter heart rate, release dangerous amounts of chemicals, increase acidity level in your digestive system, and cause constriction of blood vessels, just to name a few.

When searching for potential signs of stress on your physical body, understand that these are only the ones that we *know* exist. There are likely many effects from stress that go unknown or are inaccurately diagnosed as being caused from something else.

Pay attention to your body because it is there for a reason! Whenever it's not functioning well and you see odd things happening with your body, then review your thinking and you will likely find stress or your behavior issues at the source. The same goes for your marriage, stress will occur when you are being violated by anyone, and this effect is even worse when it's your own spouse who is violating you. Stress harms your body and your marriage.

Our bodies were Created for joy, not for stress. Stress is a consuming darkness that is intent on devouring you, your marriage, and your family. Stress affects your health, and your health and stress affect your marriage.

Should You Distract Yourself to Joy?

I once heard someone say that you should "Distract yourself to Joy". Trying to achieve joy is good, but distracting yourself is *not* the answer. Distracting yourself in this way is like distractive meditation methods. Doing so will not root out the *real* underlying problems from your life.

We can use relaxation techniques to regain our mental or emotional balance, as mentioned earlier, so that we can think clearly enough in order to find the way to destroy or remove our stress sources. But beyond that, it becomes a crutch that you will end up depending upon. Doing so will only serve to allow more stress, and it will continue to hide the real problems that plague you. We must be able to achieve joy while in a situation that could create stress. Our joy should not be dictated by stress. Where stress resides in you, joy is absent.

Trusting *in* your spouse and trusting together *with* your spouse, is the way to destroy stress and receive and retain your joy in marriage.

Distractions are distractions. If you have to *distract* yourself from stressing, the stress will again be demanding your attention the moment the distraction is absent. By using any distraction technique, you gain next to nothing except for the brief illusion of a reprieve from your stress and problems.

Using distraction techniques to reduce stress is only a feeble attempt to copy the result that occurs from *actually releasing* the root cause of your stress. It is likely that some people do manage to release the source of their stress through such techniques, but if you need to repeat this over and over, then you have failed to release the *source* of the stress. And in doing so you are only hiding the problems that are causing your stress.

Releasing and removing are the only two methods for eliminating stress from your life and marriage. Distracting stress is only a mask that hides the stress until you have regained enough fortitude to face your stress again.

Don't spend your time distracting stress. Instead, rid yourself of the source of the problem, and do it in harmony with your spouse. We do not need to distract ourselves from stress. It is stress that is a distraction from what is good. It's important to release and remove the stress and its source when possible, and then see and embrace the good.

Change the Stressful Situation Whenever Possible

Seeking harmony with your spouse, in itself, reduces stress a great deal, and actually achieving that harmony will crush stress altogether. Attacking the root of stress, together as one, destroys the stress and permanently removes it from your life. Make the decision that you will not allow stress into your married life.

When you see stress rear its ugly head, crush it! People try to do this and often only half succeed, if you can call half "success". All too often, we try running from a situation that is stress inducing. When doing so, we keep away from the stressful people as best we can when we must be anywhere near to them. We even go as far as to take vacations to "get away from it all". These common stress reduction techniques are no better than the distraction techniques mentioned earlier. When used for that purpose, a vacation is either hiding from stress, or it is a distraction from stress. Running or hiding from stress is a poor way of dealing with a problem. Doing so is like having a leak in your roof, but then going into a room where there is no leak so that you don't have to deal with the dripping water.

There are only two ways the leak will stop: The first way is when the rain stops, then the leak will stop pouring the water into your marriage house. Ignoring a problem until it goes away *does not* remove it. The problem with the ignoring method is that the moment the rains of stress pour down on your marriage again, then the roof will *again* begin to allow the stress to leak in to your marriage. The other way to stop the leak is to remove the hole by actually fixing it. Once the leak is fixed, then the rains of stress can no longer seep into your life and damage it.

Since there are no places in this world that potentially stressful troubles will not at some point rain down upon us, we must patch the leaking roof as soon as possible! Don't hide from stress, and don't ignore it. Rather, crush stress with trust and understanding. Push stress out of your life and patch the holes through which stress seeps into your marriage. You do this by trusting in each other, and then, together, trust the Creator's promises and do as instructed by removing the cause. Stress dissolves quickly when people discover this simple little secret.

Inappropriate People Behave Inappropriately

There are times when even the most confident, sure, and trusting couples will still not be able to entirely overcome stress, or rather, the cause or root of that stress. In this type of situation, the root cause of the stress is usually a persistent scourge to you and your marriage. And it is not a *what*, but rather it's often a *who*.

Most people have at least one of these people in their lives, and often it is a family member. These are the type of people who are somewhat parasitic and will consume your joy. They want to be able to say what they want, to who they want, when they want, and to do it all without any consequence to themselves. They care nothing of your beliefs, feelings, spouse, children, family unit, or truth, and they are typically inaccurate in much of what they say.

They will do or say anything that suits them, regardless of the negative effects on you, your family, or anyone else. These people are inappropriate. They may not even drink, smoke, swear, or use drugs or have any other particular vice, but they are nonetheless dangerous to your family and will induce a great amount of stress on your family.

They demand more from you than they would ever imagine offering to you or to anyone else. And while they are demanding of you, they will make you feel as if you are not doing enough for them. These people will consume you until you are utterly destroyed if you allow them to do so.

When you're faced with this sort of consuming parasite, remove them from your life, do not invite them in. Depart from them. Stand strong in your marriage, and do not allow this type of destroyer into your life. It is likely that you have already given them far more than is required of you as a human being, and that is more than sufficient.

If someone is making requests of you that are not appropriate, (you know... the kind of request that makes you scratch your head and say, "What the...?"), then consider that person to be inappropriate for you and for your family, and depart from them.

You need only deliver the message of your new limits to them once, and then it is fair for you to move on in your life without them. If you exhibit this type of behavior yourself, then you need to eliminate it promptly because it is affecting your relationships and your life whether you realize it or not. And it is an offense to you and to others.

We become so accustomed to our own behavior and our way of life that we are unable to see that our life could be more robust than it is. When we behave in this way, by stressing or causing stress, we cheat ourselves and those around us out of a great deal of joy. We become *takers*, consuming the happiness of others and, ultimately, of ourselves. While we are taking, we feel fulfilled because an immediate lust is being satisfied within us. But soon after, we are again empty and lonely, causing us to repeat the behavior in order to feel satisfied again.

Do Not "Tolerate" Bad Behavior

People ask: What if it's my spouse who is the parasite that consumes my joy. Should I depart from them? Well, that's going to depend upon you and your level of commitment.

If you recall, earlier, we discussed *tolerance* versus *intolerance*. That section was about the proper reversal of what is typically perceived by us regarding tolerance versus *in*tolerance. We also discussed the need for your *in*tolerance of their poor behavior.

When a person behaves poorly towards us, then we must stand up and oppose the behavior and *not* accept it. In passing someone on the street it is not required to do so, but in a good marriage it *is* required. If you cannot mention an error that your spouse is making, then there's a problem within your marriage. You need to understand that *now* is the time to stop tolerating poor behavior.

Does this mean that you should always correct your spouse? Not necessarily. If their mistake is harming you, then confront them about making the correction. If they are harming or violating you, then stand up to that violation.

But if they are doing something like putting a puzzle together, and they are attempting to put a piece in the wrong place, then what has that to do with you? Allow people to make some errors.

You can make the offer to assist them, but beyond that, it is in their hands to accept or decline your offer of assistance. As for them coming in and trying to improperly put *your* puzzle together, that's another matter, and in that case, it is within reason to suggest a correction to them about their behavior, just as they should do to you if you insist that they are doing their puzzle wrong. Insignificant things that do not concern us are not for us to interfere with when no one is being harmed.

When someone is violating your reasonable expectations, do not tolerate it! Stand firm in truth! When you stand firm, one of three things will usually occur: One, they will sulk away in humiliation. Two, they will attack you. Or three, they will realize their error and correct it. In all three cases, they have seen the answer because of your willingness to confront them. We are so accustomed to being able to violate others without challenge because we have an incorrect understanding of "unconditional love". We might not even realize how often we are frustrating and brashly intimidating other people. Only standing firm and challenging violations can help others to realize how often they violate people.

Truth cannot be easily hidden when people are willing to stand for truth. Do not tolerate people's poor behavior. Stand for what is right and for what is true. Be intolerant of lies and bad behavior. You need not cause a fight, but you can reject the behavior or simply remove yourself from the situation when it is not your concern. Accepting someone's bad behavior only serves to reinforce it, and causes it to become worse and even more unbearable for you in the future.

Keep all forms of stress out of your marriage and be united with your spouse as one mind, intent on living in a stress-free marriage. There is no reason that either of you need to tolerate the stress induced by outside people. Depart from those parasites that cause such troubles and refuse to stop. Allowing any outside stress into your marriage will eventually cause stress between you and your spouse, which will only further deepen your troubles. But, removing these outside stresses removes the stress that they cause between husband and wife.

Chapter 18

Understanding "Faith"

Standing for what is true is difficult for many of us because we don't actually know what *true* is. This presents a problem: If we can't see what is true, then how do we stand for what is true?

To know what true is, we can look at the word *faith*. *Faith* is another one of those types of words that is widely abused, misused, or misunderstood just like we spoke of earlier. So, what is *faith*?

Many people hear the word "faith" and think of religion, as in, "What faith are you?" But connecting religion to faith in this way is a perversion of the true meaning of the word "faith". *Faith* and *fidelity* have the same root, and that root is *trust*. This brings us to the question: What is "trust"? *Trust* is to be *true*!

Truth is something that is self-explanatory, so when people cannot understand the word truth it's difficult to explain it to them. This seems silly, but this is true! Truth *is what **is***, regardless of our perception of truth.

To have faith is to have trust in something or someone. When your spouse is *faithful*, then they are trustworthy for you. If you have *faith* in your spouse, then you *trust* them, or you put your *trust* in them. And in doing so, each spouse will be true to the other by honoring one another and caring for one another.

Few people never break their marriage vows. "What?" you say, "I have never cheated!" The marriage vows are far more than a set of rules dictating who you can or cannot sleep with. That's only a small and even insignificant part of the vow set. For better or for worse does not mean for the worse toward each other. In our references to marital trust and faith we are not referring to foolishly trusting your spouse to go on dinner dates alone with people of the opposite gender, or other situations where they would be alone with someone of the opposite gender; rather we are referring to your *overall* trust and faith with your spouse.

You are being bound together and committing to enjoy or endure life together, which is exactly what we are discussing in this book—"together". This point seems to get buried in all of the stresses that we encounter in life. When we *look beyond* the physical fidelity of not being physically intimate with anyone but our spouse, then we begin to see what real, true faithfulness is.

If you do not trust your spouse, then you do not have faith in them whether it is intimacy-trust issues with others, trusting them to balance the checkbook, or even trusting them to correct your errors in the way you balance the checkbook.

Anytime we use any tactic to hide our errors from truth, we are being unfaithful. And when we do this to our spouse, we are being unfaithful to our spouse. Physical infidelity is easily seen, but the other means of infidelity are far more damaging and subtle because they undermine many marriages without being realized by either spouse. It is these other reasons that are often the root-cause of any physical infidelity.

When physical infidelity occurs in a marriage, it is seldom the cause of the problem. The real problem is more likely what caused the physical infidelity to begin with. When we are content, then we are content, and we will joyfully go about our business. Few people go out and look for someone else to be with when they are content in a joy-filled marriage.

Physical infidelity, or even the desire for it, is a clear sign that the marriage has other underlying issues that are far more unfaithful or untrusting. Often, the spouse who is being physically unfaithful is reacting to their mate's lack of trust and long-term violations of faith and trust done or held by that spouse. People need, want, and desire trust and to be believed in. It is the way we are designed. And remember we are not talking about what is right or wrong regarding physical unfaithfulness, but rather we are trying to understand what that person might be experiencing.

People often cause this lack of trust in their relationships because of their own actions—untrustworthy people are untrusting. And, typically, those same untrusting people will unfairly treat a trustworthy spouse, as if the spouse is not trustworthy.

Faith and trust are one and the same thing. And trust and true are the same as well. If it is not true, then it has no faith. But many people believe that if you believe it, then you have faith. I suppose by definition, if you put your faith in something, then you are trusting in it—but that does not make it true. We call this blind faith, and blind-faith can be wrong if what you blindly follow happens to *not* be correct.

What is Childlike Faith and How Does it Affect your Marriage?

Blind-faith is often promoted as a good thing. In the Bible it says that we should have faith as a child does. But what does that actually mean? Anyone who has ever spoken with a three-year-old knows that they will believe almost anything that you tell them. Considering this observation about children, many of us understand the statement of "Have faith as a child" to mean: believing whatever someone says. In other words, do as he says and trust him, and then whatever he says we will believe. Most people understand "Have faith as a child" in that manner and will fight to the death based upon the principle of believing that it is good to have blind-faith in this way. However, doing this in a marriage is very bad for the relationship. We also wrongly believe that blindly following the "Good Shepherd" in this way is what was meant in a passage in the Bible.

That means that if we believe via this blind-faith way, then we could be wrong and still have "faith". But some will argue by saying, "If I follow what was said in the Bible, then I'm in good shape by following those words." This is largely true, but what if *you* are understanding those words incorrectly?

What if the position you're taking in your relationship is not good, true, or accurate? What if "having the faith as a child" is intended differently than we choose to understand the statement? What if? Well, that would make us *wrong*, and then our blind faith is incorrect and *not* true. If it is not true, then it cannot be trusted, and then it is not really *true* faith, because then, ultimately, your belief is a lie. We commonly use this flawed blind-faith approach when we passionately dialogue with our spouse about our position in any particular argument. This is both foolish and dangerous, and will never bring about joy or harmony in any relationship.

So what then was meant by "Have faith as a child"? It is the believing part and the lack of doubt that was being referred to. Children trust their parents with all of their heart, so when they ask their parent a question, the child then accepts the parent's answer as fact and true. It's not that they accepted the answer, but rather the *way* in which they accepted the answer that the attention was being drawn to in the phrase, "faith as a child". This goes back to the trust issue in a relationship that was discussed earlier. All too often, a spouse has done absolutely nothing to cause distrust, yet the other spouse will not fully trust them. When a child has faith, then they believe it all with no doubt in their heart. A couple who works together and gets on the same page and fully trusts one another in the absence of doubt, will experience a far more robust relationship than they will if doubt permeates one or both spouses' hearts.

To better illustrate this problem, let's examine the exact opposite: Some people can be shown all of the evidence unto perfection, and can even have demonstrations as proof, but they will still *not* believe something to be true. They reject it and refuse to accept the truth. Where, with childlike faith, they would see all of the perfect evidence and accept it as true with every fiber of their body and being. "Childlike faith" is not *what* we believe; rather, it is the *way* we believe. It is to accept something completely and live by that, not doubting it at all. Come together with your spouse and be as one, so that you can trust each other in complete faith, and, through that, have the joy that you desire in your marriage.

Chapter 19

What is Truth?

We touched on this question in the last chapter while discussing faith. It's difficult to discuss one without discussing the other—that is to say *faith* and *truth*—but the last chapter differs in that it was pointing out the *way* in which we believe, whereas this chapter is about *what* we believe. There is only one gift that will keep a marriage joyfully going, and it is the gift of *truth*. *Truth* is the foundation that everything should be built upon in a marriage and in life. If you fail to do so, you will constantly have to shore up your foundation every time difficulty rains down on your marriage home.

Truth is that rock on which we are supposed to build our home. When you base your life upon lies, like an occupation that you hate, or a house that is only a status symbol, then the sands of that foundation *will* wash away when the rains of difficulty pour down. Then your home will be in need of constant repair. Without truth, you will not be able to endure the rains of trouble whenever there is a downpour of trouble in your life. The stormy rains of troubles will wash away your foundation that is built with the sandy grains of a lie, and then your marriage-house will come crashing down in the stormy weather.

At least one of you must have some truth in order for your marriage to have any possible joy. Without it, imminent destruction will eventually be on the horizon. The good news is that if you do not have truth right at *this* moment... you can have it right now at *this* moment! You can choose to bring this into your marriage anywhere and at any time. You just need to invite truth into your life and accept it, and then commit to truth and pursue it with all of your heart. The choice is yours alone!

Understanding Truth

Some people think that understanding truth need not be discussed with regard to marriage, but in reality it is the single most important thing anyone can do in life. Understanding truth is more difficult than most people typically think, and our own understanding of truth has a profound impact on our marriages. Being inaccurate, dishonest, or wrong is what causes most troubles in any relationship. Most of us seem to miss the mark when thinking about what *truth* actually is, *if* we even think about it at all. Yet, we all have it within us to understand truth.

Culturally, we have been conditioned to believe things that are not true. Sometimes we see the more obvious aspects of this, like political advertisements where truth is often absent. It is when lies are veiled in bits of truth that we get lured in to the traps of their lie. You can see this happen in cults and various religious sects, where a whole doctrine will be built upon one single aspect of their religious text, or is built upon only a few words of the leader. This sort of belief is easily shaken and easily defeatable for those who seek and embrace truth.

The twisting of truth goes far beyond religions and has seeped into the secular culture. If all of "science" used the same method as is used in the naturalist method in its determination of "the origin of man" when testing its hypotheses, little would ever be learned or accomplished in life. And we would find a great deal of information, but we would be unaware of what to do with it and how to analyze the information correctly.

Two plus two equals four is honest, but two plus two equals five is not honest. Accepting truth is a choice, and it is tightly connected to the blind-faith issue. If you thrive on blind faith, then let it be your hope that you have found the right leader to follow. Truth is not blind. Truth knows all. Truth *is*!

We all have been conditioned to accept labels and the cultural meanings that come to be attached to those labels. These labels, or words, are how we communicate. They are our language. When the concepts that we attach to the labels are altered from their original root and true meaning, then we lose the truth of those words, and along with it, our understanding of them. Our ability to see becomes clouded and hazy. Then, when someone comes along and tries to explain something to us using the words in the actual correct manner, it causes us confusion. One of these words is the word "truth" itself.

Some religious sects have decided that they can "create their own truth", but this is contradictory thinking in regard to the idea of truth. We don't create truth and we *cannot* create truth. We are either created of truth, or of *not* truth—it is our own choice as to which we are created of, and that is based upon our willingness to embrace truth. Truth never changes and is the one single concept we have that will not ever let us down. We can trust it. Truth does not ever change—truth *is what is*.

Doubt is Uncertainty

What we are familiar with, is often what we trust in. We rely on familiar items such as environment, people, and beliefs to protect us, but seldom can they dependably deliver us from trouble. We are often disappointed by everything around us, including the people. Having placed our trust in our beliefs, in people, and in things, we have come to understand trust in a way that is contrary to its true meaning. Many of us have come to understand trust to be a sort of uncertainty because of where we have placed our faith.

Uncertainty permeates nearly every one of us, and this uncertainty is doubt. Doubt creates uncertainty, but what causes this? It is largely due to the way we have been raised and is partly due to our culture, both micro and macro culture. Having placed our reliance on something that will not reliably deliver as we expected makes us familiar with the all-too-dependable *let down*. And then we begin to question if the thing or person can actually deliver at all; this is where we begin to doubt.

This nature is so deeply embedded in world culture that we are barely able to, and rarely notice that we practice doubt and uncertainty on a regular basis. Yet, because we are familiar with it, we seem to like it. This is one of the worst infections in a marriage and it's all that most of us know. It seems that we do not know any better—or do we?

Confused Words

Our culture has become so proficient at distorting the meaning of words that many good words have become bad, and many bad words have become good, and some have come to mean entirely other things. Consider some of the following.

That's nice!
He is very gay today.
That's a wicked awesome car!
This sucks!

It has gotten to a point where we can't even carry on a conversation without having it sound like a sexual innuendo because of the way we use words in our society.

If a woman was to make the statement, such as, "I like the longer sausages...," she would likely get smirks before she could utter the remainder of sentence which is "-for parties, because I can make all of the sandwiches with a single stick of sausage." I am not opposed to people likening such items to body parts, but when this gets to the point where words have been altogether high-jacked so that you can't even use them for their *original* purpose then the problem has gotten out of hand. Some words have taken on altogether different meanings. There are many such words in the lexicon. This is especially so with the American-English variations of words.

Because of the cultural diversity of America, many words have continuously been entering the culture and have entered as labels only. Take for example the term "nigger", often referred to as the "n" word. This word has been wrongfully perverted by society. It is derived from the word or name *Niger, nigrum,* or *negro* meaning *black.* The problem has gotten so bad that using this word has become thought of as extremely offensive. In truth, the word is fine and is not a problem. Rather, it is the fact that when it is used, it typically is used by people who are being unfair and mean to another human being. Perverse meanings or connotations of words should not be allowed—it should never happen. Let a word be a word. For a somewhat older example consider the word Bible, what does it actually mean? Do you know? The actual word has little to do with the book's contents. To test your curiosity, know that there is an answer to what the word really means.

Labeling in this way is not always necessarily good or bad, but it causes confusion for us. Listening to people from the Middle East and the Far East speak English, reveals many of the American language inconsistencies that we are so comfortable with that we don't even notice the inconsistencies. Similarly, when Americans try to speak a foreign language, these same issues are brought out in those languages. The impact of these altered meanings can be doubled when the altered words and the foreign word used to translate the altered word both have altered meanings.

When we don't understand the underlying meanings of words, we lose an important part of our ability to effectively communicate to our spouse and others. When the real essence of a word is lost, then its underlying concept and understanding becomes very difficult to convey to another person. This is a serious problem for us when there are no other single words to explain the true underlying concept. This causes us to have to try to explain the concept using many words. When you're trying to communicate with your spouse about a problem, it is of no assistance to have to *re-explain* the meanings of words that you use during your discussion. And what is worse is that if we fail to grasp a base word such as *truth,* then we are unable to convey anything with any amount of certainty

Improperly used words, or substitute words, cause much misunderstanding in our world and marriages. In life and in our relationships, it is not so much the word itself, but rather the lack of understanding of the underlying meaning and concept that presents the problem for us.

"Pride" is a word that is often used incorrectly. When true to its meaning, if you have pride in your work then you are willing to stand for it and are willing to show it off. But the word *pride* is often confused and wrongly used instead of the word *arrogant*. "Arrogance" is to make yourself out to be more than you actually are; where pride does not do this. We addressed arrogance in previous chapters.

Joy is a word that is often substituted for the word *happy*, or vice versa. *Joy* is to receive or welcome; it is to enjoy! *Happy* is to be pleased because something happened by chance, meaning that good fortune came your way. But happiness might not have been from any deliberate action on your part, in essence it is by *chance*. While this happenstance can bring joy to some extent, joy is by-and-large deliberate, where happiness is chanced good fortune. And as mentioned earlier "jealousy" is often misused and is mistaken for *envy* or *covetousness*, or *covetous-jealousy*.

The word *truth* has done well over the centuries in this regard, as is apparent in some of the founding documents of the United States of America. For instance: "we hold these truths to be *self-evident*" sums up a great deal about the word "truth". Yet when people say things like, "That's your truth" and "This is my truth", then the above statement gets discarded. They are in essence saying "I will do whatever I damn well please!" And thus, truth has no place in their lives or heart; eventually this attitude will destroy their marriage.

The Quest to Understand Us

We are designed to seek. Everything about us is there to help us learn. Eyes are not there so that you can see as we think of the word "see". Our eyes and ears are devices that can sense and monitor unfathomable amounts of information. And all of this information is retained in the storage device of our brain.

Things that are sensed with our taste, smell, and by touch are also stored in our brain. This system is so sophisticated that it has its own heating and cooling system and it can self-replicate. We are

Created to seek and to learn. We all have an unquenchable desire for this, which is especially apparent in children, most notably in infants.

If we are designed to learn, then what is it that we are supposed to be seeking? As a married couple you will go through life together and learn, for better or for worse. And the "for better or worse" part is up to each of us as to which it will be—*better* or *worse*. Since the fact that we have been Created to seek and retain information is so prominent in our design, it's fair to draw some conclusions based upon this model and its consistent and reliable results.

With the evidence of—the reliability of billions of repeated instances called humans—we can likewise look at the nature of our human body and realize that since our body was designed to seek and learn, that it *must* seek and learn. And when the body fails to do so, it risks atrophy. When we don't use our muscles, they diminish in size, but we can rebuild them by using them again on a regular basis. And so it is with our marriages. We have been designed with certain intentions in mind. These intentions are made obvious when considering our five primary senses. When we fail to use these gifts to improve and maintain our marriages then we risk atrophy of the marriage. Exercise your marriage to keep it strong and healthy!

Since you will likely spend many years with your spouse and grow old together, it's likely that it is a desire of yours to stay strong of mind, and whole, until the day that you both die. A strong mind is a wonderful thing, but often people do not understand how to keep their minds strong and healthy. Then late in life they are burdened with a spouse who needs constant assistance and care twenty-four hours a day, seven days a week for many years.

When we stop seeking and learning, our mind becomes weak, and eventually our brain loses its ability to function as intended. Consider dementia or Alzheimer's disease: Can we revive or reverse this? I believe we can. You and your spouse will age over time, and often the mind follows by diminishing itself. Why is this? You can put your trust in mental exercises and medication, but that has not proven to solve this problem and it will let you down in the long run. So why, then, does a mind that is being deliberately exercised still often lose its abilities? Consider that it may not be *that* you exercise your mind, but rather *how* your exercise your mind. Or better stated, what you seek. You can learn more about working to preserve your mind in the cornerstone book *Understanding Prayer*. As a couple, keeping both of your minds fresh and sharp by seeking truth will add many wonderful quality years to your marriage.

The Right to Joy is God-Given

A "strong mind" is often thought of as a determined person who is going to get what they want, but in this book, we are speaking of a mind that is healthy and powerful, not one that is demanding.

Each one of us has a right to joy. This is the type of "right" that we spoke of previously. This right is stolen away by those around us. And often, it is stolen away by ourselves.

The right to joy is given to you by the Creator. And you have a right to protect that right, and you should protect that right. But this is where we get into trouble, especially with our spouses. Reflecting back to the violations that we commit against one another, we must understand how to protect ourselves without violating our spouses. This is far easier said than done.

The first step is to accept and understand truth. With truth comes a great deal of power over your own life. Stand firm in this and defend your right to joy. This freedom, in itself, is joy, and from it all good things come. This particular freedom is where creativity stems from. If your spouse is repeatedly a violator, then stand firm in what is true and right. Do not bend to their incorrect ways just to "keep the peace". Doing so will end in disaster for you.

The right to joy is God-given, so everyone has the right to build walls against injustice. But there is one catch in this—you must adjust your thinking! It might be you who is the violator; and often it is the violator who is building the walls. The walls of a violator are usually forged against truth, which is *not* a good thing to do.

If you are the violator, then change your thinking right now. The sooner you change, then the fewer mistakes you will make and the fewer regrets you will have to pay for later on in your life. Your spouse may forgive you, but you could end up living with the potential permanent damage done from your own errors—damage that might follow you for the rest of your days. Fewer mistakes are better, and the sooner we change our thinking, then the fewer mistakes we will make. This means that we violate less and live more joyfully.

When You are Not Allowed Freedom, Everything is a Lie

When your freedom is stripped from you and you are forced to follow those who steal away your freedom, then you too will be living their lies. If you choose to accept an unstable foundation that lacks truth, then everything that you build upon it is at risk because a building is only as strong as its foundation. This is a choice that only you can make. But few people fully understand that this is *their own* choice.

When we allow our spouse to violate our expectations, or if we violate theirs, it is when we submit to those violations that our problems occur. All problems begin with our submission to those violations. The more you allow the violations, then the more the violations will be repeated, and the *offended* spouse will bind and trap themselves in the ill will of the *offending* spouse. Even when these seemingly insignificant mini-violations are done inadvertently, submitting to them still holds you captive and steals away your freedom. When we allow things that are incorrect in our marriages, then we have opened the door to excessive corrosion that builds and builds until the continuity of our marriage fails.

Only When Truth is Spoken Can Freedom Exist

Truth is the only thing that can resist a corrosive marriage. When you allow your spouse to be wrong and unopposed it does them and yourself tremendous disservice. And you being wrong yourself does both of you a tremendous disservice as well. Standing firm in truth helps this, but standing firm in an unshakable position of truth will not always fully convey the message to them.

When you're correct, you should not make admission that you are wrong because that would be a lie. You do not need to force your point. But remember this: only when truth is spoken can true freedom truly exist! When you lie, then you have bound yourself and you are trapped in that lie.

If a person is violated and stands firm in their understanding of what is true, but says nothing due to fear of conflict, then they are held in their own prison of fear. Confronting violation with truth breaks down the walls that people build around themselves to protect face. Some people have become so afraid of losing face that they will protect their position even when they know that it's wrong. When this is the case, they have rendered themselves un-teachable. There is little that can be done for that person aside of simply stating the truth to them and praying that their eyes be opened.

When the deliberately ignorant behavior of a person is approached with truth, the truth is typically seen by them as an attack, causing them to lash out. Only long-term gentle love and truth can hope to help them—you must gain their trust. When we lash out at truth, it is usually because we were hurt, or because we have been taught to do so as children. We have been trained this way and are trying to defend ourselves because we have lost our trust in people at a very early age; and it is each our own responsibility to overcome that.

When our expectations are violated during our youth, we learn to *not* trust people. Not trusting becomes the only thing that we know and is how we behave in return. This means that we too, often treat others this way by repeatedly violating *their* expectations.

Only When Freedom Exists Can Truth Be Found

We are no longer free when we cannot trust. Freedom and trust are an inseparable pair. You cannot be free without trust and you cannot trust without freedom. This pair is the most important part of a good marriage, and lacking this is why so many marriages struggle and even fail. When you continuously violate your spouse, you rob them of the freedom to trust you. You, in essence, become untrustworthy, that is to say—unfaithful. Anyone who violates their spouse in any way is unfaithful.

The terrible catch in this is that it is the lack of truth that is the root of the violations. So when we violate others by way of our lack of truth and understanding, then we cause them to not trust us, just as others have done to us. It strips away our freedom; and where there is not freedom, truth cannot be found.

It's up to each of us to remove the nonsense from our life and stand firm in truth. And in doing so, obtain our freedom and then teach that freedom to our spouse, our family, and our friends. Be true and give your spouse the freedom to trust you. It is when we each declare our independence *to* the Creator (not *from*) that we will find the freedom of truth.

What Is

The topic of truth is so integrally important in any relationship that failing to address it produces only bad results. Any marriage that is lacking in the truth department will experience much unpleasantness. If truth was not so often misunderstood, then the divorce rate would be far less than it is—even nonexistent. Truth must be understood in order for joy to exist in your marriage, but many people do not grasp the concept of what truth is. If you fail to grasp truth it causes problems in your marriage and in your life. Of course it's important to understand *what is true*, but without first understanding *what truth is*, you cannot begin to understand *what is true*. This all-too-often-misunderstood topic is incorrectly understood to where we tend to think of *what is true*, rather than *what truth is*. Consider the difference between those two perspectives because it is a very important distinction to make with regard to your marriage and general life.

Truth is not some obscure concept with a clouded meaning. It is *what is!* Our individual interpretation of the "what is" part is what gets clouded. In an earlier chapter we talked about the fact that we like what we are familiar with. In addition to this, we have the bad habit of altering the definition of "truth" to get what we want. In other words, we will allow ourselves to be deceived and we will believe what we want in order to get what we want and also to try to feel good about our bad decisions.

This happens in our belief systems when we invest a great deal of our life in believing things to be a certain way. This occurs to the point that we are willing to overlook sound evidence that runs contrary to our erred beliefs. When we do this with concrete physical items it's easier to detect and to see our error. Yet, even in that, our society often chooses to overlook the facts. This problem becomes even more dominant in the abstract realm of our feelings; and this intangible part of our life often dictates our actions and greatly clouds the "*what is*" of truth.

In our marriages, we want to see things from the vantage point that best serves our own selves, rather than what is best for both spouses and the marriage all as one aspect. Sort of in between the two, *tangible* and *intangible*, is the example of the eye witness. Often, in court, the witness is sworn in with the question: "Do you swear to tell the truth, the whole truth, and nothing but the truth?" But then when the questions are asked by the prosecutor, the witnesses are often *not* allowed to tell the *whole* truth. The person cross examining the witness understandably only wants to hear the parts of the story that benefit their client's case.

We are no different. We are the defendant, the witness, the Judge, the lawyer, and the Jury, all wrapped into one person. When we cross-examine ourself, we often make sure that *we*, the witness, cannot tell the whole truth, because that would defeat our misguided cause. When we do this in our marriages, especially when in heated debate, then we have limited our remedy to a point of only dissatisfaction. This of course, applies to everything else in life as well.

This graying of the "*what is*" of truth perverts what we societally call "the truth". Be honest with yourself in all things, be honest with your spouse in all things, and then life will flow much more smoothly for you in your relationship. Even though you may have a few tough spots to work through, remove yourselves from the trouble that the graying of "what is" is bringing into your marriage.

To Know

To make sure that you keep the "*what is*" within you clean and pure, you need to unceasingly seek to *know* and seek to be *honest*. Many of us imagine that we are honest, and we look at others and see them as being dishonest, yet we fail to test ourselves in the same way that we test or judge them. We should always strive to be that witness who was sworn to tell the *whole* truth—and then tell it. Tell everything that you know about your feelings and actions and your spouse's feelings and actions. But be *accurate*. Tell what you know and only what you know with no extra speculation—be *honest* with yourself and with your spouse. Embellishing your feelings for emphasis will not go well with your spouse, and it amounts to lying to them. Lying breaks trust, and broken trust *always* causes damage to a marriage and stirs up needless strong emotions of anger.

Often, we think that a witness's purpose is to end the case and incriminate the defendant. But this is not really the purpose of the witness. The accuser, which is the plaintiff, does that to the best of their ability. The witnesses are there as a fact-gathering mission. As a witness, you are supposed to tell everything you know and *only* what you know. Even if you don't know the entire story, you are still supposed to relate the parts that you do know. You tell what you know, not more and not less. If this would actually occur in the court system, then many more of those who are guilty would be jailed and many fewer innocent people would be jailed. The same concept is true of marriage. When we argue with our spouses, we tend to play the part of the *prosecutor* rather than the *witness*. A witness's testimony that is filtered by the Judge is intended to lead the Jury to the facts. In the case of marriage, the Jury is your spouse. When you decide to become the prosecutor, then your spouse will almost always assume the position of the defense lawyer, which is *not* a good thing. When a relationship is about prosecution versus defense, then it has become a rivalry of wits till death–or divorce–do us part! Being a reluctant but honest witness is what we all should be.

When all of the witnesses come together in a case, then the Judge is supposed to decide without prejudice, what has bearing on the case and what does not. Many judges are very good at this, but even in the Supreme Courts this sometimes fails. After all of the testimony is heard in court, which is supposed to be the truth, then the Jury is supposed to put these pieces of truth together and be able to have a picture of the whole story as it actually occurred.

However, seldom can the Jury do so with eye-witness testimony alone because people often alter the "what is" due to prejudices and what they think they saw.

To *know* something is a skill that must be developed and cannot exist without utter objectivity. To know something, you must be willing to hear and process the information that others have to offer—all of it—even if it does not agree with your current thoughts, beliefs, or perspectives. If you violate your spouse and they correct you (they, being the witness), and then you're angry with them for doing so, then it is *you* who is the problem. Further, we should not add speculation and assumption to our presentation as if it is part of actual truth

Any person who won't allow correction can never be true, and they will frequently be wrong and will always continue in their wrongness, thus they can never be trusted. That is, until they have decided to freely allow correction. To be true is to *know*, and you cannot know without being true. It is a decision that you must choose on your own and it is the only path to freedom. It takes courage to stand for what is true because truth offends those who will not abide by it, and they will attack you for being true. Being true is a decision that *you* make, and it happens fast! When both spouses in a marriage have chosen to embrace the correction to truth, then they will quickly achieve bliss. The path to truth happens in a moment, in a split second! It is an instant decision that we each make on our own.

Do What You Have

An aspect of truth is lack of it. This lack devastates marriages, and is often due to working at the wrong job. Many people go through high school without direction from their parents. Others go through high school with too much direction from their parents. Then, midway through school, the student is coaxed into selecting a "career". After selecting the supposed golden-morsel of success, we embark on an expensive journey through college, and then we marry and live happily ever after... Right?

Wait, that's not true. If it were true, then all who have gone to college should be living in marital bliss and have the career, life, and happy marriage promised from college. Yet it seems the percentage of college graduates who are unhappy in their life is similar, and maybe even greater than the percentage of those who are unhappy and did not attend college. Why is this?

Even if there were a smaller percentage of unhappy people amongst the college graduates versus amongst the "uneducated" populous, there should still be next to no dissatisfaction in college graduates if that is the true path to success, but this is not the case.

If you have something that you have a great passion for, then you should pursue it with your whole heart. If you do not have a passion for it, then let someone else pursue it who does have a passion for it. This is especially true when selecting a mate. Getting into a relationship in a ho-hum manner is unfair to both people in the couple, and the "ho-hum" will inevitably get passed down to the children and/or end in much dissatisfaction and often divorce.

If you're a parent who is hell-bent on sending your child to college for some specialty degree of *your* choosing, then you're wasting your money and *their* life. It is you who should attend college for that degree. People should do what they themselves each choose for an occupation. It is not a parent's job to choose their child's occupation. It is the parents' job to instill desire in their child so that the child seeks an occupation that the child will have their own passion for and find joy in doing. The same goes for you. Living a ho-hum life is not why you got married. And having a ho-hum relationship is not why you got married. Embracing your passions and gifts enhances your life considerably, and when you support each other in doing so, it will also enhance your marriage considerably.

This applies even if your passion is to be "only" a mom and a wife—which, by the way, being a mom is the toughest and most honorable job on the planet. It's time to embrace the true woman and allow her to choose to be a mother and let her enjoy it if she so chooses. To bring forth a Creation much like yourself and your husband, and then to teach that *being* all that is good in the world and what to watch out for, is the single most important task that any woman can choose to do. Guiding and caring for a wife and the children is the single most important job any man can do. And guiding and bringing up a family is the most important job that any couple can do. This does not mean that you must do it. Rather, note the importance of the job of being a parent because without a parent, you would not exist or be here to read this. Failing your children puts a great deal of stress on your marriage as the children grow. Doing it right will enhance your marriage considerably. Do what you love, and teach your children to do this as well. You need not look far and you will quickly see how many people suffer the pains of stress and dissatisfaction at home because they are doing work they don't like. This way of living will run through everything you do and will affect your family, which will affect your relationship. Always be on the lookout for outside attacks inside of your marriage.

Being true to yourself means to do what you have or what is natural in you. When you live outside of truth, then you fall short of truth and of your true self, and by doing so you cheat yourself out of your own joy. Bullying your spouse or condemning them in an unrighteous manner is unfair and amounts to ridicule. This sort of violating stops people from being the way they really are meant to be—true! Make the decision to be who you are. Regardless of what your spouse or anyone else says, be yourself, be true, do what you have as natural in you, and do it well. It is your gift, and that gift is Created in you.

Stay clear of allowing people to redefine *your* life in *their* version of various shades of white when what you really want is pure white. When tensions in a marriage grow strong it's easy to forget your own true passions and then settle into the negative influences around you believing them to be the new standard of the way to live. Outsiders often tell us what to do in our marriages, and that influences the things we say to our spouses. These outside influences include co-workers, counselors, movies, etc. You'll find varying shades of white in relation to marriage when you observe these influences. Some people believe the blackness of divorce to be white, and some believe the murky gray of marital dissatisfaction to be white, but in the end we all know what good really is when we are honest with ourselves and each other. In a marriage, our graying of rationale often appears within our arguments. It is usually unintentionally done by the one who is confused. If you fall prey to a progressive inaccuracy, it is difficult to realize that you're being drawn into it until it's too late. You begin to notice it when you become frustrated with the other person in their unintentional tainting or graying of what is true and evident, in essence turning pure white into murky gray. When this occurs, stop and refocus to regain clarity and make sure that you yourself are not graying things.

If Your Wife Doesn't Trust Your Decisions, then She Will Feel Unsafe and May Go Elsewhere For Her Guidance

Another aspect of this subject demonstrating the utter importance of truth is the ramification of a lack of trust within your marriage. We discussed the violation issues in-depth, but there is still another aspect of this problem. In much the same way that a man may choose to find trust in the arms of another woman, or other visual stimuli, so too, a woman will seek security in another man or from other means.

If a husband's decisions are not wisely laid down and the decisions falter, a wife may seek her guidance elsewhere. A married couple should seek their guidance from truth together, and only from truth. Anything less than that is bound to end up with the couple following lies and misinformation.

Repeated violations through bad decisions from either spouse will cause problems in your future. When we make decisions based upon our renegade emotions, we are in danger of losing sight of truth. This clouds our view of the facts about the decisions we need to make, and it often causes us to make a wrong or poor decision. When this is done repeatedly to ourselves, by ourselves, then for good reasons, our spouses will not be able to trust our decisions.

When we dupe ourselves by making decisions that are unstable, we then have robbed our spouse of the right to trust us— we have stolen freedom from them. When this behavior is frequently exhibited, it's common for the person who has been making the errors to not allow correction from their spouse. You will find this to be true in people in general. This is often seen in friends or other family members, but it is especially damaging when this happens within a marriage.

Always seek the truth and make wise decisions, then at least you will be trustworthy. Even if your spouse or others do not trust you, you will know that you are correct based on truth and will welcome correction in your thoughts so that you are thinking rightly. That is true freedom. That is Truth!

Be In a State of Pure Joy

Obtaining freedom is done quickly. And when you achieve true freedom, then the world becomes a great deal less intrusive to you and your marriage.

While someone can steal away your ability to trust them by them being untrustworthy, they cannot steal away your ability to trust yourself, your ability to trust the Creator, or your own ability to be trustworthy. It is in this where your pure joy will reside. When you have obtained the freedom of truth, then you become a beacon of light to those around you. While it may seem to sting a bit if they ridicule your new understanding of living within the boundless confines of truth, their ridicule will not easily bring you down. In a marriage, this can be a painful time if your spouse refuses to seek truth. But in the end, it is likely less painful than what you have been experiencing up until now.

When you bear the pure light of truth, eventually you will become an index to others and to your spouse. Often this index is undesirable to them, because when you wear the pure-white gown of truth, then they are forced to see the various dirty shades of white that most people live within. Any person who chooses to defy truth will bear dirtier shades of white than those who love truth. The soiled shades of white that they bear become very noticeable when compared to the pure whiteness of truth, and the darker those shades are, the more it seems they will want to tear you down to make you appear dirty so that you don't look whiter or better than they do. Truth has a tendency to expose our own folly. If we are forced to compare ourselves to anyone with truth, it quickly becomes apparent that we have fallen short. This is a real big problem in marriages when it is both people in the couple who are doing this.

In many cases, those of us who have had much error in our lives, and in our thinking, will get close to accepting the truth. But then when we are ready to grab hold of truth, we glance into the mirror of freedom and see the light of truth exposing our own errors, and then our dirty dark white reflection frightens us. When this happens, we pull back from the fear of our own reflection and fail to obtain truth. This is a very common occurrence that keeps us in slavery to the things that are not true that we currently experience around us.

Think about this: If you *choose* to believe something that is not real and not true, then you have trapped yourself in an inescapable lie. If other things in your life are dependent upon that lie, then those things will fail when the lie fails. All of it will fall down together and pull you down into the deceptive abyss along with it, often ending in divorce.

We Must Share Truth

The pursuit of truth cannot occur without sharing that truth. Sharing truth means to allow others to see it in you. This cannot be done without you opposing the violations that you experienced in your life. If you stand strong in your true belief, but then back down and hide away when violated, then you are extinguishing your truth causing it to not be seen by others.

Truth is the loving strength that arrogance tries to emulate. It is the thing to which both men and women are most attracted. Truth is a certainty and confidence that is unshakable, and it desires and invites scrutiny. When you have truth, then there is nothing that you fear! Fear is the lack of truth. Truth illuminates fear and drives it far from you, but the consuming fire of fear devours your truth *when **you** allow* it to.

Bridging the gap from fear to truth is the only "leap of faith" that you will ever need to make. Once you have embraced truth, your fears begin to quickly depart, and the more you embrace truth, then the more your fears will disappear.

To keep truth alive and well within you, you must share truth by allowing others to see it in you, and also by offering the direction towards truth to others. It is your job to get the message to them, and then to point them in the direction of the light of truth so that they too can choose the freedom of truth. This is especially important to share with your spouse.

If you allow your joy of this true freedom of mind to shine brightly to those around you, eventually they will want what you have and will be drawn to you. When they draw to you, then you can show them this truth so that they, too, can choose it for themselves. This action will draw you to those who are willing as well.

When we deeply invest our minds in the false life that we have built up around ourselves, and then go near to people with truth, then we instinctively feel attacked and are repelled by their truth. Truth will drive away those who are bad for you and attract those who are good for you. But you must also understand that there are those whose sole ambition it is to destroy *true* people. These people are covetous of your certainty, and they will do anything they can to destroy you so that they can look better to themselves and, as they wrongly think, to others.

When We Decide that God is on Our Side

The goal of marriage is to be drawn into the truth that one another bears and to both become one into this truth and share that truth through your children so that they can do it all the same in, and for, their lives.

Individually, and as a couple, truth is a decision that only you can make. No one can make the decision for you, and you cannot make the decision for anyone else. But you can make it easier for others when you allow them to see your truth in confident love. Stand against violations, and state your case in a kind and loving way. Be strong in truth and let it guide your way.

You are Created a certain way for a reason. When you utilize that reason, you will flourish in truth, and others will be drawn to it from your example. In embracing truth, a good way to start is by realizing that the Creator is never "on your side". *You* must *choose* to be on the Creator's side. That means *you* must choose to join the Creator's team.

The choice to be on the Creators side requires nothing more than your embracing of truth. People often believe that if they attend church and pray, that they are doing all that is required and all will be well. But that is entirely wrong. The church building structure could be for the worship of any "god" and the prayers could be being requested from a carved idol. So, attending church alone does not meet the requirements needed to join the Creator's "team" of truth.

When you're in alignment with what you are Created for, then there is little that will get in your way. And often, the struggles begin to vanish, and assistance seems to come to you as it is needed. As a couple, choose to be on the Creator's side, and then watch what happens—you *will* be impressed!

The more we understand our connection to the Creator, and the more that we understand about the technical aspects of our Creation, then the easier it is for us to repair our personal and marital problems.

Chapter 20

Conspiring Couples

Over the years most of us have seen marriage dynamics portrayed in books, movies, and on television. Regardless of how sweet the couples seem on these shows, many of us are bothered when they're not working together in harmony as a couple and are instead at odds with each other. They frequently portray the couples at odds with each other as they spitefully try to harm or demean one another. But in entertainment, where they conspire in harmony, it seems better, even when the portrayal has the couples doing wrong or illegal things. This type of *harmony* is attractive to most people, though we don't condone partaking in illegal or improper activities because conspiring for a bad end will end badly for everyone.

It's not *what* they're doing that appeals to us. But rather, it is *how* they are doing it that we like. The fact that such harmony appeals to us is the reason why they write the scripts for the shows and movies in this way. Although in many cases, the writers may not specifically realize that they are doing so.

Businesslike Harmony

We can learn many lessons from well-run businesses that function with internal harmony, but business lacks the warmth that marriage is supposed to thrive on. We can also learn many business lessons from a warm and joyous marriage. In resolution of their differences, many marriages use methods similar to a business. Often, people don't see it this way or even realize that this is occurring. What I am referring to is "compromise".

We discussed compromise several chapters back, and spoke of the difference between *what we see as* compromise and what compromise *really is*. Compromise is to co-promise. It is an agreement, but it is frequently used in the context of a disagreement where people will adjust their own thinking and end goals, and then make their co-promise to work together. For business this works well, but this is altogether wrong for marriages in that context. If we need to *compromise* in our marriage in this way, then we're making a statement that we have agreed to settle for less than we desire, and often, for less than we signed on for. This is the wrong approach.

It is unfair to one, or to both spouses, to have to compromise in this way. Let's look at it in a more tangible way. We can use favorite pastimes as an example. If a wife's favorite pastime is to watch romantic movies and a husband's favorite pastime is to watch sports, and then the wife watched sports with her husband, but the husband refuses to watch romantic movies with his wife, then there is a bit of an unfair imbalance in the relationship.

Or, if the husband goes shopping with his wife, but the wife refuses to ever go fishing with her husband, then there is also an imbalance in the relationship. Even if one spouse does choose to partake in their mate's favorite pastime, but is not enjoying it with their mate, then there is a slant in the relationship.

It's fine to have these sorts of leisure activities, and to do them alone or without your spouse, but what we are referring to here is the desire of one spouse to be a joyfully active participant and be a part of one or more of their mate's favorite activities. At times, each of us will likely want to do certain activities alone or with friends, and that's fine, but again that's not what we are referring to here.

Being a part of your spouse's favorite activity, but then not putting your heart into it, or not wanting to be there, cheats the other person and robs them of a full and robust experience. Often this is done in this negative manner and is done for only one of three reasons: You are doing it for manipulation so that they owe you one; or one spouse may agree due to the demands and manipulation from the other spouse; and finally, it is being done out of complacency—complacency being the least offensive of the three.

When we partake in this behavior, if we are the spouse who is either being manipulated or the one who is doing the manipulating, we are prostituting ourselves—we are selling our affection and attention for a price. If it is us who demands or bargains for our spouse's companionship, and we promise them favors so that they come along for the activity, then we are trying to buy or force their love and companionship.

Marital prostitution in this way goes on to some extent in nearly all relationships, but it does not create a picture perfect relationship. Where manipulation of any sort exists, trouble lurks. You may be together "until death do you part" and not really feel manipulation has affected you, but it has. Manipulation has cheated many couples out of a robust life together. Yet, we are so accustomed to this in our culture that we barely notice that it occurs.

Many preachers, teachers, and counselors preach that a marriage is all about compromise. If it is in the sense that the word compromise means to agree to be true to each other, then it is acceptable. But typically, when we speak of "compromise" in marriage, we mean reducing our expectations to adjust to the violations that the other person is perpetrating against us. This is simply ridiculous. We do not need to bend to the manipulative will of others no matter who they are. What we need is to be honest and kind.

Now someone can say, "Well I honestly don't like to go shopping, so I am not going to go because I don't want to compromise in that way". This could be a legitimate position, but if your spouse is excited to partake in your favorite activity but you are not excited to partake in *any* of theirs, then there are selfishness issues in your relationship that *you* need to work on. If you only partake in the activities of your spouse that you like, but they are partaking in activities that they find rather boring that are your favorites, then there is an imbalance. In saying this, I mean that if she is normally bored with sports but watches or goes to games with you and is excited and cheering with you, but she would never do this without you, then if you fail to offer her the same in return, you are certainly being selfish. If your spouse can get into your activity with excitement when he or she is with you, but is otherwise bored with that activity without you, then you should also be able to find it in your heart to mentally get into whatever they like to do, and share in it with them.

The manipulation subject is a difficult one for many to see their way clear about because tit-for-tat comes into play, where one spouse will withdraw in an effort to hurt the other as retaliation for the hurts felt in other areas of their marriage. This muddying of the marriage waters makes it very hard for both spouses to see their way clear to what is truly going on in their relationship.

If a wife likes to watch a romantic movie now and then, and her husband reluctantly agrees to watch it with her, but then he's playing video games and ignores his wife during the movie the entire time, then the wife will likely settle for what she can get with regard to his companionship. But if this is the case and she has to settle, then she is probably going to "owe him one." This is a horrible thing! She didn't desire for her husband to watch the movie with her so that he could immerse himself in playing games that are of no interest to her. She wanted him alongside of her, so that she could share her passion together *with* him. The same would be true if the husband desired to have his wife along to a ball game and she then decided to bring a book and read instead of cheering with him for his favorite team.

What is being illustrated in the examples of these types of situations cannot truly be considered "being together", at least not the way it is wanted by the spouse who wants to share that part of their life with their mate. This sort of interaction is forced love. Of course, we can't expect our spouse to want to do everything that we want to do. But often this pattern is commonly done throughout all aspects of the relationship, and it is often very one-sided, having one spouse always feeling alone.

Trying not to be too harsh here, this behavior is selfish and cruel. If you are going to be there, *then be there.* This door swings both ways. If you are going to have your spouse accompany you, but you have no flexibility in your plan to accommodate any of the likes that your spouse has, then you are being selfish. This type of inflexibility is common in many relationships, and usually goes unrealized by the more offensive spouse. If you really do not want to partake in something with your spouse, then you need to look in the mirror and be honest and ask yourself—are you being fair? We also must consider that when we *begrudgingly* concede to something, we are taking away from our spouse's enjoyment of that activity. We are stealing from them! We all fail on this somewhat, but we should work to focus and be there for our spouse when we are there.

"Fair" is a deceptive word with regard to a marriage. Fair indicates that you are trying to be equal. Fair expresses that my spouse will not come with me, so in return I choose not to go with my spouse. It's partly a tit-for-tat tactic, and partly a businesslike agreement. It's cold and self-serving. We can't be expected to want to do everything that our spouse wants to do, but we can expect that we can get more than a lame "compromise" out of a marriage (recall where we discussed *enemy* or *rival*).

In a joyous marriage, you will desire to be with your spouse in those times where they want *you* to be there with them, but there needs to be something in it for you, too. This sounds awful, but it is not meant to be taken in the context of "what's in it for me?" Anytime someone acts in a manner that is one-sided, they are in the habit of taking, and taking is not true love. The "What's in it for me?" part is your spouse's love and companionship.

Each couple needs to work these things out on their own, but in doing so, it is important to be honest with yourself and make sure that both of you are considering your spouse's desires. If you refuse to do something as simple as watch a movie together because you don't like romantic movies, but your spouse does, then there are real problems that *you* need to deal with within you and within your relationship.

Pulling Together

The most difficult thing for any person to do is to obtain desire for another person when the desire is not automatically in them. When desire is natural, it typically is initially selfish or for self-serving purposes. Thus, our first attraction to someone is often physical, but usually, it quickly and beautifully transforms into a desire to better know the other person in a truly deep way.

Our desire to get to know the object of our affection causes us to do a great deal of investigation and observation by learning all that we can about our new girlfriend or boyfriend. It is our automatic intrigue that is attractive to our new friend. Simply put, it feels good when someone takes a true interest in us. After our curiosities are satisfied, we tend to have our attention drift to other areas of our own individual interests. The natural flow of our change in interest is, to some extent, usually in violation of each other's expectations, and in many cases it is often heavily one-sided.

When waning desire is balanced between the spouses, it is less of a violation to each, but when it is heavily out of balance, then one of the spouses will suffer a great deal of loneliness. When one spouse fully satisfies their desire to understand their mate, then due to their lack of attention towards their mate, their mate is no longer going to feel as if they are desired. Additionally, when the satisfied spouse is busy doing other things, there's a tendency for them to feel as if their mate is bothering them whenever their mate wants to know them better, which only serves to compound the problem. Is there a solution to this?

So long as the satisfied mate is not desirous of fulfilling their spouse's desires, it is unlikely that the problem will go away. A satisfied mate has no reason to alter their behavior. If the deprived mate makes any attempt to balance the marital scale by withdrawing a little bit, then the satisfied mate will likely take that withdrawal as an offense, or worse, be happy that their spouse is not bothering them as much, or worse yet, not even notice their spouse's withdrawal at all.

At other times, withdrawal might be received as an attempt at punishment. When a spouse withdraws because they feel violated, it is often a form of punishment directed at their mate. It is a form of vindication—a way to get what rightfully belongs to them. In essence, we are *jealous* (true to the word) for our spouse's attention.

A healthy desire to be with our spouse is often wrongly mocked, made fun, or demeaned by the spouse who is the less desirous spouse. This is typically done through accusations of calling the person names like "needy" or "clingy", etc. This unfair position will end badly for them because, in the long run, the violated spouse will likely seek satisfaction elsewhere. If you make your spouse feel unwanted, then they will feel ever greater need. The only way to reduce someone's need is to satisfy their needs, getting this right will restore the proper balance in the relationship. Of course on the other side of the coin, it is possible that showing excessive desire for someone will make you come across as "needy"—the skill needed here is *balance*.

Sports and shopping are both fine pastimes, and we cannot expect that our spouse will want to do everything together with us; yet, it's not wrong to do most everything together. To combine yourselves to be as one is the whole point and foundation of marriage. It should be each your own desires—to have as your desires—many of your spouse's desires as well. Mutual desire is applicable to each spouse, and it is the two-way street of marriage. Anytime two or more people have a common goal, then that goal is far more easily achieved together, than it is by one person alone.

It's okay for people to have solitary activities apart from their spouse that they like to do alone or with friends. But this can end up being bad if their spouse wants to be with them but must barter to get the companionship they desire and deserve. If a person has a desire to do most things apart from their spouse, it is a clear indication that there are deeper underlying problems hiding away within the relationship and within the person who is wanting to be away from their spouse. Please do not misunderstand this. It's okay for each spouse to have some of their own activities that they do without their spouse. Doing so often gives you both much more to discuss and learn from each other when you're together.

Combine Your Thoughts

Couples often struggle and have problems in various areas of their lives. The struggles might be in regard to finances, child rearing, possessions, political views, spiritual beliefs, your relationship, etc. Regardless of what part, or parts, of your married life are left wanting, the *cause* is always the same. The cause is lack of ability to want to do it together, in harmony, as one.

Couples frequently bring contaminations from the pasts of each of them into their marriage. In regard to these contaminations, our childhood families are often an enormous strain and the primary source of the contaminations. This strain puts pressure on the couple and often draws away one or both spouses to their childhood family rather than to each other. Attention should be focused *on the married couple's* joint goals and their own combined family of them and their children. Their parents and siblings must be limited in contact if that contact is dividing or trying to draw from the couple's end goals. It's okay, and even good, to depart from anyone who causes your family or marriage undue and unjust stress. Your errors are your own to make, but be attentive to separating *good advice* that someone gives you, from them *unjustly stressing* your marriage. If you're making mistakes, it's probably good that someone kindly points out those mistakes to you.

But unreasonable external pressure suffocates a marriage and divides the spouses and causes strife within the marriage. Sometimes outside pressure demands that the couple do things the parents' way or their siblings' way. This could be in manner in which one or both of the external families' desires are exercised. For instance, if a spouse's family had no ambition or understanding to accomplish much, this is often passed to the spouse who came from that family, and it will divide the goals of the couple.

Complacency is very bad for a marriage and will seek to destroy it. Complacency is a particularly dangerous human behavior. The difficult part of complacency creeping into a marriage is that neither spouse understands that this is happening because it's usually not intentional. The result is that one spouse will have goals, and the other will have very few or no goals and, typically, won't desire to share any of the more ambitious mate's goals. This mismatched complacency is mostly unintended, but can greatly hinder a marriage and deeply hurt the spouse who is not complacent nonetheless.

People with complacent and goalless personalities often come to the unintentional expectation that their spouse will pick up the slack in the workload, and for that matter, in the goal-load as well. Seldom will complacent personalities have even small goals, if they have any at all. Their complacency is fed by those who are goal-oriented and ambitious. The ambitious like to work and are passionate about it. This allows their less ambitious counterpart to continue to do little without any resistance, thus feeding their complacency even more.

While complacency is not done with malicious intentions, it is, in varying degrees, nonetheless damaging to the relationship. We think of "damaging" as being a downgrade from where we currently are. But in truth, it is a downgrade from where you should have been. This means that if a complacent behavioral pattern exists in your marriage or in your life, then you are living in a damaged marriage or life.

Your marriage will be greatly improved when both of you are able to combine your thoughts and energies into the same goals and dreams, and then share in them *together*. The power of two is more than double. This is because with one person alone, a goal often cannot be accomplished. An example would be if one person needed to lift a heavy object and could not do it because it was too heavy for one person alone to move without any help. No matter how hard or how long that person tries, he or she simply will not be able to ever move the object by themselves if all they have is their body to do the work. Adding the extra force from a second person allows them to easily move the object to its intended position. The difference is having it moved exactly as desired, versus not having it moved at all. You simply cannot be as successful as a couple when you are not working together as a single mind.

Some people wonder how it is that evil can exist. The reason is that people doing bad things conspire *together* and pool their energy or resources in an effort to take from others in an evil manner. Working together is a very powerful approach and is the point behind the phrase "United We Stand" The gift of unity is being wasted and is diminished when the unity is abused and occurs for evil purposes. In the long run, evil unity decreases the value of humanity. We might not want to think of it this way, but when a couple is intent on discord within their relationship, then they have ultimately unknowingly conspired for evil in order to destroy *their own* relationship—and succeed they will!

But when unity is present in marriage it builds and increases the value of humanity and it makes the world a better place. Evil must be separated, and good must be unified. Evil unity devours and eventually defeats itself, but loving unity increases and grows—it is self-sustaining. People unified for truth and good always have far more power in the long run than people who are unified for bad, for cheating, or for destructive purposes. When you see bad behavior succeed, then know that the reason it succeeds is that they are unified and they know it.

When you see troubles in your marriage, realize that you are not *unified* as a couple. Whether emotional, spiritual, financial, physical, or other troubles, those troubles are from a lack of unity. In a sense you are unified in disunity and you will succeed in disunity which brings about failure. Instead, be unified for good and harmony and joy.

When you break your marriage unity, you have broken your marriage contract. Remember: a contract has the primary purpose of revealing violations of one or both of the people named in the contract. It's a sad case, when a marriage commitment is made, but then is not pursued with full love and devotion. Allowing yourself to devote yourself to your mate's goals and dreams, and they to yours, is truly the most loving thing you each can do. But your goals and dreams must be rooted in truth and goodness if you expect your mate to actually want to become a part of your goals and dreams. Believing wrong things or wrong ways, lying, cheating, or arrogance will not attract your spouse to you. Rather, doing so will usually drive them away from you.

Combining your minds, as one, to accomplish all of your goals and expectations, will allow you to keep yourselves well-grounded and synchronized, thus, allowing both of you to be successful and joyful. When your thoughts are aligned with your spouse's thoughts, then life will go more smoothly as a couple—We cheat ourselves when we fail to do this. The best example of the need for unity is in raising your children. If you are not of one mind while raising your children, then expect problems in bringing them up, and expect problems with them as adults in the future. And finally, understand that any of this will affect your marriage in a negative manner.

The answer to all problems is very simple. But humanity's problem is in our failing to achieve this simple answer. Unify as a couple and you will both be stronger, and so will your marriage, your children, and your family unit!

Chapter 21

Your Children and Your Marriage

Many marriages struggle as the children grow older. When the children are very young, life often seems mostly in order. Then later in life, as the children reach their teen years, their behavior creates unwanted stress in the family and in the marriage. Understanding how to properly handle and teach your children is crucial to a joyful and stress-free marriage and family life. Your children, and your examples and words to them, are the only things you will ever have that are truly lasting in your life. Everything else you do in life has little lasting or real value for future generations. If you want deeper insight into family, and bringing up great children, the cornerstone book *Strong Family* goes in-depth and discusses bringing up children and offers many unique insights for creating a strong family. When we fail our children, then we fail ourselves. And when we fail ourselves, then we have failed our children.

As a couple, being of one mind when raising children will reduce your strife. When done well, it will make life pleasant! Being of one mind is very important, but having the right goals is equally important. You must choose to raise your children in truth if you ever hope to have lasting joy in your family.

For those couples who don't want to have more children, be diligent when using any means of birth control. People often decide to take chances in a moment of passion commonly resulting in unintended pregnancies. This is fine if you both truly do not mind having more children, but if either one of you does not want to have any more children, then being very responsible is the wisest course of action in this regard. Most people will still dearly love their children even if the child was not intended, but it can put unneeded stress on a marriage when the child was not intended and the parents are not in agreement on such matters in the future.

It is much better for the children and for the family, if the children are desired from the beginning, before conception, and loved throughout. When this is not the case, it often causes tension in those relationships. Children bring much joy when they are well brought up. Sometimes people fail their children and then don't want more and/or don't like the children they already have. If this is your situation, then consider promptly and properly addressing your children's needs. When parents choose to fail their children, and then choose a selfish lifestyle, they cheat themselves out of much joy and companionship later in life.

Married Couples and Birth Control

Having children is best after a couple is committed to each other and willing to commit before family and friends at their wedding. Having children is also best when the children are wanted by both spouses. Birth control is a touchy subject for many people, and misunderstood by many as well. Is birth control okay to use?

The Bible or the Church or a Pope or worse, some person who read a book and has an opinion have words that are often called upon when this subject is contemplated. But let's be clear something up right now. This topic is often conflated with *premarital* sex, which in general is a bad idea that causes much grief for the participants, especially the women. So let us separate those who are not married from those who are married. People who are not married and are not committed should not be having sex for all of the reasons being discussed in this book, but married couples should be having sex to their own delight! So now that we cleared up who should be having sex and who should not, we can discuss what is permissible regarding birth control *within a marriage.*

The subject of controlling birth by any means is often written about with great passion for or against any means of it and any degree of it. Often the Bible is used to discourage people from using birth control. But what really is "birth control" and what does the Bible really say about it? Birth control is any method of reducing the probability of unwanted pregnancy. So what is permissible regarding birth control?

The Bible has a couple of references that are often *misused* by people who foolishly take the stand against *all* forms of birth control. The first one is about a woman whose husband died and the husband's brother was supposed to give her a child so that she would not be barren. During the act of intercourse he withdrew and spilled his seed on the bed or ground. For this the Creator was not pleased with him. This situation is often understood as if we should not control birth in this or any other way because the Creator did not like the fact that the dead man's brother spilled his seed on the bed or ground. However, the Creator was not angry that he spilled his seed on the ground, but rather was angry that the brother-in-law did not fulfill this basic need for the woman. And worse, the man took the sex but refused to give her the seed and therefore the child. He in essence raped her and that was the offense that angered the Creator. This has nothing to do with married couples that do not want to have any more children so they use birth control. Within a joyful marriage birth control is not offensive to the Creator unless it is used for abusive purposes.

Then we have a second Biblical interpretation error, which is that people in the Bible had large families—there were not many, depending upon your definition of "large family". Since the Bible follows the descendants of Jacob (known as Israel), people often use Jacob's family size as a gauge for birth control. They just keep having children until they no longer can because Jacob had lots of children (thirteen in all as far as we can tell by what is written—twelve sons and one daughter).

But let us get something straight about Jacob's situation. Jacob was duped by his father-in-law and cheated out of his true love due to the father-in-law's traditions of marrying off the oldest daughter first. He tricked Jacob on the wedding night with lies and deception and gave him the oldest daughter first. But eventually he allowed Jacob to also have the younger daughter—the love of Jacob's life. Both daughters came each with a servant woman, so Jacob now had four women to care for.

In a sort of odd jealous competition, when the sisters couldn't conceive then they had children via their servants as surrogates. Each of the four woman did not have thirteen children, but all together all four woman had thirteen total children. The point here is that having thirteen children is fine if you want to put your body through that, but it is *not* "Biblical" for one woman alone to have that many children. It's not wrong, but *it is also not* **Biblical**. And when Jacob had thirteen children there were four women working together to care for those thirteen children and there may have been a pretty good span of years between some of the children, all making the care much easier than it is for only one woman to have many children.

If I recall correctly, of the four women, one had seven children and the other three each had only two per woman. Both of the sisters had a servant woman to help them. So, in the case of the oldest daughter Leah who had seven children, she also had her servant who had two children. Between the two of them they had nine children which averages to four and a half per woman. And for all four women the average is only three and one quarter children per woman. So the workload was very likely shared somewhat. This is not the case when one woman has many children. A good indicator of how many children a woman should have is the average for the women of Jacob. It was a good rate to keep the population increasing slightly, which is why the average for the women of Jacob is close to the average that people have when married to one spouse their whole adult life.

Now that it is cleared up that the Bible *does not* instruct us to have as many children as is possible in a lifetime, we can discuss types of birth control. We are not going to dwell on the types of birth control but rather the general types. There is natural control, such as abstinence, and withdrawal where the sperm is not deposited inside the vagina. Then there is obstructive such as condoms and diaphragms. And there is chemical such as the pill or spermicides. And finally there is the infamous "Morning After Pill".

The morning after pill is the equivalent of an abortion, so that one is actually offensive to a newly created life, thus we will remove that one from discussion. The other chemical means of birth control will kill sperm cells before they are able to make their way to the woman's egg, or chemistry can stop the woman's eggs from taking their normal course and thus avoid the potential pregnancy. The problem that some people have with chemical birth control is that it increases the risk of birth defects in the event that pregnancy occurs regardless that the chemistry was actually used. Also it can have negative effects on a woman's body. But these are risks that each couple must decide upon for themselves.

The simplest means of birth control that have little or no physical risks are barriers such as a condom, withdrawal, sex without penetration, and of course the always faithful abstinence. And abstinence is the only perfect way to guarantee that pregnancy will not occur but can be offensive to a spouse who desires intimacy.

It is highly unlikely that sex is *only* to procreate with reckless abandon and have more children than you can handle. If you have too many children to where you find no joy in life because the burden is more than you can handle, then birth control is a good option. But things get even worse if the mother dies in child birth; let's say on the seventh or eighth child then who will be mother to the remaining children?

If you want children then go ahead and have them, but if your done then be done and find joy in your family at the size you want it to be. Disregard the words of fools who will make you feel guilty for using birth control if you are a married couple. If an extra child comes along, you will still love them, but having more than you can handle because of foolish erred beliefs about what people wrongly interpret the Bible to say or mean has worked out badly for far too many families over the centuries. Sex is not between you and the Church, or the Pope, or some author, or a friend with a foolish opinion. Sex is between you and your spouse. And unless the

Church or the Pope, or some author or other person who tries to impress their foolish opinions on you are going to come and care for *your* children whenever things get out of hand, keep their opinions out of the intimate parts of your marriage and out of your bedroom.

Your marriage-sex and family-life are yours to enjoy as you both see fit in accordance with the Creator's Creation. Don't let fools foul your marriage with their ignorance of the facts.

Having Children Will Not Help a Bad Marriage

When discussing having children there are often varying opinions. Some couples are afraid to have children but are jealous of couples who do. Some people are very self-focused and do not want children because they don't want to give up their lifestyles. Some people physically can't have children. Some people keep having children and don't specifically want them, and most of the rest choose to have their children because they truly want them.

But there is another reason people have children—they do it to "save" their marriages. Having children to save a marriage is *not* a good idea. A bad marriage is a bad marriage, and any attempt to make it better by having children is only placing a bandage on a wound that is already badly infected. This will only cause the bandage and wound to be neglected, further serving to increase the original infection that happened before the children came along. Resolving marital issues *before* creating life is the wisest course of action for any couple.

If you have a troubled marriage, then consider that it is a *confused* marriage that is out of sync and in a fog, rather than being a "troubled marriage". A confused marriage is a marriage that is not functioning with clarity due to the lack of unity between the spouses. The lack of unity is often inadvertently adopted from the parents of both people in the couple and will be passed down to the couple's children if ignored—this is not good.

The resolution to troubled and confused marriages is simple in concept, but often the selfishness that we each possess inhibits our ability to have a full and robust desire for our spouse and their dreams. Having children to fill this void *is not* the answer. Doing so usually only perpetuates the problems and delays the inevitable failure of the neglected marriage. That is of course, unless having children is the actual problem in the marriage. It is sometimes even worse if the problem is not a physical inability to have children, but rather, one spouse desperately wants a child and the other spouse does not. Having a child in this case is unlikely to solve anything and may make matters far worse. Being in this situation is another good example of being unequally yoked to your mate. However, for some, the added responsibility of a child has awakened them from their blind slumber and thus improve themselves as people.

Two Steps Forward and Three Steps Back

Any patch to solve marital problems is only going to result in more problems down the road. And the future problems will often be worse and deeper than the initial problems were.

Having children to patch a damaged area in your marriage is a mistake unless the damaged area is you not being able to have children to begin with. These kinds of attempts to patch a marriage are taking two steps forward and *three* steps back, ultimately leaving your situation worse off than before. These attempts are reverse progress, and with each child that you have you will be further from the joy that you are aiming to achieve in your marriage. That is, of course, until you resolve your *real* underlying problems.

When having children for the purpose of patching a marriage, you will likely still love the children, but you will have contaminated them with your lack of unity. This lack of unity will almost certainly have infected their lives, causing them to have similar problems when they marry. You might even have seen this in your parents with regard to your own life. Whatever the condition of your relationship with your spouse is, it will inadvertently be taught to your children, and it will be emulated by them because it is all that they know—this emulation *will* occur whether your relationship is good or bad. You must have your foundation built, and in place, before you can move on to a joyful state in marriage, then children are a joyful gift!

Having children can end up being similar to using *things* as a patch in attempt to fix your marriage. If your marriage is in peril and your spouse wants a better or bigger house, and that is one of the points of contention in your marriage, then acquiring that house is unlikely to solve your problems. Few people have the available funds for paying cash for their home and they will need to borrow the money to make the purchase. This causes the couple to have to make payments on that house for the next fifteen to thirty years. This is an example of the two steps forward three steps back action, and it will cause you financial strain for years to come because you are obligating yourselves for something that cannot possibly solve your true underlying problems. Such attempts to sooth a wounded marriage might temporarily sooth the problems of the marriage, but it is more like putting a local-anesthetic on a wound to mask the pain. No one in a marriage is ever truly satisfied without *proper* unity.

Filling our marriages with children or things is the way of many marriages. We haphazardly place a patch on a damaged area and never actually remove the problem's source. If you cannot be in love with your spouse while living in nothing more than a tent in the woods, then your marriage has problems that will keep reoccurring through the duration of the marriage, even "until death do us part."

Whether you are trying to correct your marital problems by obtaining riches, having children, or any other false method, your efforts are futile, as so many people have come to discover. It's when you have children for the right reasons that you will find joy in them and in your relationship. When we have children for the purpose of patching our marital shortcomings, it is often our children that suffer most from our lack of ability to see our own errors and our failure to correct the problem by removing the actual source of the problem. If we are actually able to correct our own errors after having children, then it is often too late and the children have already been exposed to a great deal of our bad relationship-examples during the most important time of their upbringing. This adversely affects the remainder of their lives if left without repair.

Respect Your Spouse

Children have a peculiar ability to sense problems in their parents' marriage, though the children may not be able to specifically describe the trouble they sense. Parents often intentionally, or inadvertently, lie to their children. Through these deceptions, the children come to understand these problems and lies as an acceptable part of life and an appropriate way to live. So, what exactly is it that they are seeing?

They see the inconstancies with respect to their expectations of their parents' marriage. For whatever reason, children expect and desire harmony in their world. By nature, a lack of harmony upsets children. While the parents offer loving-kindness to the children, that same loving-kindness may be absent from the relationship between the parents. This sort of void will be noticed by the children and eventually adopted by them as normal, and very likely repeated by them when they get married.

Children can see a void in their parents' relationship, and when it goes on long enough they adopt and mimic it. This behavior is reflected back towards the parents, and then the children go on to disrespect their own parents, thus disregarding them—that is to say, disregarding you. When the disrespect is shown between spouses, or even from only one spouse towards the other, then to some extent, disrespect will also typically be shown towards the children by one or both parents.

It's bad when children see examples of disrespect between their parents. But when the disrespect is exhibited towards the children, then serious problems will most certainly arise. The resulting behavior patterns generally do not stop within the family, and those patterns follow the children throughout their lives, causing them, in turn, to do the same thing to their own children.

Few people grasp what this void actually is. We call it lack of respect, but in our world "respect" has come to mean: we do what our elders say we should do. This is incorrect, and age has little to do with "respect".

The word *respect* contains within it the word *spect*, as in *spectacle* or *spectator*. *Spect* or spectacle means to look, and in the case of *re-spect* it means to **re-look**. It may be easier if you think of it in terms of observing something. So what then are we observing, or *re-looking* at? We are looking at the other person, their thoughts, hopes, dreams, questions, and conclusions.

Respect means: To hear and consider another person's thoughts, and then to actually mentally process those thoughts with consideration and actual contemplation. It means to share in those thoughts and reply with sound reasoning and compassion, and then be able to clearly explain your own point of view without disregarding theirs. It means to add to their thoughts, and then, together, to share a common goal of seeking justice and righteousness.

Respect is *not* defined as demanding that others hear your own point of view and then not allowing them to express their own. The idea of respect goes all the way back to the beginning of this book and includes everything we have been discussing so far. When people have chosen an arrogant approach in life, then their **dis-respect** of others is the result.

An arrogant person's view of respect is that *others* must listen to *them*, and at the same time the arrogant person does not feel that they need to hear other people's thoughts. The arrogant nature in people is often very demanding and cruel in both the delivery of their own opinions, and in their rejection of other people's opinions.

Arrogance is common in anyone who has an "I am elite" type of personality. What they are doing has nothing to do with respect, and what they are intent on is the servitude to them from those who they interact with. This is not *respect*, it is **disrespect**, and is an utter violation of the expectations of those around them. When arrogance exists in a marriage in this way, it will be seen by the children and perpetrated on to the children, and then it will be mimicked by the children right back to the parents. If it is only one parent who is arrogant and disrespectful, it still has the same effect on the children, but often the children will also show the same disrespect against the spouse-parent who is innocent.

"Disrespect" means: *apart* from *respect*, it is *non* respect or to not look or consider. It may seem harsh to say this, but in truth, by accurate definition, disrespect is *hell* because it *conceals*; hell means to conceal. Disrespect never allows honest and full opposition to the disrespecter's thoughts. This is done because the disrespecter is afraid.

Arrogant people are always disrespectful and are afraid to have their own thoughts challenged. They are afraid that they will be proven wrong in their thinking because deep-down they can tell that they do not fully understand their own position. All of the emotional investment that they placed in their false belief will suddenly be stripped away if they are challenged, leaving them feeling naked and foolish for believing wrongly. This is why many of us fight so vehemently for our opinions and conclusions, even if those opinions and conclusions are incorrect.

When you take from others in this way, you adopt disrespecting others as a primary method of communication—You are dooming yourself to error. Both your spouse and your children have much to offer you in knowledge and understanding. To refuse their collective wisdom is to choose to be a fool. Respect your spouse, your children, and others, and then your children will do the same back towards you.

Words are Cheap

If by this time you have not realized that you are a repeat violator, then you are either already an awesome person, or you are incredibly blind and will likely suffer the consequences of your stubbornness until you choose to change. If you have come to the realization that your offenses are vast and wide, then now is a good time to change your behavior. The choice is yours and yours alone!

The best part about life is that it is not so much what you did yesterday that matters as much as it is what you are doing right now and what you will choose to do tomorrow that matters. Continuing in bad behavior will get you a whole lot more of what you are currently trying to escape from. Holding on to such an arrogant attitude keeps a person bound in their own chains of misery until they change their thinking.

If someone only verbally states that they have changed it is meaningless. To improve your marriage and bring harmony to your children and family, you and your spouse *must* make changes. Change must be shown in *all* actions, words, attitude, and in the person's thinking. Apologizing to others is a good start, but it too can become an offense to others if, after the apology is made, the person proceeds to continue in their offensive behavior, thus making their apology a lie and an insult to the other person or people.

If you truly want to apologize, then change your actions *first*, *and then* offer the words of a true apology. Offering words of apology without changing your actions amounts to a lie, and that makes the one doing the false apology the liar and very offensive. Children have this amazing ability to learn from and repeat our behaviors, good or bad. We can only expect them to do to us and their own spouses and children what we teach and do to them. This applies to the bad things as well as the good things. Changing first, *and then* apologizing and explaining your errors to them will alleviate much future pain for everyone. Make your changes sooner rather than later and in doing so you will change your future for the better. Only when changing our course of life by embracing truth can we accomplish true and lasting success in life. Once we have made these changes then we can offer true and meaningful confessions of apologies for our past offenses as we realize each of them.

Signs of a Good Foundation

When our lives are corrupted from a void of truth, our truth is replaced with a great deal of inaccurate thinking that becomes apparent to others as they see our shortcomings. Often, those around us have been passionate enough about us to endure our bad and foolish behavior.

An apology is more than saying, "I am sorry." A true apology is being able to convey exactly what it is that we are sorry for. An apology to our spouse and our children is our admission about what we have done wrong to them—it is our admission of our offenses against them and it is our promise to no longer offend them. Our recognition of what we have done wrong and the subsequent admission of our violations are only the blueprints for our new foundation. The blueprints or instructions for a foundation are worthless until they are *actually used*. If you don't properly repent and apologize to your spouse, then you are a fraud. If this is your case, you can change your behavior *right now*, and offer true apology for your offenses against them as you begin to realize each offense.

Using your own blueprint instructions means that you will follow the pattern laid out by your own recognition of your errors. It means that you will diligently make all efforts to no longer offend your family because you now recognize that how you had been treating them was not good. All of your actions towards them will be loving and peaceful from now on.

Understanding the terms *loving* and *peaceful* is also very important because "loving" and "peaceful" have come to be improperly understood as well. We are instructed to stand for justice. To do so, we must take a stand against violations from others. This is a delicate balance for most people to learn. When we stand against violators, we often appear as if we are making waves, and are seen as being not loving and not peaceful and are viewed as violators by the actual offenders.

Additionally, fear and hate often sneak into people's lives, and the resulting arrogance gets in the way of them being able to see themselves clear of the dangers of their own arrogance. Fear and hate become a problem when standing against a violator. A good example of this would be a policeman or a government official gone bad.

When a person comes to understand truth, it becomes physically and verbally apparent because they will no longer seek to harm or violate others. Our actions change when we choose to not violate other people. Our intentions are always reflected in our actions, even those intentions that inadvertently violate others. Imagine, with regards to your children, that you are a policeman or government official who has gone bad, and then you can more clearly understand how your negative actions are affecting your children.

When we accept these truths and remove arrogance, fear, and hate from our lives, then everything we do changes for the better. This is seen and felt by everyone around us. Our past conspirators, who had previously benefited from our violations against others, will likely angrily resist our change in direction.

When you change direction, then your children will see your new ways and they will automatically adopt this behavior over time. You must teach your children about *respect* and *truth* because if you do not, then they won't understand *why* they are behaving as they do. In turn, this lack of understanding causes them to inadvertently pass those errors on to their own children. Your children are bound to repeat your past mistakes when you fail to teach them your new way of living with the words of your mouth as well as with your actions. You can avoid being responsible for and having your children repeat your foolish errors by embracing and sharing truth with them—deliberately.

Your Family

In general, the term "family" is understood as those who are related to you through blood. While this is true, "family" extends beyond that for many people, to the extent that it is the people that you live with or are very close to. Often our birth-parents and siblings are considered "family" even after we have children of our own. But, it is really *your own* spouse and children who are your family in the possessive form—they are under *your* care.

For good or for bad, the people around you who are blood related or very close in friendship *will* affect your family. Your family (you, your spouse, and your children) and your words and examples to them are the only things of real value that you are in charge of in your life.

Your Greatest Concern is Your Family

We have been given the task of the care of our spouse and children. They are our greatest concern and we will be held responsible for our part of their safety and upbringing. There is no "out" for this responsibility. Separation and divorce will not remove the responsibility that *we chose* to take on when we married and had children, or if we are not married but still had children the same is true.

When you make the decision to give your seed to her, or to receive his seed from him, through intimate contact or through artificial insemination, then it was *you* who made a commitment to be true to that life. When you fail in guiding your children, then you fail that life—you unnecessarily fail your children.

It's time for us all to accept responsibility for our actions and stop blaming our children's problems on genetics or other "bad" kids. When you bring your children up in truth, they learn to see errors for themselves and will generally not associate with the so-called "bad kids". Since "bad" is relative to our perception of life, your children might be considered "bad" in the eyes of others, and their children might be considered "bad" in your eyes.

Many parents place the blame on other people's children for their own children going wayward, but sometimes it is our own children who are leading other children astray. We must ask ourselves in utter honesty, "Are my children influencing others for good, *or* is their influence for bad?" *Every* person has some amount of influence on others. Even the most introverted people affect others. What have *you* given to your children?

To compensate for all of the *bad* in the world, we, as parents, often over-compensate and turn our children into cynics. We turn them into people who have no sense, we turn them into dogs. We teach them to not trust anyone, and in our concern for their safety and in our blindness, we destroy our own children. We press them to seek higher education for a job that they have not chosen, and we send them off to be educated by people who often do not reflect our own understanding of life or our own values.

Many of us even send our infants away to be raised by others at daycare for the sake of a few extra dollars we can earn, or for the insurance policy we can get. This makes no sense! Ask yourself, "Is it worth it?" Of course not everyone has a choice. For instance, a single mother may be trapped in this sort of financial muck and will have to work when her children are young. But it should be made clear that if the principles discussed in this book would have been instilled in her by her parents when she was young, then it would not have become an issue for her to begin with. If you're a single mother who is stuck in a situation similar to this, then remember this as you teach your own children, so that they can avoid what happened to you. For women whose husbands died it is an entirely different story.

No extra money or insurance can bring you lasting joy. No higher education can bring your children lasting joy. People who have been educated and believe this lie, have become *products* who are expendable and will lose their jobs at some point later in life, only to find that they are now no longer "employable". Then that golden morsel of "education" (that gave them their false prestigious degree) gains them little because they lacked the most important element of life—Truth!

Your family (your children and your spouse), are all that should matter to you. They, along with your words and examples to them, are the only lasting tangible elements in your life. Your children will reproduce, and their children will, in turn, reproduce. When you fail yourself, you fail your spouse, and when you fail your spouse, you fail your children. If you failed your children, you have likely failed your grandchildren. And on it goes through each subsequent generation. Your own spouse and children are the most important elements of your life as a family. Treat them as such, and teach them to be desirous of truth. Doing so pays you and your spouse great dividends throughout your marriage and beyond.

Always Encourage Questions

Teaching children to be ambitious can be a difficult task. The later in their life that you do it, then the more difficult it is. Some children acquire ambition on their own, but many need the guidance of their parents because ambition is partly a taught behavior. So how do we teach ambition?

Ambition starts with you! Children look to their parents for everything, and you are all that they know. This means that if you sit on the sofa watching football or talk shows and eating junk-food all day, then they will see this example and will likely repeat the behavior. Sometimes parents need to push their children forward in much the same way as a mother bird might push the baby bird out of the nest.

When you talk to your children, on occasion tell them a good story about your workday with passion and excitement. Show them ambition in your work. Show them in the way that you talk to them. And show them in the way that you talk to and about others. If you are an ambitious person, chances are that your children will also be ambitious if you allow them to be. "Allow them?" you may ask.

Yes. As parents, we often work so hard that we lose sight of our family. We hand everything to our children on a silver platter, thus, not allowing them to experience the need to quest for something on their own.

In giving them everything, we often rob them of desire, ambition, and an understanding of the worth of working. Wealthy people often will not give their children a large inheritance. Why is this? It's because they understand and have seen what typically results from having everything automatically given to someone. It usually destroys people—but why?

In withholding somewhat from children, you can teach them to find their own way and earn a living rather than them living off of what you have created. But this is no guarantee that they will be well-balanced humans when they are adults. Often, wealthy children turn out just as badly as the parents feared might happen even when the parents decided to not to offer much of an inheritance to them. Money is not the problem and money is not a bad thing. The problem with money is that it has a tendency to hide bad parenting.

If giving money does not work, and withholding money does not work, then how are we to instill desire into our children?

Children must see that your desire is *real*. Money is not real, it is a fleeting nuisance with regard to family. Money is merely a marker for your time. Money is handy and it makes life more comfortable, but money is not the make-or-break in life even though many wrongly believe that it is. It is *truth* that your children will recognize and emulate that gives people true ambition. If you don't teach them truth, then expect divorce, despair, and doom at some point in your blood-line. So much more control than we realize is in our own hands.

Encourage your children's questions. Many people become frustrated with their children when the children ask, "Why Mommy? Why Daddy...? why... why... why...?" The frustration might be because the child is doing this incessantly, but just as often, parents become frustrated because they don't have answers to the questions that their children are asking.

You encourage questions by answering questions. Do not lie to your children! If you frequently lie to your children, then you will pay a price for lying by having children who are blindly susceptible to believing lies and eventually become cynical because they innocently believed those lies.

Be patient and never lie to your children, lying is simply unnecessary. We often take this as meaning that we must explain everything to them. Children are happy with the simple, but true, answers that fit their age.

We often end up struggling with, and ultimately lying about, common questions such as, "Where do babies come from?" When this is asked, simply answering "from mommies" is often enough of an answer for the child. Sometime later, the next question typically is, "How did the baby get in there?" This is a good time to explain that babies grow in there when a mommy and daddy decide that they want to have a baby. And usually that is enough of an answer for them.

Children are easily distracted from the part you feel that they are not yet ready to hear. Too many parents begin making up ridiculous lies to tell their children about "where do babies come from?" and other such subjects, and in doing so, they teach them how to believe lies.

Answering questions in a certain way can reduce follow-up questions. For instance, saying that daddy planted a special seed in mommy might provoke the question "How did daddy get the seed *in* mommy?" Where, simply saying "Daddy gave mommy a special seed" is far less likely to provoke that question. Or simply saying "Mommy and Daddy wanted a baby" will often suffice. We offer too much information but don't realize that we are doing so. It is the extra *un-requested* information that typically invokes the follow-up questions that make us so uncomfortable that we are willing to lie to our own children. In this case it was the fact that the child was told that the seed was "planted in" rather than "given to." And further it was the fact that the term "seed" was mentioned rather than a desire being expressed.

Be aware that this seemingly insignificant difference in your answer allows you to answer their questions *without* lying. And with regard to lying, it is important to say things such as "gave *special* seed" so as not to be putting yourself in a position that they are picturing a planting a *plant* seed if you choose to use the seed explanation. But even if they do picture a plant seed, at least you have still told them only what is true. Yet, how much better to not get into the seed substance part at all at too early of an age. Oh the troubles we would save in life if we all only chose our words with care.

As parents, we need to teach our children the truth about life— as they are prepared to receive the information based on their ages, but we should not lie to them in the meantime. We need to teach them how to detect truth. This is easier once you learn how to do it for yourself. If you were lied to as a child, then you likely inadvertently learned how to lie to your children, but did not specifically realize that you did so. It might sound harsh to call these minor deceptions "lies", but a lie is a lie.

Protect your children from lies; not from the truth. Children are your most important concern, do not lie to them. Instead, encourage them to ask questions by allowing them to hear the whole truth as they are ready to receive it as they age.

The Four Cornerstones of Family Life

There are four cornerstones to a great life. Just because you have one of them in place does not mean that all four will automatically be there for you. In fact, if any one of these is missing it can make the other three almost useless.

The four cornerstones are yourself, your marriage or relationship, your family and friends, and your prayer life.

All of the cornerstones have equally important aspects. They are all very different, but they all overlap. Understanding that these cornerstones exist is the beginning to securing joy in your life.

In this book, *Red Hot Marriage*, we are addressing the very important cornerstone of relationship, but if we do not get the other parts correct in our life, then our marriages will still suffer greatly. There are three other books in addition to this one that deal with each of these cornerstones of life that you have probably noticed mentioned. When you have each of these cornerstones in order in your life, then your life can, and will, go more smoothly and will be very joyous!

The first of these cornerstone books is *Hot Water*. Hot Water deals with our own self and how we come to be the way that we are. The second book, the one you are reading right now, is called *Red Hot Marriage*. The third cornerstone book is *Strong Family*, which details how to strengthen your family and create wonderful children. And the fourth cornerstone book is called *Understanding Prayer*.

Misinterpreted scientific information discovered over the last couple of centuries has caused many people a great deal of doubt, and this has led many away from prayer and the Creator. To have your prayers reliably answered you need to understand prayer and how and why it works.

Properly establishing these cornerstones is the only way to experience true joy throughout your life in all areas of your life. Without having these four cornerstones in place in your life, you are sure to suffer self-doubt, strife, and will greatly lack success in most everything that you do.

Wherever you see true success in your life or anyone else's life you will see the corresponding cornerstones in place. Examine these books to learn more as they each tackle one of the all-important cornerstones of a sound, robust, and joyful life.

Regardless of the way you choose to go about obtaining your cornerstones, getting all four cornerstones properly placed in your life will make a very big difference to yourself, your spouse, your children, your future, and your marriage.

Chapter 22

Passion is The Key to Your Joy

All that we do in life has no meaning if we have no passion for it. It is as simple as it sounds—our passion is the meaning of what we do. In other words, if we have no passion for something, then, in general, we do not care about it. And if we don't care about it, then it has no significance to us and is meaningless to us.

Passion is the key for everything. People even use negative passions to live their lives. Negative passion is no less passionate than positive passion, and often it is even more intense than positive passion. This sad but true phenomenon drives many of us to do amazing things, and when hatred is involved we do cruel things as well. It would be better for us, and far more productive, if we did our passionate works from a positive perspective. We experience this sort of negative passion when we argue with our spouses.

Negative passion is usually competitive and tries to subdue others, where positive passion will strive to excel no matter what negativity comes our way. Positive passion is not dependent upon beating or defeating your spouse. There are two types of passion: *Hateful* passion and *Joyful* passion. Hateful passion always seeks to harm, to bring low, or to destroy. Where joyful passion always seeks to build up and increase. Passion is why, in the Bible, it says, "I desire that you were either hot or cold, but since you are lukewarm I will spew you out of my mouth." "Lukewarm", meaning the people lacked passion. The most boring people to be around are those who lack passion. They will sit still, seeming to care of nothing, doing nothing, and improving nothing. All too often, passionless people become parasites to society by consuming more than they contribute. If complacent people are not just plain old lazy, then they're usually afraid to seek anything because they have fear, and they are afraid because they don't want to see the answer that they *think* they will find in any quest they might have otherwise undertaken. In other words, they fear failure. Doing this in our marriages will not bring any amount of joy to our marriage.

The Trouble With Complacency

Complacency is a danger, and it is a very deep marriage rut that we get stuck in. We live, we work, we eat, and we sleep, repeating the same routine over and over, and in doing so, we often forfeit our *real* passions. Our Creator, our spouse, and our children should be our primary passions. After those first three, the work of your hands is next in line, but often it is the work of our hands that gets top billing. When we place our work before our Creator, our spouse, and our children, then we get bogged down by all that is *not* important. You can think of it in this way: Your family is your primary job and they should be your primary passion besides the Creator.

As adults, we take a job just to make ends meet, but often that job has nothing to do with our real passion for the kind of work that we would actually prefer to do. When we work at a job that we do not have passion for, then we must put forth more effort to do that which we were not Created for. We spend our time doing something that we typically hate and then we complain about it. This leads to a great deal of frustration for us. Working in the wrong job steals away our focus from our family, and places that focus onto the problems we incur at the job we hate, which we chose in order to pay the bills and feed the *family* that we love. Our family is why we took the job to begin with.

When we move our focus from our Creator, spouse, and children, then *they all* become nothing more than background noise in our perception, and thus, we become complacent with regard to them. In doing so, all of our energy goes into a job that leaves our family wanting, and consumes the best years of our lives.

After many years of this misdirected focus with the wrong job or maybe better stated as a job we really do not like, our complacency towards our family rubs off on them and then they begin to ignore *us* as well. All of this complacency ends up being a learned and deeply embedded method of life. Our complacency permeates everything else in our lives except the one place that we waste excessive energy—the wrong job. Seldom will a hated job pay you or your family back in any long-term or equitable manner, other than to pay the bills and mortgage. (As a side note, you may find it interesting to know that the word "*mort*-gage" is from *mort* meaning *dead* and from *gage* meaning *wage*.)

When our spouse and children experience our complacent and lukewarm nature they will typically either jump on the bus of complacency and ride along with us, or become very frustrated with our complacency.

It is the complacent people of the world who have allowed terrorism to increase throughout the centuries. Complacency is perhaps the most dangerous weapon on earth. When an ambitious, but villainous, person wants to be in power, they will prey on the complacent people because they know that the laziness of complacency is the best way to manipulate their intended subjects.

When complacent people blindly follow their new evil leader, they strengthen the power of the villainous leader and trap themselves in the bondage of misery because of their own fear and/or laziness. It is only when people, who are good, are passionate enough to rise up and fight against the villainous leader that freedom can once again prevail. Complacency lacks truth and it is lazy and mis-focused. There is nothing good about complacency. The silence of complacency hands power to tyranny. When you are complacent in your marriage you will suffer these same misfortunes by allowing an oppressive spouse to become a tyrant.

We tend to confuse *complacency* with *contentment*. We can be passionate and still be filled to contentment with what we have and where we are in life, but with complacency, we choose to be ignorant and are self-pleased.

With marital *complacency*, we stop and sit lazily by in our lackluster way and watch as the world goes by, allowing any good or bad thing to befall us without much thought and little or no effort to change our own circumstances.

However, with *contentment*, on the other hand, we are satisfied with what we have, but will still work for an improved life. If we are satisfied and someone tries to steal away our freedom, then we will fight to stop their theft of our freedom. But with *complacency*, we accept our loss of freedom and follow our oppressor's demands. This is true about complacency whether that oppressor is our spouse or an outside person.

We cannot be passionate and complacent. Those are two utterly opposed ideas.

If You don't Look You Won't Find It

A complacent nature seldom, if ever, strives to learn more or seeks out new information. Complacent people *choose* to have a low capacity to learn and retain information. When we choose to be complacent, we choose to be stupid or stupefied.

Complacency has a tendency to cause us to be amazed at cheap magic tricks. Thus, we are choosing to believe that something physically impossible is actually occurring when it is not. This same attitude is the birthplace of idolatry. When we fall away from what is real then we fall for what is *not* real. Our often complacent nature allows us to deceive ourselves. We are Created for a purpose and with a function. And that purpose and function are *not* there so that we can believe things that are lies.

If you have a true desire to understand, then it will not take you long to unravel the illusions of a cheap magician. The problem that arises when we are complacent is that we cast away our passions. When passion is gone, we accept what we see as an amazing trick, or magic. In the end, we understand that there is something fraudulent about magic, but *we* accept it as real.

When we complacently accept what we see as if it is amazing magic, then we allow ourselves to compare that deception with what is real, and we then believe it to be the real. In doing so, we lose sight of truth, and then things like the belief that humans are of little value creep into our hearts and minds, causing us to begin to believe the naturalist theory, and that our sustenance only comes from the earth. These evidences that we have decided to accept as "true" about our origins are severely misinterpreted. And when we allow this sort of thinking into our lives in the *science* versus *Creator* dilemma, then we very likely are doing it in *most* other areas of our lives as well.

Our complacent view is small-minded and self-centered. It focuses on our own pleasures and we become contented with that pleasure. Our dangerous complacency then stops us from being able to ask questions. The longer we dwell within complacency, then the more intricately woven into our being it becomes. When we allow this in our marriages, then we pass our complacent lack of passion on to our children, on to our spouse, and on to others around us.

In the end, the result of complacency is that we lose our ability to ask the right questions. Our quest to *seek* is our true passion. Without our quest to seek, there is nothing good that would exist, and all things in our world would be chaos until humanity is utterly destroyed. There would be no shelter, there would be no children, and there would be no spouse. Our quest to seek is everything to us—it is truth! But, just because we have passion does not necessarily mean that we have truth.

If You Refuse to Look, You Will Never Find It

There are many of us who are "passionate" about politics, religion, and human rights. But we face a dangerous problem with this when we have any level of complacency within us. Sometimes complacency is a deliberate action.

Religion, politics, and freedom are the most prominently passionate topics. When we are fully complacent, we often tune out and end up ignoring the discussion at hand. Thus, we *learn* nothing, *advance* nothing, and *do* nothing. When we are even partially complacent, we are often deliberately ignorant. Politically, this is demonstrated on a regular basis and is highly prominent in society, and has been so for thousands of years.

What we tend to do is to choose a particular path of belief, and when we think that we have learned all that we can about that path in life, we invest all that we have in that path because it is our passion. When someone opposes us, then from fear of being exposed that our way is incorrect, we vehemently debate them on the subject. This is prominent in political, religious, and naturalist views, and it filters into our marriages.

When we're passionate, our passion shows through and is often admired by those who are complacent. It seems that the louder we shout and the more "educated" about our case we pretend to be, then the more it attracts complacent people. They are impressed by our passion even when we are entirely wrong. If we passionately discuss what we believe to be the horrible behavior of our spouse it will almost always persuade people to our side of the problem. This is often true whether or not you are correct or accurate in your complaints against your spouse.

The more often and the louder we make our deceptively crafted points, the more convincing our argument appears to be. When we manipulate facts, we do it with an agenda to serve ourselves. Then, when challenged, we are unable to adequately defend our well-crafted, but poorly-backed, beliefs and choices. At that point, we attempt to defend our incorrect position either by resorting to insult and mockery, or by attempting all-out destruction of our opponent—in the case of marriage, that "opponent" happens to be our spouse. When you are wrong, you can hold onto your erred belief and be the only person alive on earth and have no one left to disagree with you, but you will *still* be wrong. When we have this sort of misguided passion in our own marriages, we suffer from our own actions, and we torment our spouse and ourselves in the process.

A truly passionate person will hear and fully consider *all* of the facts from their spouse, *and then* base their conclusions upon all of the facts. When we are truly passionate, we will maintain an open conclusion, thus allowing us to obtain even more information as it becomes available to us—we will invite it. When we are truly passionate, even though any forthcoming information may jeopardize our current conclusion and all that we currently know, we are still pleased to receive the information so that we can believe correctly. This is true passion!

True passion does not fear to correct its own errors or fear to have those errors challenged or corrected by others. In fact, true passion revels in the opportunity to do so. True passion speculates only enough to get a view on what might be, and then observes until after the truth appears about the speculation. When we argue with our spouse and don't have a solid foundation for our viewpoint, then we tend to get louder and more aggressive in impressing our point upon them. But when we have true passion we will remain silent as we hear them out completely in an effort to seek and discover what they think, and how they feel about the situation.

Complacency refuses to look. When you have chosen a path in life of being complacent by not seeking, then it is nearly impossible to *find* something even if it sits right before your eyes. How many times have you driven down the streets of the city and not noticed certain vehicles, yet when you buy a new red car, you quickly find that you frequently see many vehicles the same color as yours. That can happen with anything, clothes, hair style—anything. You drive around, and it seems that you see it everywhere once you have bought it. Why is this? Those items were there before you had your own item, so then, why did you *not* notice them before you bought yours?

When we *don't* look for something specific within our marriage problems, then we have no index of what exists. When we *seek*, then we already know what we are looking for, and our quest is to find what we seek. It is the *evidence* of the *truth* that we have the desire to find while in our quest as we seek. When we see it, we will recognize and embrace it and work to change our circumstances. It's similar to the red car effect where when you see another vehicle like *your* new vehicle, then you recognize it because you are aware. So, too, is it with problems in our marriages and also with the good things. When we see and then actually notice something, we obtain the power to properly address what we see and then correct the problem through truth and love.

Desire to Know the Mystery

What is it that we want to seek when we're passionate about something or someone? This is one of those all important questions to understand *and* to get the true answer to. One of the mysteries to a great marriage is hidden in this question. Backing up a section or two, consider *complacency* and the ramifications of it with regard to your relationship and violations.

We often have this ridiculous notion that we know our mate extremely well, when in reality we do not. In many cases, we only lump their behavior into unfair labels that we created from observing them through our own complacency.

We often say that our spouse is picky or temperamental, grouchy or moody. Sometimes it has nothing to do with us, but more often than not, it is *we* who are the cause of a great deal of our spouse's "bad" behavior.

Thinking that you even know the tip of the iceberg of your spouse is an absurd notion. Your spouse has lived a different life than you, they see things from a different point of view than you, and they understand things differently than you. It is not possible to ever entirely know your spouse, or anyone else for that matter. You will need to spend the rest of your life getting to know your spouse and then you still will not completely know them. While you will know them well by the time you are both gone, you will not know them *completely*. Even if you try to know them all of your married days, it still is not possible to ever know them *completely*. If anyone thinks that they can ever know their spouse completely, then they have chosen to be a fool; this is especially obvious when we realize the most of us do not even fully understand our own selves.

This is the beauty of a marriage, and it is often entirely missed. The quest to know your mate is what attracted you to each other when you began courting. Your quest is what gave you that wonderful feeling of complete satisfaction in those early days of dating. It wasn't already knowing your mate that was a thrill, it was your passion to *discover* your mate that was exciting, and the discovery need not ever end.

The intrigue you had towards your mate attracted them to you and you to them. And the intrigue they had towards you attracted you to them and them to you. It is a match made in heaven! There is usually something that sparks this truth to seek the light of your mate; things such as looks or some common passion are usually the initiator of your early quests for one another.

Your desire to know the mysteries of your spouse and your Creator is the most important thing in your world. Nothing compares to it and nothing surpasses it. Our world thrives on this very premise—to know and to understand.

When we seek to know something, we ultimately want the truth about it, and no substitutes will be suitable or acceptable in any way. We should only ever accept and receive utter and total trueness. Our desire to know the mysteries of our spouse are what gets overshadowed by the real "background noise" in life.

The *real* background noise makes our spouse and children appear to be the background noise—but they are not! We must keep our desire set upon knowing our true spouse, and when we begin to know them, we begin to recognize that which we quest for within them. Share yourself and your light with your spouse just as you did when you first met, and desire to know the mysteries of your spouse, now and in the future, so that you see their light as well.

Don't Do This, Don't Do That

There are many wrongs that occur in life, and these wrongs come in at us from all angles and from most people. We suffer these wrongs and endure them unto utter frustration.

In our frustration, we will deliver our message to our offender only to find that we have offended them via our frustration and poor delivery. Yet, when the same is done to us, we behave similarly towards them. However, when we finally chose to seek the truth, then we joyfully accept any *justified* criticisms and the accompanying justified pain.

We often get or give instructions from or to others, "Don't do this" and "Don't do that". Because we have been blinded, we need our instructions to be told to us. We each should quickly set our wrongs aside and then focus on being better than we previously were.

If we have not had the greatest of environments in our youth, then typically, we have been trained to fixate on our wrongs (the "don't do this or that"). Thus, we focus on the immediate correction period rather than focusing on the future. A classic example of this is the laws of the Bible given to the people. The laws became a point of great contention and still are to this day. The people focused on the laws and on debating about what was meant by them rather than abiding by those laws. These debates and battles still rage on today in many religious circles and negatively affect many marriages. Often, one spouse will attack their mate and shame them for making an error, instead of working with them in a kind and loving manner while teaching them a better way. We add to the problem when we do wrong. We often mistake someone correcting us for them trying to unjustly shame us.

Being legalistic and imposing many relationship rules in your marriage is a very common and destructive behavior, and specifically in marriages it is devastatingly destructive. Many books have been written that lay out all of the dos and don'ts for a happy marriage. When we read these books in a selfish manner, then a litany of rules is laid down for us and our spouse to follow and abide by.

Rules place our focus on what is being done wrong. Initially, this is fine because people do need to become aware of what they are doing wrong, but it should end quickly and then the focus should be placed on the future. It might seem simple, but it is very difficult to get this point to be properly received and understood by others. From our youth on, we are frequently taught to obey and "do as we are told" and to believe what we are told. We are taught complacency.

The horrible practice of complacency has been perpetrated on all of humanity from the beginning, and has infected each subsequent generation. When we don't understand this, then any questioning of the instructions or rules is utterly unwelcome by our taskmaster. Our complacent nature not only stops us from learning new and wonderful truths, it also stops *others* from learning the new and wonderful truths.

The rules of law are a brief index that should not even exist, but they need to exist because our complacency blinds us from seeing the obvious. Think of such rules as a wakeup call.

A functional railroad crossing signal is there to tell you that a train is coming. You are not supposed to focus on the signal. The signal is only a warning about the potential danger, it is to alert you of the coming train. It is the train that we must respect. If we do not respect the train, then it will harm us when it hits us, which could possibly also derail the train and cause harm to many others who are passengers on the train or are near the train.

If you sit in your car parked on the tracks arguing about the meaning of the signals in your marriage and who should follow that signal or rule, then you are going to be overcome by the train and are likely to be destroyed because you failed to address and *follow* **what** *the rule was for.*

Seeking to know your spouse will be far more passionate than focusing on rules from books that may be helpful in the short term. Focus on tomorrow and focus on your spouse. Seeking to know your spouse means to know both the physical and the spirit or inner person.

Ask Questions

When you have true passion for something, you will want to know all that there is to know about it, and you will often keep up your quest to do so.

The quest to know all about a hobby is why most hobbies often fall by the wayside over time. There's nothing wrong with a hobby, but there is often an emptiness felt with hobbies once the quest is completed. This emptiness does not make it bad or wrong. It's just that the completion of the quest is the reason for your sudden lack of interest. Once we have exhausted our quest of something, in our heart we tend to lose interest in it—including people.

When we desire to know someone, such as our spouse, we seek to understand them and want to know all that we can about them. When we build a wall around ourselves, regardless of its justification, then those who seek to know us are hindered from being able to get their answers about us. This makes it seem, to them, that they know everything about us, and thus, they lose interest in us. Remember, we can never know everything about another person, including our spouse.

While the protective walls that we build around us have usually been built for a good reason, at the same time the walls also become our downfall and our prison. When we fear to have our spouse ask us questions that penetrate our walls, we cheat ourselves and our spouses out of their passionate purpose.

There are likely to be people in your life that your walls are meant to keep out, and it may be well to do so. But if the person that your walls are trying to keep out happens to be your spouse, then you need to reconsider who gets the keys to your city gate.

Not allowing your spouse to ask questions, or fearing to ask your spouse questions because of their own defense wall, is *not* good for your marriage. Also, if you are afraid to ask questions because of your own walls, then that is not good for your marriage either.

Both people in the couple should feel safe enough to be free to ask their spouse any imaginable question and not be attacked, mocked, belittled, or concerned that the question will be made public. Your spouse has a right to know your heart. If you refuse them that right, then you have stolen a great deal from them, and you can likely expect that they will eventually find satisfaction elsewhere or in another form. But your spouse should respect your right for those things to remain private, and the same goes for *their* thoughts.

Ask questions and allow questions to be asked with regard to your spouse and your marriage. In a friendship with outsiders it's not a problem to refuse answering an inappropriate question. But, in a marriage, there are no inappropriate questions, though there may be inappropriate demands or requests.

Within a marriage, spouses are privy to each other's hearts. But, when this is violated by one spouse, then the other spouse feels the right to do the same and often will. The burden of reconciliation should be held by the violating spouse. If reconciliation takes too long to begin, then the other spouse may well decide that reconciliation is no longer an option; although, with *true* repentance this is seldom the case. While the burden of reconciliation *should* rest on the initiator of the violations, in reality, the burden of correction rests on the spouse who first becomes aware of what is occurring. This is usually the person who is being violated. Yes, it's *unfair*, but it is the reality.

How do we Get People to Ask Questions?

The question of questions: How do we Get People to Ask Questions? This is easy with little children. You simply kindly answer their questions and then more questions will arise. You teach children to ask by answering. But with adults it's much more difficult of a task due to our well-fortified walls that we have constructed throughout our lifetimes.

This question is essentially, How do you get someone to be interested in something? Or, How do you get them to have passion? Good luck on this one, even the Creator could not quite pin this one down to get us to have passion about some things. Getting someone to care about something that they have no interest in cuts to the core of their complacency, selfishness, and laziness. Then how do we instill interest or curiosity in people?

Look at the word "interest". The word *interest* could be replaced with the word *concern*. *Interest* is also used when speaking of someone's *share* in, or *portion* of something. Complacency is why there has been such a tremendous departure from the Creator. We have chosen to be complacent, and we fail to seek answers because we lack our own ambition. By failing to have our own ambition we have allowed others to dictate our lives and tell us what is and what is not.

In our complacency, we have allowed others to blindly guide us and we have been incorrectly told that we have no share in the Creator and that we are not worthy. Thus, we feel that we have no interest or stake in a Creator who we are inaccurately told is imaginary, and so now we don't even bother asking questions any longer. The continuing naturalist-origin beliefs have only served to add to this problem. There is not a single one of all of mankind who cannot have a share in the Creator.

The lack of interest we feel in regard to our spouse occurs when we feel that we do not have a share in our spouse, so we end up no longer trying. This problem is intensely imbalanced and unfair when *you* have not been the cause of your spouse's complacency and lack of interest. Understanding that we all have a share in our Creator also helps us understand that we can have a share in other people such as our spouse.

If you have been the cause of problems, simply alter your attitude and allow *them* to know *you* by putting yourself out there for them, and then invite them in to know you. Give them a stake in you, a share of you, a reason to want to know you. Become their desire!

The passionless complacency problem becomes much more difficult when someone was taught as a child that they have no value. When we have a poor self-mentality, then seldom will we feel worthy to fully receive a share in someone else. We also don't want to give up any part of ourselves because we incorrectly believe we have little value to give, and so we want to keep it all for ourselves. When this is very deeply rooted in a spouse, then their mate will end up being as a parent to them rather than a partner in the relationship, and this will strain the marriage.

The unhealthy complacency situation is sad, yet it frequently exists. This problem goes beyond marriages and well into everyday life and readily transfers to your children. It is nearly impossible to teach those who are caught in this trap when the example was set by their parents as their parents were raising them. Those who are trapped, simply do not see it as a problem, but it will ultimately destroy them regardless. And often, it destroys their children if no corrective action is taken.

When, due to our parents' example, we have come to be caught in this trap, then it is mostly invisible to us and goes unnoticed.

When we do choose to take a step toward claiming our rightful place, then we are often slapped down by someone, causing us to resume our lowly position and thinking. The cornerstone book *Hot Water* explains this in detail. When attempts are made to explain this problem to someone who is in this situation, they usually look at you in utter confusion or in utter contempt, and, typically, they reject your information, rendering themselves un-teachable.

Only a grand amount of patience and perseverance can win the battle. In the meantime, you need to decide to either tough it out, or leave. A spouse's awakening must be of their own making. It is not possible to force this sort of thing because desire is a personal *choice* that each of us makes, and no one can force us have desire—not even the Creator. We can drop hints, or even attempt to explain, but often that ends in strife for us. Patience, loving-kindness, and prayers for their awakening are all that you can do. The rest is up to them. You getting frustrated and then angry will not make things better, and it often only serves to make matters worse.

If you are coming to the realization that *you* are one who has no desire, then realize that you have a stake in your Creator, and in your spouse, and in your family. When you fail to have desire, then you risk permanently losing your stake in all of them. As it is with the Creator, so too, is it with our families and our marriages. There are no free-passes in life; eventually your lack of passion will catch up with you and destroy you, and it will destroy those around you as well—if they allow it to.

It is at our point of awakening where we often get stuck because we attempt to fake our passion, and faking passion is not technically possible. We can offer cheap imitations of our feelings, but faking feelings of passion in this way amounts to prostitution or harlotry. It is empty and transparent and they who wonder why people distance themselves from them can take their hint to a solution here. When we fake things, then we are doing something that we don't really want to do in order to get something that we think want in return. In doing so, we are cheating our spouse out of the robust love that they deserve.

Importance of Your Thoughts in Your Marriage

Choosing to be passionate is not something that comes easy to most of us. Typically, we are either passionate about life, or we are not. Some of us are only passionate about one or two things if anything at all. At one point, you were probably passionate about your spouse. If not, then my condolences to them.

True passion comes from the way that you use your mind and body. It's something that you do as habit. True passion is the manner in which you approach life. And true passion can be taught to children in the rare cases where it is not natural in them.

Some people, for whatever the reason, are naturally highly inquisitive. Whether their inquisitiveness is entirely natural, or only taught, is not fully known or understood. The idea of natural passion or inquisitiveness has been the underlying substance of much thought and discussion for thousands of years. It seems unfair if someone automatically has a passionate nature about them, when another person is rather stagnant and without desire or ambition about their marriage.

A lack of passionate desire very well may be an attribute that is partially passed through spirit at conception, and then compounded through learning by example after the child's birth takes place. This seemingly unfair situation is in fact, very unfair to a child, and is discussed in-depth in the cornerstone book *Strong Family*. However, rightfully labeling it as "unfair" will do nothing to change the situation for that person other than to identify the problem. In the end, it all comes down to a choice—your choice! Even if you had a poor upbringing, *you* get to choose how you will live the rest of your life. And how you choose to live, profoundly affects your marriage.

This is better understood from a perspective of assuming that the Creator *does* exist. Recall the story in the Bible about the woman who gave her last two bits; she was considered to have given more than all the rest even though it is only two bits. In this way, so too, is one who has been given little ambition and rises up to offer all the ambition that they can in order to come to know and understand their spouse. When you rise up and truly offer something from your heart and of your own free will to your spouse, it will be highly valued by them, as long as you have not already irreparably damaged your union.

It is promised by the Creator that if, with all of our heart, we give an offering that is pure and free from deceit that it will come back to us many times over. It is *you* who must make the first move. It is *you* who must decide to passionately offer the little passion that you do have to your spouse, and then to offer it with love and truth and anticipation so that it will come back to you abundantly from your spouse.

When you fail to utilize your *true* passion, you are at risk of forfeiting everything in your life, including your health, marriage, and life itself.

Your Brain

Many people get married and probably don't ever think about seventy years from now. We meet our spouse-to-be and court them for about a year or two, and then we get married and have children, work our job, pay for our house, get old, and then die at an average age of about seventy-eight years old. As you age, you will be dealing with the health of yourself and your spouse. It's a lie to believe that you must get decrepit and senile and then wind down in a painful demise and die at the age of seventy-eight.

Since at least the end of the eighteenth century people have been looking at life from a personally and physically very dangerous perspective, but in reality, this has likely been going on since the dawn of man. We have placed our trust in the wrong hands. Too many of us are looking for that magic pill that has been the quest of man since the early 1900s. And many people believed, and still believe, that they have found those pills near the end of the twentieth century and into the twenty-first century.

Since the dawn of time there has been an understanding that the brain and the less tangible mind are somehow linked. Knowledge on this topic has come and gone over time, but the naturalist ape-to-man perspective has served to destroy a great deal of understanding about our brains' connection to our souls. Yet at the same time, that futile naturalist quest to prove something that is not completely accurate has allowed us to uncover a wealth of truths about the human mind and brain.

Throughout history, the importance of the way in which we think, or use our minds, has been central in understanding our bodies and the health of those bodies. Since the advent of our highly sensitive electronic lab equipment, we have been given the wonderful opportunity to see in the brain *while* it is doing its purpose of working and thinking.

There's relatively little known about the brain, and much more insight is yet to come on the subject of the brain-to-mind connection. And there will always be much more to come no matter how much we learn. Taking care of your mind *now*, while both of you are relatively young, will greatly assist you when you are older, and might even eliminate the grief-filled downward spiral of dementia that far too many couples suffer from in their later years.

There are many tests being done to see the brain's reaction when partaking in various mental tasks or exercises. One prominent area in the brain that seems to react with particular types of mental usage is a small inner part of the brain that is low and central in location. Recordings of brain images and activity have been made while people were doing various thought exercises and it is clear that during certain types of activities that this area was highly active as were other parts of the brain. This in itself may not mean much or seem to prove much, but when we consider that those who have certain degenerative mental complications, such as dementia, seem to have degraded brain structure, then we must take a serious look at it this.

In tests, the subjects' amygdalae were activated during vigilance and self-vigilance, or meditation (prayer and self-reflection), and when witnessing acts of kindness. This may well be an indication that if we pray, then our amygdala will activate and stay healthy. But what is equally important is that when we have truth and true love for our mate, and our minds are void of all malice and lies, then it may well be that our minds will be strong for many more years than when we are mean at heart. It is important to note here that just because you outwardly appear to be loving and not malicious, does not mean that your heart isn't feeling mean and malicious inside of you. Check your attitude carefully within yourself, rather than using only your outward actions to gauge your life with.

Our scientific community has a tendency to be blinded by the same complacency spoken of a few sections back. The brain is often blamed for the problems that are occurring in the mentally ailing patient, rather than searching for the real reason that the brain is deteriorating.

Faking your prayers, your vigilance, your meditation, or your love for your spouse and others, will not make the deterioration to your brain stop or go away. Your vigilance must be *real*—it must be *true*—and it must be *passionate!* The way you think is not determined by your brain. Rather, your brain is determined by the way you think. A brain without passion will experience atrophy and *you* will be left dealing with it in a matter of decades. This choice is in your heart. You cannot escape it with any amount of reasoning and you will be rewarded for the contents of your own heart. This reward may very well come to you when you are alive on this Earth and the "reward" will be equal to what is in your heart. If you are filled with malice for your spouse and others, then expect a bad future. But if you fill your heart with only truth, love, and love for your spouse and family, then expect a good future.

What we think and say has obvious effects on marriage, and usually those effects are noticed quickly, like when you say something mean or stupid to your spouse, or they to you. But our mind is also of immense power with regard to our bodies, our health, and our longevity. Some people take the mind-over-body idea too far, and others refuse take it far enough. To better understand what is good or bad for our bodies, we need to look at what is good or bad for our minds. Understanding this requires the single leap of faith spoken of earlier, *the decision*—which is that instantaneous point in time where you have made the choice to understand with open heart and mind and embrace Truth—the *what is*. Not only will doing this enhance your marriage and life in general, but it will also enhance your health. The very same health that you will, or will not, need to deal with when you and your spouse are well along in years.

When you understand that you have been Created, then you're able to detect *purpose*. Without this understanding you have little chance of ever truly grasping *what **IS***.

While it's true that you must realize that you were Created, this is no guarantee that you will use your mind correctly for its intended purpose, especially with regard to your spouse. We can still lie to ourselves by believing things that are not true about the body, and expect more from it than it was designed for. But such self-deception takes its toll on us by causing us to take wrong action with regard to the care of our bodies, thus, abusing it outside of its intended purpose.

Alternately, when we do not properly understand our body, and our expectation falls short of its abilities, then we will also err in our judgment with regard to our body and risk its atrophy. Both of these are key reasons that much disease exists in our society. Our thinking affects more than most people and science are willing to admit or want to know. We like to think only in superficial concrete terms where we can immediately see the result of our actions, but that is not how things really work underneath it all.

Your mind is the controller of your human body and that body is designed for all things good—including love. Anything less than *what is true*, is not good and will harm your body in the long run. Your body is designed to love and to desire truth. More of your being is wrapped up in your relationship with your spouse than you will ever realize. When you have irrational anomalies (lies and non-truths) in your marriage life, then you are impacting your body in ways so negative that you have likely never imagined them possible.

Accepting or believing things that are not true, abuses your design and harms your body. This ultra-simplistic view is so base, that to deny it is choosing to be deliberately ignorant of the evidence that we all experience every single day.

Our minds—those things that we utilize in order to think and wonder—causes our brains to create reactions. And these reactions cause chemical chain reactions throughout our entire body all during our life, thus, causing all of our physical functions, both inner and outer, to be affected. Negativity brings on more negativity, and it is a choice we each make on our own. The tit-for-tat we've been referring to causes this to become worse in many marriages.

The only part that is in question is, what exactly is good, and what is exactly is bad for the body. There is no question as to whether or not these chemical reactions occur. As a couple, you are a team. Failing to bring each other to the things that are good and true, and failing to have true love for your spouse, causes adverse effects on your marriage and on your health. You will have to deal with these adverse effects more and more as you grow older each day.

How to judge what is bad can be done through the use of observation. If something causes our bodies or relationships to decline, it cannot be good. But this must all be considered in a long-term view to get a proper picture of the severity of the problem you face when you fail in your passion towards your spouse. Using various body enhancing substances, such as pharmaceutical drugs or medication, can cause an increase in the body in the near-term, just as money can quickly enhance your status and appearance of harmony in your relationship, but you will pay a heavy toll in the long-term if those are what you rely upon for your health and happiness as a person and as a couple.

Additionally, if what we do with our bodies and our minds and our relationships does not add to ourselves and our marriages and to those around us, then are we really living life properly? If you are not adding to something, then you are certainly subtracting from it so long as you have the breath of life in you. Do not abuse this wonderful system that we call our bodies. And don't abuse your marriage by means of low desire and lack of love, or it will all come to ruin for you. This is not a punishment of some megalomaniacal god. No, rather, the damage to our bodies and relationships is the result of using a wonderful machine for something for which it is not intended, and the gift of a union as if it were a case of contention in a court of law.

Your desire and passion are abused when you use them for anything less than increasing your spouse, yourself, your family, and everyone around you. Any passion to any other end is ultimately bad and will negatively affect your body and all of your relationships in the long-run. In our contemporary time, we have become extremely shortsighted, just as many other cultures have become shortsighted over the years. Our shortsighted view of life tells us that we must live for today with no regard for tomorrow. We fail to imagine and forecast that we will live many decades after we first meet our spouse.

Having a shortsighted view of living only for today is a fool's way, and it will destroy your mind, your body, and your marriage in the long-run. When living only for today, you may happily have things your way for the immediate period doing things that cause long lasting consequences, but eventually your *things* will vanish and you will be left alone holding your fragile defiled bag of bones, which will be of little use to you or your spouse later in life.

When you have no desire and you are lacking passion, especially with regard to your spouse, then you have chosen to cut yourself off from all good and you will subsequently feel the physical and emotional effects. Having desire for good is good and it serves to build up your spouse and others around you, and will bring them and yourself higher.

When you desire your spouse, and they and your Creator are your passion, then you are fulfilling a great portion of the purpose of your design. Children inherently understand this fundamental function of design, and have tremendous desire and passion. But sadly, it is us adults who destroy this desire and understanding within our children just as our parents and society did to many of us. Make sure that you don't crush your spouse's desire. And especially make sure that you don't crush your children's desire. In this way, when your children get married they do not need to face unwanted and unnecessary struggles and strife. Realize that this could have happened to you while you were growing up, and then make sure to remove this crushing force from your own life and enhance the passion of others, especially your spouse. It serves to make the world a much more beautiful place!

If you would like deeper insight into the issues of the mind and body-health and how to work to avoid degenerative disease of your mind and brain, the cornerstone book, *Understanding Prayer-The Prayer How To Manual*, shares more insight on the subject.

A Woman's Role

Women: You hold the keys! Men generally will patiently wait for you to make your move in passion and desire. This places some of the burden of passion onto your shoulders. There is a role for you wives that you must fulfill in order to utilize your purpose to completion, just as there is for your husbands.

Even if it is the husband who is lacking in desire, it is still somewhat easier for a woman to fulfill her purpose than it is for a man. A husband's desire is for his Creator and for his wife, but, he must be invited into her. This places the responsibility on her shoulders and gives her all of the control. This is the control we spoke of earlier that is so often abused by women.

It is the wife that must *invite*. Ladies, if you doubt this then do a close observation of your physical body inside and out, and also research the chemistry of the fertilization of an egg and you will quickly see that a woman's body and essence is clearly designed to receive. If a husband forces himself on his wife, uninvited and unwanted, then he will be violating her.

A husband has made his offer to his wife by choosing to marry her. He can ask to come and play, but she still must invite him to do so by saying "Yes!" when he asks.

What most men really find attractive, is a woman who is sure of herself and who knows that she wants to know her husband, and who is not afraid to invite him into her physically, emotionally, mentally, *and* spiritually. Sometimes people see this as somewhat dominating, and while at times domination may be attractive to some men, this is not what I am referring to.

A wife needs *to invite* her husband, *not force* him—it is as simple as that! Her sole role is to properly invite him, and then all else will freely flow from that point, provided, of course, that her husband is willing to accept her invitation. He cannot accept anything without her asking him. She must seek him and he must be her passion. Once she has done her part, it is very likely that, in time, he will come around and respond in a very positive way. It is then the husband's task to fulfill his purpose and design by going into his wife and sharing with her. If any husbands doubt this purpose, then make an observation next time you stand in front of a mirror and you will quickly see how you were designed.

It is likely that the invitation and subsequent acceptance that I am referring to here is being understood by you as physical intimacy. While that is certainly true of the physical part, it is not what is being relayed to you now here in this section. Rather, I am referring to your *being, soul,* or *mind.* We and our bodies are "Created in the image of". Thus, we are in that body and we are like it. We should follow the obvious design by which we are made.

Both men and women can learn from one another, this is certain. Some women will say "I am from a line of strong women." or "My family is full of strong women." This typically means that they are bragging on the fact that they feel that they are in control, when in reality, they are actually *controlling.* What often follows those comments is a long path of sad tales of sorrow, strife, and discord. It is never a good thing when women try to be men, or when men try to be women. It cheats both genders out of the beauty in which they both were Created. A self-assured woman who is dignified and lives by truth need not brag about her strength, because it is obvious in her.

When a woman's desire and passion is for her husband, and she truly seeks to understand him and his Creator, then the chance that he is going to respond to his wife with a great deal of enthusiasm is very high, even if he foolishly serves another god. If he does serve another god and will not acknowledge the Creator, then he has done both himself and his wife a great disservice, and it will cost them dearly because they will both be believing things that are not true. But when a wife does her portion of the relationship well, she will be able to easily guide him to the one Creator.

Wives: Do your part and invite your husband into you, and then the rest is up to your husband.

Husbands: It is your function to offer yourself and accept your wife's invitations and then share yourself with her.

In general, a husband supplies an offering to his wife by marrying her and supporting and protecting her. Beyond that, if his wife does not invite him in she may as well be his child and be treated as such. What is the difference to him if there is nothing special for him in her? Sadly, in troubled marriages men often get more satisfaction from their children than they do from their wives. The reverse is often true as well, where the wife gets more satisfaction from her children than she does from her husband.

It's not bad that satisfaction is gotten from your children; what is sad is when the children give a husband or wife *more* satisfaction than the spouse does. You two were intended to become as *one* and you should get great satisfaction in your children *together*.

Passion is the excitement that we feel. If we have lost our ability to be excited and passionate about life, then we have doomed ourselves to a droll, mundane, lackluster life that is filled with troubles and strife—or worse, loneliness!

Ignite your passion for your spouse and partake in not only their body, but more importantly partake in their heart, mind, and soul—be passionate *with* them!

Chapter 23

What "Sex" Really Is

This is the part that some people will read this book for—the sex! Saving the best for last, I suppose. What is "sex" anyway?

Sex is perhaps the most misunderstood term: Is it a function? Is it a thing? Call it what you will, but what is it? Seldom do we stop to consider what sex is all about while in our eagerness as we explore sex with our girlfriend or boyfriend. All too often we see a person who we feel is attractive, and we lust over that person, wanting to make our score. This behavior is not exclusive to men, though men seem to be more stereotypically prominent in that regard.

Our unhealthy urge to "jump the bones" of the object of our affection, as soon as is possible, has caused many difficulties for the citizens of this world for thousands of years. Age seems to have little to do with a reasonable mind in this regard. Once puberty hits, we get stupid and practice little sense with regard to making wise sex choices.

With so many people having adopted the naturalist belief system over the past several centuries, it is surprising that we have not become more judicious in our mate selection by selecting the "fittest." So it seems that natural selection's survival of the fittest is of little or no help in our quest to understand sex. And apparently, the theory does not apply in the real world given the actual choices of mates we sometimes make.

The naturalist belief has sex as nothing more than a mere instinctive reaction or desire to reproduce strong offspring. If that is the case, then that makes many animals much smarter and wiser than most naturalists and many other people are because many animals are somewhat selective in their mating rituals, where humans on the other hand, are not very selective with regard to sex.

We use the term "sex" in two main ways. The first is with reference to our gender, as in: What is your sex (gender)—*male* or *female*? The second is in reference to the act of copulation as in: Did you have sex with him/her?

A large portion of the population suffers a great deal in regard to sex. Often, when we make the choice to follow the urge to have sex with our date within the first few dates, and we have not really gotten to know the person very well, sometimes these sexual rendezvous result in unintended pregnancies.

It Started When We Were Children

If you have experienced an unwanted pregnancy yourself, then you know the troublesome price that is usually paid in these situations. Having children in an environment that lacks the consideration of the potential conception of a child, typically, has negative effects on the child, and the behavior often is repeated by the children resulting from those unions. This in no way means that a happy life is not possible when these circumstances occur. But not having made well-thought decisions often leads to divorce and broken families unless the couple can see beyond their urges and into the hearts of one another as they move forward together in life. Thankfully, in this case they can live a joy-filled life just like any other well founded couple does.

What we call "sex"—the act that sometimes results in the conception of a child—is typically not explained to children adequately. It is not explained adequately by the churches, it is not explained adequately by the schools, and most sadly, it is not explained adequately by the children's own parents. In many cases, children learn all they know about sex from the schools and the schoolyard—is it really good that their information is lacking in this way? Other children glean their sex information from friends and society, and then school rounds them out on the subject and explains all of the different ways sex can be done, but is this really good? Even more surprising is that some children never really learn about sex at all, and they have no clue about reality when they hit puberty and decide to experiment with the sexual aspects of mating in their teen years.

Some churches, and some people, have a tendency to make sex out to be evil. This is a foolish and dangerous lie. If children are lied to about sex by the people who they trust the most, then when other information arises that proves contrary to what they were taught, the children lose trust in their mentors who lied to them or were inaccurate in what they taught about sex. When the children are a bit older and try out this new "sex" thing, they will likely think to themselves, "Hey, this feels pretty darn good!" which disproves the proposed evilness or "yuckiness" of sex that was wrongfully taught to them earlier in life.

Schools, at times, have been closer to reality with regard to sex than some in the church have been, but regardless, the education system seems to be blind to the truly important parts of intimacy. Based upon many schools' teaching, children are often left to think that they should have sex whenever they please and with whomever they please, and that everything is okay so long as they have "protected" sex. This dangerous and very foolish method of sex education is the gateway for generations of misery and disease in those families, as was made evident by the progressive escalation in unwanted pregnancies and disease in the later part of the twentieth century. Schools and the schoolyard, along with society, tend to take away our inhibitions and are the catalyst for many children to make very costly long-lasting errors. But, let us not solely blame the schools, rather, it is the parents—us—who fail to properly teach this to our own children.

With regard to children, parents are often mysteriously absent in discussions about sex. Why is this? Mostly it is because all of our lives our knowledge about sex was lacking. Then, because of our own personal sexual errors, we are often brought low, and thus, we are inhibited and afraid to properly teach our children about sex at their proper ages.

We wrongly feel like hypocrites when we consider teaching our children about sex and other things where *we* erred. We know that we should tell our children what is good and what is bad, but our own errors run contrary to what we wish to teach our children, thus we do not teach as we should be teaching because we fear being hypocritical. Being a hypocrite means you pretend you have not fallen short and then you judge and condemn others and expect *them* to live up to something that *you* yourself refuse to even try to live up to.

It is *not* hypocritical to teach your children that you made mistakes and why those mistakes were mistakes. If we do not do this, our children will experience trouble through our lies and errors, and a price will be paid by them in the long run. All of our errors can be useful lessons if we choose to properly use them as lessons for our children at the correct times and ages. Children do not need to know *all* of our foolish deeds, but we should not be afraid to teach them the right way when we ourselves have seen the light.

Adult Perspectives

When religion manipulates our marriage-sexuality through the fear of hellfire, it does a disservice to the citizens of the congregation. Having a church leader screaming about sexual immorality and hellfire only serves to inhibit our sexual understanding. While the hellfire perspective with regard to sex-abuses has a fair amount of Biblical documentational backing, the fear of hellfire should not be the reason that people choose to be good. We should choose to be good and make wise choices because it is good for us all, rather than only because "the Bible told me so".

Only when we *understand* are we able to make decisions based upon truth. Anything short of full understanding will cause our decisions to be based upon—*not* all of the facts. Physical intimacy is a private activity and it should remain so and should be reserved for *after* you have decided to be fully committed to each other in marriage because physical intimacy is sacred. This is why it is regarded as something that should not be discussed freely with others, and should be done in private with your spouse. But, this does not mean that sexuality should not be taught about by us to our children at the proper times.

Our dangerous parental, social, political, and religious approach to this topic destroys our children's ability to see sex with a healthy, decent, safe, and good perspective. When epidemic problems eventually arise with regard to sexuality from our poor approach, sexual intimacy will once again gain the respect that it deserves. But sadly, the then desperately needed respect for sexuality will come through socially uncomfortable and physically painful means.

The certainty that we will repeat history is sealed so long as we continue to repeat the mentality which caused the problems of the past. When we duplicate past thinking and behavior, we can reasonably expect that the *result* will also repeat.

What is sex? Sex is a cold term that is either misunderstood or misused. To get a grasp on "sex" we again must look at our physical design. By looking at our design, it appears that sex should only happen when we want to reproduce; at least that's how it appears when strictly adhering to natural selection. But then, why does the urge to have sex after multiple children or even after one child still occur since our naturalist desire for replication should have been fulfilled? The Creator wants us all to create within the parameters of decency.

The term "copulate" is probably a better term for the act of sex because it means to *join. Copulate* and *couple* both have the same root, and the base meaning of the root is to *bind* two together. To get a really good grasp on sex, let's revisit the purpose of design. Women are clearly designed to accept, and men are clearly designed to offer.

Since we are made "in the image of", as mentioned in the Bible, then what exactly are we *accepting* and *offering?* In the physical realm, the husband is offering his seed, and his wife is accepting that seed, but is there something more behind this? After all, we are Created in the image of the Creator, so exactly what does this act represent?

The Joys of Sharing

Our word "share" means to *shear* or *cut*, that is to say, to get your *cut*, or *part*, of something. It is to *divide* what is there and distribute those parts so that we each get a portion. The joy of sex is the sharing of yourself, meaning: when you get your part of the completed transaction, then it is your *share* (your portion) of the connection or coupling that has been made.

Reflecting on where we spoke of the violation of *hopes* and *expectations* earlier, it is clear how easily we can violate our spouse. With regard to sex, it is even easier to make such violations. Sex has come to be, perhaps, the most notorious area of manipulation in all of human history.

Manipulation through sex surpasses money, political power, religion, and just about anything else you can think of. In fact, if you take the time to study history, you will find that sex was a driving factor that has contributed to the downfall of various cultures. I am not speaking of the morality or the immorality of a culture, but rather the way in which sex has been able to lure pivotal powerful community leaders to their own demise, and how it has done the same to the citizens. But is it really sex that leads us down the road to error?

Since sex is typically only seen as a physical act, the more meaningful deeper realm is mostly ignored. It is our ignorance of this deeper realm that causes our errors with regard to sex.

Sex is easily manipulated because of its intimate nature. Intimacy is a particular time that people are supposed to really let go and submit themselves to their spouse. And many people do let go, only to be emotionally hurt through sex. This frequently happens when there is no real commitment or trust. Any violation during sex touches the deepest part of us whether we are willing to admit to this or not. We literally bare ourselves to our spouses and are completely exposed—we are vulnerable. Being violated in this situation can break the trust that you had placed in your spouse even if you are joking or playfully teasing.

If a couple is working towards the act of physical copulation, and in the process they are completely physically exposed by being naked, and one of them (stereotypically, this is the wife) covers up under the blanket or insists that the lights be turned off, so as not to be seen by their spouse, then they are likely violating their spouse. When we physically bare ourselves for our spouses, we are literally exposed, and when one spouse won't allow themself to be seen, then it is potentially a violation against their mate's reasonable expectation. We generally have an "I'll show you mine, if you show me yours" expectation with regard to sexuality.

When a spouse chooses to hide from being exposed in this way, it is usually not done as an intentional violation. It is done in a feeble attempt to avoid being violated for fear of having someone notice that they have let themselves slip physically—it is *shame* that holds them back. When a spouse won't reveal him- or herself for fear of ridicule or because of self-shame, then they clearly do not trust their spouse. Their self-focus of hiding themselves is a selfish behavior. Their concern is for their own well-being rather than for the joy of their mate. But you must make sure that your past words have not violated your spouse and broken their trust, causing them to want to hide their body or heart from you. If you find that you have violated your spouse in this way, then immediately work to reconcile the situation.

In some cases, the spouse needs to be coaxed out, but when the refusal to expose one's self to their spouse goes on indefinitely, then this lack of trust deeply violates their spouse. When we choose to engage in sex, we are trusting the other person in a very deep way. If that lack of trust is unprovoked, and a person still does not trust their spouse and refuses to allow themself to be seen during this most fundamental and intimate situation, then it is likely that the hiding spouse cannot be trusted in other parts or aspects of the marriage. This is a base behavior and it is the way in which a person functions. When a spouse violates a transaction within a particular aspect of their married life, then the way in which they violate their mate ripples throughout all other parts of their life. Whether deliberate or inadvertent, any situation where the same behaviors can occur, they likely *will* occur.

If you always hide yourself under the covers while in your bedroom with your spouse, it is almost certain you do this same sort of thing in most other areas in your life with regard to connecting with your spouse. It likely goes beyond your interaction with your spouse and, to some extent, it probably happens with just about everyone you know.

Again please note: if you are facing these sorts of troubles and cannot draw your spouse out, then make sure that you have not previously violated your spouse in this regard. What you said at the mall while shopping can affect what happens in the bedroom at night. It is part of the inadvertent tit-for-tat that we spoke of throughout this book.

If your spouse has not violated you in the intimate settings of your life together, and you still continue to refuse to expose yourself, then you are being unfair and cheating your spouse out of an important joy of marriage. They would have been better off marrying someone else who would not withhold visual, physical, or spiritual intimacy from them.

Physical intimacy is a gift that has been given to humans, and it is best used in a faithful, true, and committed relationship. A relationship that is riddled with violations is not a true relationship. You are designed to share and to become one with your spouse. The sooner you choose a path that utilizes your design for its intended purpose, then the sooner you will find joy in your marriage.

If you are the spouse who is withholding yourself from your mate, then your job is easy because all you need to do is let go and allow yourself and your spouse the enjoyment of uninhibited marital intimacy. It is important to remember that this goes beyond the bedroom. So make sure you allow your spouse to share in you in the other parts of your life as well.

If you are the one who is having your life stolen away by a spouse who has no trust in you, then the task that you are facing is far more difficult and all you can do is your best, and hope and pray that your spouse wakes up before you have had enough and choose to withdraw, rebel, or leave them.

We are designed to share and shine our light, for and with, our mate. This is our purpose with regard to our spouse and our intimacy with them.

The Deep Significance of Sex in Relationships

Physical intimacy is often taught and thought to be a bad thing, or at least interpreted to be a bad thing. Often parents, in their own clumsy way, tell their children about sex, but then have a tendency to make it sound bad when trying to convey that it is only bad outside of marriage. Sadly, we often fail to illustrate that it is not the act that is bad, but rather it is the recklessness with which the act is often practiced that is bad.

Culturally, we blind ourselves with regard to sex. We abuse something, and then we call it bad when it is actually the abuse that's bad—and not the act itself. Let's take water as an example: You cannot live without water. At some point, you will expire if you have no water. This means that water is a vitally important part of our survival. Yet too much water, or water in the wrong place, will promptly put an end to you. When we inhale too much water we drown. So, is water then good or bad?

This means that water is neither good nor bad, it simply is. It's what you choose to do with the water that harms or helps your future. When used for its intended purpose and for its design, water will always be a good thing. Water was not intended to be in our lungs, and our lungs are not designed for water to be in them in that way. Sex is no different. The physically intimate act is designed to be utilized within a committed and truthful relationship because it is so intimate knowing the deepest parts. Using sex for anything other than that will eventually end poorly. So we get to *choose* what we will do with regard to our sexual interaction with other people, but we also must realize that we have to live with the results of our actions.

Again, we must go back to our design. What is the significance of our design with regard to sex? That is to say, what is *he* really designed to offer, and what is *she* really designed to accept? The *full joy* for either spouse is felt *only* when the transaction is properly completed. Sex is supposed to be the climax of that transaction, but because we have worked so hard to emotionally disconnect from sex, our disconnection causes sex to become a service, much like you would get from a prostitute or a fortune teller.

Wives: do not prostitute yourselves to your husband just to get him to say what you want to hear.

Husbands: do not be fortune tellers for your wife by telling her what she wants to hear just so that you get your share in her.

Be honest, be physically intimate in truth.

So, how then, do we be physically intimate in truth? There are some things that cannot be explained to you without you making the choice spoken of earlier. The choice is that moment in time where your life changes and you seek *what is*, this includes seeking your spouse. Our understanding comes at that moment when the choice of truth is made deep in our own hearts, then the world of understanding and insight opens up to you in a way that was previously unknown to you. Selfishness disappears and you will want to please others and offer them joy by being true to them. With your spouse, this includes the uninhibited explorative freewill offering of the physical act of sex, as well as the deeper aspects of heart, mind, and soul.

God, the Bible, and The "Sex" Topic

Having spoken at length with people on the subject of sex, I have come to understand that sex is perhaps one of the most difficult topics to properly convey to people due to incorrect preconceived notions about it. Because some people are all too often set into a rage at the mere mention of the Bible, I try to not mention it if possible in discussing any potentially controversial topics; but because marriage touches deeply and so closely to the relationship between mankind and our Creator, it would do you injustice if such comparisons were not drawn in this book.

There is a saying that "The heart wants what the heart wants." I suppose this is so, but what is the heart, and what controls the heart? We are often told "Invite the Creator into your heart." What then is the heart? Can we actually receive something into our physical heart?

When we hear someone say something to us, it actually physically becomes a part of us because the receiving of those words alters our biochemistry. This is undeniably evident, but to what extent it alters us is somewhat unknown—or so we like to believe.

When we hear the words of someone or see those words in writing, we choose to either *receive* or *reject* those words. When we reject those words, we have made a personal choice to not heed those words of information or advice. Rejecting such words can be either incredibly wise or incredibly foolish.

Only you get to choose for yourself whether to receive or reject someone's words. No one else can choose this for you. When we receive our spouse into us, especially when women do so, our spouse becomes a part of us and we are becoming one with them—we are getting our share in each other.

I am going to place women in the Creator position for a moment, and men in the women's position. If a husband offers to his wife that he will have sex with her, but he does not really want to and she can see his apparent reluctance, will she delight in his offering? Is he truly giving her his best love? If he makes his offer of intimacy out of mere duty, then will she be able to be fulfilled in him? Be assured that she will not.

If a wife has come to know only the physical part of a relationship, then she will always feel empty or shorted even when she is completely physically fulfilled by her husband. In such cases, she may not notice that he did it only as a *duty* offering, and so she may be momentarily sated in her desire of sexual fulfillment. But because this type of fulfillment will not satisfy her for long, her satisfaction will only be for a fleeting moment.

Now, on the other hand, if she is familiar with proper and fulfilling love, and her husband makes his offering only as a duty offering, then it will most likely be taken as an insult by her. However, if she is starved enough for deeper companionship, she will likely take what she can get even if it is *only* "duty" sex. When her husband does this, it will make her feel that she is forcing him to some extent; and anything forced or done as a duty is *not* a freewill offering. It is the *freewill* aspect of an offering that makes sex special, and without it, you are, for the most part, buying or selling sex.

To turn things around a bit, the same is true of men. When a woman approaches her husband out of a sense of duty, then he will feel it, and as is often the case, he will accept it because, to him, it is better than receiving nothing. This is the sort of love he can get from a prostitute, can he not? Prostitutes offer only a physical service that is void of the true bond that we truly seek. When the true bond is stripped away, then we only have the physical part remaining and it becomes devalued and cheap because there is nothing deeper with it. In this case, the husband gets a better exchange from the prostitute because the prostitute is more likely to be better at pretending and at acting out the part that he so desperately seeks from his wife but cannot get, and the prostitute is more likely to be physically uninhibited for him.

This was the same problem that occurred in the Bible with the people and the Creator. They withheld their best from their Creator, and then when they did give the best of their crop as an "offering", they did it *begrudgingly*. And as far as the destruction and dispersion of the rebellious people is concerned, world history proves this to be consistent. This self-destruction re-occurred with people throughout the ages whenever we failed to understand, and then failed to make our freewill offerings.

Whether our offerings are to the Creator or to our spouse, we typically fail miserably at making these freewill offerings purely and passionately. This causes us to be dissatisfied when we offer, and it also causes the one to whom the offering is being made to be left wanting. This is when and how infidelity enters our lives.

In our selfishness, we fail to fully give ourselves to our spouses and often have "better things to do" than to fully submit during our poorly offered and feeble "freewill offerings" to our spouses. This is true whether you are the husband or the wife.

In the Bible, the Creator said to the Israelites that the Creator would not be their God and that they would not be the Creator's people due to their horrible behavior and incessant violations against the Creator. Assuming that this is an actual account of things, then how foolish are the people to have denied their sustenance? As is often said, "The heart wants what the heart wants." The Creator wanted the same thing that a husband or wife wants: a pure and passionate freewill offering.

After the Israelites turned away and they were no longer considered "God's people", they tried making offerings, but their offerings were no longer accepted by the Creator. They blew it—it was too late! This same thing happens every day all across the globe within many marriages, and we keep falling short. We do not know how to passionately offer ourselves to our mates, and when we finally manage to do so, it's often done too late.

For others, they do understand how to make a pure offering of themselves to their mate, but for some unknown reason, their mate does not understand how to receive that pure freewill offering, or simply does not want it even though it is pure and passionate. This is cruel because the person to whom the pure freewill offering was made had committed to the relationship and likely accepted such offerings themselves in the past. When they don't want the offering, or their spouse, then they have unfairly bound their spouse in chains by not allowing their spouse to be able to give or receive freewill offerings of love.

Those who do not know how to, or do not want to, receive freewill offerings also are usually the those who do not want to offer the freewill offerings themselves—unless it suits them. Let us add to the old adage, "The heart wants what the heart wants, but must be prepared for the consequences of its desires!"

If you have ever given a gift to a person who did not expect that gift, and the person who received the gift truly loved it, then think about how good you felt when they reacted better than you had hoped for. It is very important to remember this feeling and *why* you felt that way.

Now, suppose the person that you gave the gift to, had instead looked at you after you had given them the gift, and said with an odd somewhat rejecting look on their face, "Thank you?" You would likely recognize the look on their face to be one where the person did not know what to say about a gift that they did not care to receive from anyone. Another example would be if you had hoped that someone was going to give you a gift, but they did not, or they gave you the wrong gift. (This often happens with people during the holidays.)

These gift-giving examples are the simplest way to see this problem for what it is because we can disconnect our thoughts from the emotional frustration that we often feel with the more delicate areas of our lives, such as sex. If you place yourself as the giver, and then again as receiver, in the respective gift examples just given, then you should have a pretty good idea of what is being conveyed here.

An intimate freewill love offering is the single most beautiful thing in existence. When we learn to do this, and we do it well, then the pleasure of our spouse becomes our goal, and *our* pleasure becomes *their* goal.

Delight in your spouse, know them, and let them know you. Change your heart so that their pleasure is your desire. Then you will begin to know exactly what they desire, and the two of you together will share the gifts you both have for one another. When you share together long enough, then you will become proficient at knowing what your spouse wants because you will make it your mission to find out what their desires are, and you will seek to know them better.

Wives: you are your husbands' temple, invite him in to pay homage to the Creator.

Intimate Freedom

One of the joys of marriage is intimate freedom, but this too has been perverted by the intrusive minds of foolish cultures. With each successive wave of societal "sexual freedom", a couple's intimate freedom is breached. Each generation's new-found "freedom" is a damaging counter-balance to the previous generation's damaging inhibitions. The battles between these two extremes become waged publicly to the detriment of the vast majority of couples who stand in the balance. All of the bickering about "rights" and "sexual freedom" confuse the hearts and minds of most people.

Both spouses in a couple should be able to talk openly to one another, and the information in their discussions should be kept private because it is intimate knowledge between, and of, the two. When a spouse betrays this confidence, it breaks the trust, which is very bad for the relationship, and it reveals the nature of the spouse who freely shares the private information. The couple should make their own decisions as to what can or cannot happen during their intimacy. We *do not* need to check with the world to see if what we agreed to do in the privacy of our own bedroom is okay.

It's good to include the Bible as a sort of guide for sexual intimacy, but that is your option. Looking to the past is a good way to find out what has failed. The Bible says *very little* about what *can* or *cannot* occur between a husband and wife in their marriage bed. This is a good indication that it is up to us to do what we want sexually in the privacy of our own homes. However, the Bible does tell us, repeatedly, that where other people outside of the committed relationship are concerned, that there are strict limits. People who suffer with lack in their marriage are far more likely to seek out something that suits them better, which will likely violate the wise fidelity limits described in the Bible.

While intimate freedom is yours to enjoy as a couple, it should also be respectful to each spouse and not dangerous to your physical well-being. Intimacy is the one place that both spouses can let go and express themselves, unafraid, uninhibited, and in utter safety when there is trust in the relationship. Something is wrong in the relationship if you cannot speak open and freely with your spouse with regard to intimacy and sex. The most important takeaway from the Bible with regard to the sexual behavior of two people within a marriage is physical cleanliness.

Each couple should do what they desire in the privacy of their own intimacy, provided it is not destructive to either of them or their relationship. The joy of freedom and exploration in your intimacy is your gift to each other and from the Creator. Keep public opinion out of your bedroom and keep what happens during your intimacy out of public opinion.

Seducing Your Husband

Over the course of past decades we have all been privy to the magazine-cover text that wallpapers the grocery store checkout lanes, and we have been witness to a multitude of suggested techniques for women to "please" or seduce their men. Yet, even after all these years and all of the supposed great advice offered by these articles, many relationships still struggle, suffer, and even fail while these titillating articles persist. And I dare say, it is likely that those who read the articles as a source of guidance have a higher percentage of relationship troubles.

I am not condemning these writings. Rather, I am perplexed that it is thought to be so needed year after year. If women were not complaining about those topics, then there would be no articles written about those topics because there would be no interest in them. These articles are generally written in response to queries and purchase demand. So we must ask ourselves, why are the articles about "pleasing" your man so overtly abundant? Is it not because many women cannot get the desired reaction from their man, thus they are not properly pleasing him?

This important section may offend some women because it places the burden squarely on the wife, and it is very important to your relationship for you to seriously consider. If not for the articles supported by the many women who read them, we would not know that it is the women who seem to more often seek to find a way to "please" their spouse in this way.

Since this obvious stereotypical situation is extremely strong in this regard, it would be foolish to ignore what the magazines have had the foresight to address. Thus, the ball is in the women's court.

So, just how does a woman properly seduce her husband? Some will say the way to a man's heart is through his stomach. Others will say it is done with creative techniques in bed. Yet, many relationships where these tactics are aggressively tried, end in failure or live on "until death do us part" in a lackluster and near failure of a marriage. This is mostly because they actually believed that it is the techniques, like those written about in the articles, that would properly satisfy their mates.

While the techniques found in these articles are entertaining and will likely be well received by many of the men on whom they are tested, couples who practice the techniques still will typically fail if they fail to address the real underlying issues in their relationship. This does not mean that women should discount these techniques, but this is clear indication that the techniques, in themselves, are not what the man is after.

Yes, the techniques can and typically do make things more exciting, but if you want to seduce your husband, then seek your husband, desire your husband, and be one with your husband. And *then* try these techniques. I assure you that those techniques will have a far greater impact once the rest of the relationship's foundation is properly in order.

You are where *he* wanted to live to begin with, so allow him to do so. You are his temple. If your troubles have been caused by a strong urge to control, then consider that rejecting him and trying to control him has not worked in the past, it is not working now, and it will not work in the future, regardless of what some advice might say.

What is a pure offering? It is finding what he wants and offering it to him in humility and purity and with passion. Sadly, few women understand that it is *you* that he wants. Gifts of sex are fine, but they will not last and are empty and without meaning if the rest of you is not freely included. *You* are the offering, and your body is only a symbol or vessel in which *you* are contained. Your body is one way of showing your intentions, and when your invitation is offered properly, it will be very fulfilling for both of you!

When you fail to get the first parts right, then the techniques for physical intimacy that you have read about will likely backfire on you in the long-run. A joy-filled marriage will never exist until a wife learns how to offer herself to her husband by properly inviting him. After a wife learns how to properly give herself to her husband in this way, then the techniques you may have read about in all of those magazines will be far more fulfilling for both of you. Those techniques become a bonus when you get the first parts right. In fact, physical intimacy or sex in general, is a bonus when you get things right with or without such techniques. Often your natural instincts will be far more creative *when* you allow them to be. This relates somewhat to the "spread her legs and then everything will be okay" comment mentioned earlier. The notion of opening the legs is an invitation to a man. The problem that must be addressed is that it's not the legs that need to be opened for the husband as much as it is the heart and mind in order to let him in. When the heart is open then the legs will automatically follow. The legs part is the result of an open heart, rather than the cause.

It is her choice! A *pure* invitation is a woman's choice and no one can make her do it. It is something she must choose to do on her own—seldom will this fail when done properly. It is only when a man's past has been very tainted and conditioned with wrong thinking, wrong example, and bad experience that his wife will have to work with him on this to a point where she will experience resistance in doing so.

Women: you control your own happiness and joy. There are women who experience this joy already, but many of those women do not understand specifically why they have success and joy even if they have actually wondered about it. Therefore, most women can only pass this on, unintentionally, to their children through their example, and are unable to *deliberately* pass it on. This means that they do not know exactly what they are doing in this regard, and it is only the good blessings of what they experienced while growing up that guides their habitual actions. It is important to note that most men have even less knowledge about this than women do, and that places more of the work in the hands of the person who knows more about it, regardless of which spouse it is.

Since these examples are typically being passed to the children only by pure chance, then if the children fail to grasp what is happening, it is only by chance that they will have joy in their own marriages. The chance occurrence of understanding and emulating this includes both the boys and the girls.

Anyone who takes this as a form of blame must then understand that it is *you* who is to blame. This is not blame, but rather a truth of humanity and the design after which we have been Created. The more quickly men and women realize that we need to be deliberate in our *invitations* and *acceptance* of our spouses and their affections, then the more quickly we can invite true intimate joy into our lives.

Realize in your mind, that no one is perfect in this, and that all of us should seek to understand, and thereby improve our own marriages. If you refuse to consider this, then you will continue to suffer the consequences of improperly utilizing your design all the rest of your days.

If you so decide that you have been descended through natural selection without intent of the deliberate Creator, then accept your result whatever it may be, good or bad. But, if you choose to understand that you are a Created being, then understand that you have a specific design, and that your design has a specific purpose. Go with it and in it, and find the joy that was intended for you while you use your design as proposed by its intended purpose.

Offering Yourself to Your Mate

We discussed offerings in depth, and it is my hope that you now understand what a *pure* offering void of violation is or that you will soon come to recognize it. In order to leave no stones unturned here, we will briefly review it now. Freewill offerings are difficult for us to grasp because we have been trained to want to do everything to our own advantage. Many preachers teach that if we give, then we will receive. This is true, but we must give rightly and properly. We must give a *pure* offering. But all too often, we give with the attitude of, "What's in it for me?" When a young child proudly scribbles on a paper and gives that paper to Mommy or Daddy then that paper is a *pure* offering, and we parents proudly and happily display it on the refrigerator door or on the wall at work. Now that is profoundly simple! The reward the child receives for the offering that the child made is the love and adoration from the parents.

We love our children's pure offerings, not because of what the offering is, but because of *how* it was given. They do their best and then offer it to us in absolute purity. Later in life we come to expect that same attitude from them, but it slowly erodes. And when they are older, if they do things for us, their innocent offering has often vanished and there is a reluctant attitude that accompanies any offerings they make. Parents become disgusted with these ill offerings and usually feel violated. The feeling of violation is there because the purity is now missing. It is the purity that we are seeking. Now equate the offering of a child's art to your marriage with regard to the purity of your intimate offerings to one another as husband and wife.

The following applies to both spouses: Offer yourself, in purity, clean and pure from guile. It is good to have good hygiene because it keeps infections away, but this is not the purity that was sought by the Creator and it is not the purity sought by your spouse. Wash your bodies, for sure, and be clean and without bad odor and disease, but more importantly it is inside your heart that needs to be cleaned and offered in a pure state. This is even more important for women to understand because *you* are *his temple* and he is supposed to dwell *within* **you**, and where he comes into you should be clean and pure.

Also, men must understand that a woman who is clean and has a pure heart will *not* enjoy receiving her husband if he has not washed and is dirty and has a corrupted heart. As it is with the cleanliness of our bodies, where being *unclean* can cause infection, so too is it with the cleanliness of our hearts. Generations have wrongly taken "purity" to mean things such as having sex in one position and to *not* enjoy it, and to only do so in effort to have children. This is utter foolishness! A married couple getting intimately wild in their own bedroom is their own business. And every couple should receive this wonderful gift of joy from the Creator with great enthusiasm. Embrace and explore it as you walk forward together in your intimate life and in life in general.

Wives: your heart is the joy of your husband, and if you fail to realize that, then your marriage *will* suffer the fate of that misunderstanding. Often, we equate suffering with punishment. But I ask you to consider, instead, that suffering is a *result* rather than a *punishment*. It is a result of either our blindness or our *ignor-*ance.

Wives: take delight in pure offerings of yourself to your husband.

And **husbands:** take delight in your wife's pure offerings and offer yourself, in kind, to her.

She is His Zion

Everything about a wife who has learned to offer herself purely to her husband is joyous, delightful, precious, attractive, sexy, and cherished to him. She will make herself presentable physically, intimately, and spiritually, and then she will joyously and freely offer herself to her husband while desiring to please him. Few men will ever consider rejecting this.

But be warned wives, if you have not been doing this for many years, and then suddenly make a change, it may surprise and shock your husband, and he may not initially respond as you would hope and expect. It will be up to you to regain his trust, and through it, regain your marriage. It can take time to do this and time for the emotional wounds to heal, so some rejections may occur, but don't stop trying if you want to succeed in restoring trust.

This same thing applies to husbands as well. Sometimes it takes time to reverse the damage we have caused in our own marriage and life.

Wives, you are supposed to be your husband's Zion, his holy city, his temple, where he will dwell within you. When he is not received purely because you have not offered yourself to him to dwell within, then you are abusing your design and will struggle in your marriage because of it. Call upon your husband as your joy and not by your demands.

We say, "God, I want this", and "God, give me that". "I need a better car, a bigger house, and more money, and I want it now, now, now!" If you think about this for a moment, why would anyone want anything to do with a person who has that sort of attitude?

On the other hand, if you were to go and invite your Creator into your heart fully, purely, and passionately, then you would not even need to ask for anything because the Creator would already know what you truly want and need, and thus, the Creator would be excited and pleased to do so for you and would take delight in doing any good thing you want.

So then, how much more would a husband, a mere mortal appreciate and enjoy a pure and passionate heart in a wife that trusts and loves him? To the Creator we are all special when we come in purity, but how much more of a gift is that same purity to a mere mortal? In doing this, a wife will be the delight of his life on this earth. There is nothing better, sweeter, more cherished, or more precious for a man than to be able to take delight in the pure offering for him to have his home in the heart of his wife, and for him to receive all the freedoms that go along with that. That is how a woman can turn her husband on, and *keep* him turned on! The same is true for a man's offer of himself to his wife.

Be Hot For Your Mate... Always

While it is more up to women to choose a wonderful marriage, almost everything you have read here applies to both spouses nearly equally.

Women: If you always appear hot for your husband, both emotionally and physically, then he will likely always be hot for you!

Men: If you always appear hot for your wife, both emotionally and physically, then she will likely always be hot for you.

This, of course, is provided that you have both come to understand the simple truth of offering yourself to your spouse in *purity*. We are not speaking of physical aspects here, though that is a part of it.

There is but one truth in life, and when we deny our design we then breach that truth and are left without light—we are in utter darkness. When we are in darkness, we cannot see our way clear, and we will spend a great deal of our time groping through the darkness trying to find all of the wrong answers in all of the wrong places—that is to say, we will look everywhere but in our own hearts. Those dark answers will leave you feeling void.

Wives: If your husband is not allowed into you, then he cannot dwell within you and he may eventually seek his refuge elsewhere.

Husbands: If you breach your design and do not have the truth of your Creator in your heart, then *why* would your wife want you to dwell within her at all? You must be clean and free of darkness. You are her light. Your desire should be first to have your Creator in your own heart, and then you should be eager to enter the temple of your wife physically, but more importantly, spiritually.

Husbands and Wives: You have come to the end of the road of understanding love. Beyond this, it is up to you to let go and accept truth and humility, and then be who you truly are. Be great by being what you are Created as, which is indicated in your physical form.

Continuing to seek love and acceptance as you have in the past has obviously not worked, and repeating the same behavior will get you the same results as you have gotten in the past. But, changing your focus and accepting truth in its pure form, unaltered by the lies and mistruths of society, will give you great joy and great power. Your marriage will benefit, your children will benefit, your finances will benefit, your health will benefit, and your souls will benefit! You will become a beacon of hope to those around you, and you can share this message with them.

When the world comes to torment you and tries to lure you away from these truths, stop and reread this message to remind yourself what it is really all about. Share this message with others and make this message your way of life by invoking it in all of your relationships. Then you will see the joy of your life increase abundantly!

What you have been Created for may not be your current job, and it certainly is not the darkness that most of us aimlessly grope around in.

When you are where you are Created to be in life, then you will thrive and enjoy almost every day as if it is the best ever! It is a new way of life. If you continually fail to do this in one area of your life, then you will eventually fail to do it in *all* other areas of your life. Be vigilant of the truth within you and share it with everyone, but most of all, share it with your spouse!

These are the same truths spoken of in the Bible. This idea is not new. Through thousands of years these very same messages have been at the command of humanity but are largely ignored, causing untold destruction and horror throughout the world and in innumerable marriages.

It is now time for you to forever rewrite yours and your spouse's versions of *The Shopkeeper and the Woman* so that they are in harmony as one. What will your Version 7 say? You must share and create the same desired story so that your story ends in mutual marital bliss. In the ideal situation, how should the shopkeeper and the woman behave and react to each other? That is how you should behave and react to each other. Here's the best part of life, you can write that story, adjust it, and perfect it *every* day of your life, making it better and better with each passing day. While what we did yesterday affected our today, it is what we do right now that decides our tomorrow. The best part about our past is that it is our past, and the best part about this very moment, is that you are reading this and now realize that *you* can make those needed adjustments *right now* at this very moment, and change the rest of your tomorrows forever!

You can change your tomorrows every day, and you can continue to make adjustments until you have achieved the fullness of your joy in your marriage. Then your fullness of joy will be shared with your children, your spouse, and all those who see your light!

Delight in your spouse!

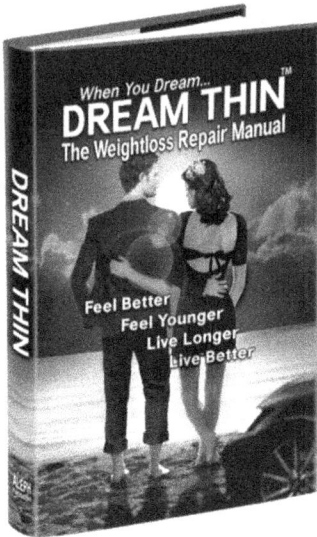

Volume 1 - The First Four Days

Is there a God? Did we evolve? Did everything start from a big bang? These questions have been plaguing our minds for many years. Only science-minded people and clergy seem to have the answers. But do they really have any true answers?

Is what we are told by science true? Is what we are told by the Church true? Or are there other better explanations for everything? Did we hitch a ride from Mars, or is that all fantasy science? Was everything Created in six twenty-four hour days, or did it all take billions of years to happen? Few people are willing to even fully consider these questions, and even fewer have any coherent answers. *The Science of God* challenges your current beliefs while asking tough questions of science and of the Church.

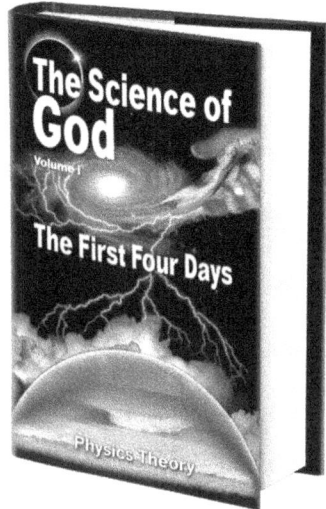

For years, Christian after Christian has attempted to argue for God and the Bible's Creation only to fail miserably. Why is this, why is it that Christians cannot seem to win this debate? Often Christians think they are winning the debate only to find themselves at a loss to answer the real questions, and then they get mocked for their poor answers.

Whether you are a scientist or an average Christian and want to discuss the Creation debate, *The Science of God* is a mandatory read for you. *The Science of God* takes you through the thought process to enable you to speak intelligibly about Creation, the cosmos, evolution, and astrophysics.

Search: The Science Of God Book
SayItBooks.com

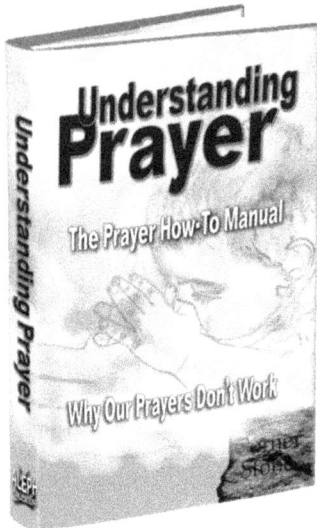

Rocking the Cradle of Life
A Decent Account of Descent

Have you ever wondered if humans actually did evolve from apes? Or maybe, if we were specifically created, then how might have that occurred? There sure are a lot of opinions on the evolution versus creation topic. And too often these views use confusing technical jargon that few people care to learn or have ever even heard.

The answers to the questions you might have are, in many cases, the same answers that many other people seek. When you have solid answers that are difficult for someone to thwart, it's good to share those answers so that others can also feel confident with their own understanding of the arrival of mankind and the level of importance that it has in their own lives.

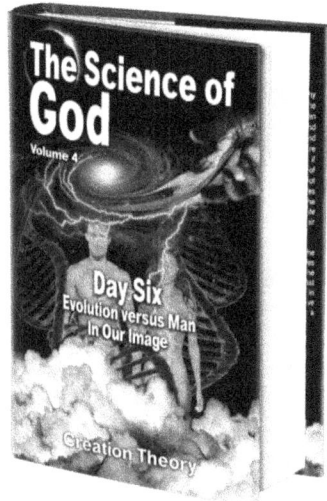

The Science Of God Volume 4 - Evolution versus Man – In Our Image takes a deep but simple dive into the human evolution versus human creation debate using simple language that everyone can understand and enjoy!

If you have thoughts that you have been reluctant to share, then suspend your thoughts for a bit and open your mind to consider the perspectives and evidence presented in *The Science Of God Volume 4 - Evolution versus Man – In Our Image*. You will acquire a much clearer view of the subject as you read the various points made in this engaging book about the arrival of mankind.

Search: The Science Of God Book Volume 4
SayItBooks.com

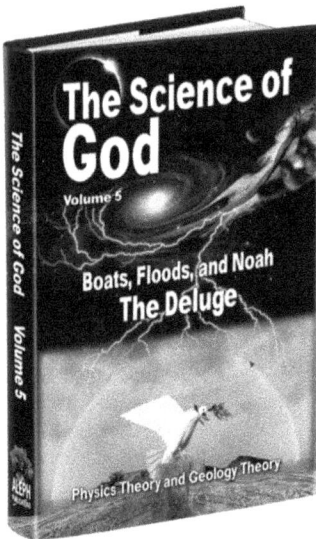

Understanding The Bible

The Bible How-To Manual
AND
The Things We Don't See

The Cornerstone of Moral Civilization

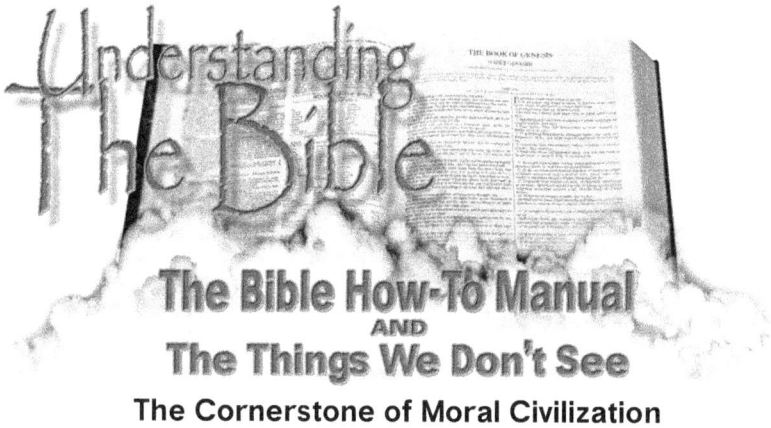

Was Jesus really the "Savior"? Did Noah really save humanity from extinction? Did Adam and Eve really get evicted from the Garden of Eden? And what does the word "Bible" mean anyway? When studying or even just reading the Bible, many questions arise to a point where the Bible can be confusing. But when you have certain information before you begin reading, it can instantly propel you to a deeper level of understanding by nothing more than knowing a few key points.

It takes people years to realize some of this information, yet it's not some big secret that only scholars and theologians know. No, this information is for everyone and it's easy to grasp these pieces of information about the Bible and some of the events described within it. Be prepared to have your current views challenged because many things are not as we have been taught.

To truly Understand the Bible, we must open our minds and toss aside all of our biases. Knowing and grasping the often-unrealized basic information presented in *Understanding The Bible - The Bible How-To Manual and The Things We Don't See* brings the Bible to life in a way that shows you, personally, its undeniable relevance to the world, to our culture, and to your very own life!

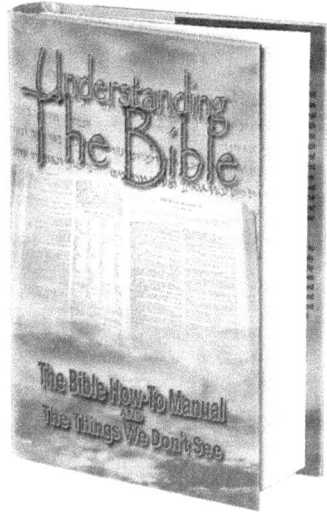

Search: Understanding The Bible Book
SayItBooks.com

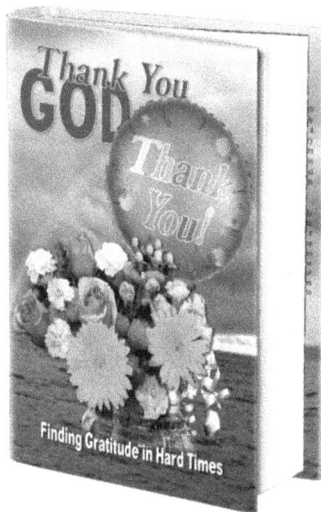

Notes

Notes

Notes

www.ingramcontent.com/pod-product-compliance
Lightning Source LLC
Chambersburg PA
CBHW021500090426
42739CB00007B/396